OVER LAND AND SEA

On completing his education, London born Mark turned down the opportunity to train for the priesthood, opting instead to travel the world. On returning home he immersed himself in the burgeoning dance music scene and its pharmacological subculture, funding a hedonistic lifestyle with a variety of jobs, including baker, DJ, seismologist, piano tuner and, most recently, mobile phone salesman. Mark Worrall supports Chelsea Football Club.

Mitch
Best wishes
Mark Worrall
6th Feb 2005

MARK WORRALL

OVER LAND AND SEA

Matador
9 De Montfort Mews
Leicester LE1 7FW, UK
Tel: (+44) 116 255 9311 / 9312
Email: books@troubador.co.uk
Web: www.troubador.co.uk/matador

ISBN 1 904744 27 3

Cover photo: Daniel Mott
Website design: Amanda Sage
Ugly John Travel: ujtravel@aol.com

www.overlandandsea.net

THE NAMES OF SOME OF THE CHARACTERS HAVE BEEN
CHANGED, BUT THE SONG REMAINS THE SAME

Typeset in 11pt Book Antiqua by Troubador Publishing Ltd, Leicester, UK
Printed by The Cromwell Press, Trowbridge, Wilts, UK

Matador is an imprint of Troubador Publishing

For the lads who enter Stamford Bridge
through Gate 17

"*WE ALL FOLLOW THE CHELSEA, OVER LAND AND SEA ... AND LEICESTER ... WE ALL FOLLOW THE CHELSEA, ON TO VICTORY ... ALTOGETHER NOW*"

Chelsea terrace anthem adapted from Land Of Hope And Glory

CONTENTS

ACKNOWLEDGEMENTS

Chelsea Gate 17 … the glue that binds my life together … Dave M, Chris M, Dan M, Mark L, John F, Pav T, Andy B, Brian J, Clive O, Utpal T, Jason H a true blue now ha ha, Roger E. Victor T … God bless you. Jonathan B and Ewan G … honorary members of Gate 17. Uncle Robert P for his profound wisdom … they will buy it with their eyes. Jeremy T at Troubador for insight and guidance through the publishing minefield. Amanda Sage … you're a genius. Charlie M for all the favours … top girl. Carole P. The ubiquitous Dave Draper … Gate 16's finest. Clive T … a decent Gooner. The North Surrey Mafia … see you in the Gamecock. The management and staff at One … the best drinker in West London. My old dear Giovanna whose timeless enthusiasm for Chelsea FC remains intact, and finally, the legend that is Gianfranco Zola … thankyou.

PROLOGUE

Someone once said that what they loved most about following the fortunes of Chelsea Football Club was the 'glorious unpredictability' afforded them by a team that could win convincingly away at Manchester United one week and then contrive to snatch defeat from the jaws of victory at home to Charlton Athletic the next.

I first had the idea for this book in the midst of Chelsea's last Champions League campaign which finally came to an end in Spain after forays into Germany, Turkey, Italy (twice), Holland and France.

In each of the three seasons that followed Chelsea qualified to play in the UEFA Cup. Unfortunately, owing to the 'glorious unpredictability' factor, any endeavour on my part to provide a literary account of these campaigns would have resulted in a very small collection of amusing vignettes, the last of these being set in a small fishing village in Norway on a very rainy October evening in 2002.

The weekly feeding of my Chelsea addiction began in earnest at Highbury in August 1984 when a spectacular Kerry Dixon strike in a lively 1–1 draw with Arsenal marked the blues return to the old first division in some style. I have ridden the emotional Chelsea rollercoaster ever since and, like many others, have a deep fund of far more colourful two word expressions than 'gloriously unpredictable' which I can draw upon to describe certain performances I have witnessed.

In the last twenty years, despite tangible progress on and off the pitch, Chelsea has remained a cruel mistress to me; her 'glorious unpredictability' capable of coupling unparalleled highs, such as those experienced at Wembley, Rasunda, San Siro and of course on a more regular basis White Hart Lane, with unfathomable lows; more often than not these days following another humiliatingly painful defeat at the hands of our dreaded bogey team from north London... Arsenal.

Highbury, Stamford Bridge, the Millennium Stadium even Las Vegas; irrespective of my location I could never understand why Chelsea always seemed to bring a knife to a gunfight when it came to their footballing

1

encounters with Arsenal. With just one relatively recent exception, when their reserves turned up without any ammunition, the Gunners always seemed to shoot us down.

Mr Ranieri had achieved much in his brief tenure as manager of Chelsea Football Club. No longer was the spine of our team brittle, no longer did we flatter to deceive on a cold winters afternoon at home to Middlesboro; no longer were we 'southern softies', tabloid fodder open to ridicule following another 'shock' FA Cup exit at the hands of lowly Stoke or even lowlier Shrewsbury.

Chelsea had confidently despatched all of these teams from this seasons FA Cup competition and, following a 2–2 quarterfinal draw at Highbury, confidence was running at an over enthusiastic all time high that the replay at Stamford Bridge would see the Gooner ghost finally laid to rest as Chelsea prevailed over Arsenal.

The confidence the team would take from this would not only result in them ultimately winning the competition, but also enable them to consolidate their current position in the top four of the Premier League making Champions League qualification, Messrs Bate's and Ranieri's key objective, a formality.

Well, that was the general consensus of the fifty odd Chelsea supporters gathered, along with myself, in the Crown and Anchor, a 'traditional' English pub situated on East Tropicana Avenue, three miles east of the legendary Las Vegas 'Strip'.

Now I know what some of you may be thinking. What was I doing in the middle of the Nevada desert some six thousand miles from where I should be, namely Stamford Bridge, at a critical time like this? And, what relevance does a trip to Las Vegas in March 2003 have with the European Champions League campaign for 2003 / 2004?

*   *   *

Every story has to start somewhere, and the reason I was in Las Vegas in the first place had a tenuous link to one of Chelsea's past endeavours in Europe. Unexpectedly, and perhaps more to the point, not only was it the place where I would enjoy the kind of ramshackle bonhomie and camaraderie that binds Chelsea fans together when following the team over land and sea, it was also to be the place where I would witness, albeit on TV, the grim spectre of 'glorious unpredictability' throwing the first of a series of very murky shadows over Chelsea's prospects of qualifying for Europe the following season.

I was in Vegas 'visiting' a gorgeous, surgically enhanced, woman by the name of Zorina. Zorina, Zori to her friends, had lived there for twelve years but originated from Bulgaria; Sofia to be precise.

I'd met Zori a couple of years previously when Sir Larry and I had made the trek out to Bulgaria's capital for the UEFA Cup tie with Levski. She was there visiting her family and was having a drink with some old friends of hers in a bar in which Sir Larry and I just happened to be celebrating Chelsea's 2–0 victory.

Captivated by her beauty, her wasp-like waistline and, most importantly, her Jordanesque chest measurements, I'd made a reasonable fist of chatting her up. Sadly, by the time she'd left I hadn't got any further than securing her email address; which considering the amount of alcohol I'd imbibed wasn't such a bad result.

Over a period of time, and with increasing regularity, the emails had flown backwards and forwards across the Atlantic until finally, with romance blossoming and my work commitments wilting, I decided to take Zori up on her invitation to spend a week in Sin City, USA.

I'd planned the trip to Vegas at relatively short notice and, having consulted the Chelsea fixture list, made an assumption that if the Arsenal cup tie being played on March 8th ended in a draw then the replay would probably be on either the 18th or the 19th. With this in mind I went ahead and booked my flight for 23rd... big mistake.

What I hadn't considered was Arsenal's participation in the Champions League and the fact that Champions League fixtures took precedence over domestic fixtures. The good news was that Arsenal lost 2–1 to Valencia on March 19th and as a result were eliminated from the competition; the bad news was that the Arsenal v Chelsea cup tie had ended in a draw and the replay was scheduled for March 25th. A date when I would be in a country where the majority of people recognised Chelsea as being the daughter of ex President Bill Clinton and, when pressed hard, thought that Arsenal were a boy band from New Jersey.

Not withstanding this, and buoyed by the fact that Chelsea had panelled Manchester City 5–0 at the Bridge on the Saturday preceding the replay, I left for Vegas confident that I would find somewhere to watch the match, and more importantly, that the result would be in our favour ... surely this time it had to be!

*   *   *

The interesting thing about being a football fan in the 21st century is that technological innovation, particularly in the field of satellite telecommunications, has brought the English game a far wider audience. Prior to

Christmas, whilst holidaying in Goa, I had enjoyed watching the full 90 minutes of Chelsea's away league fixture with Middlesboro in the company of ten 'true blue' Indian lads and four Chelsea supporting fellow holiday makers. The only thing to spoil our enjoyment was the fact that the commentary was in Norwegian, but then you can't have everything.

Up until a few years ago a crackling shortwave radio tuned into the BBC World Service was the only means available to keep abreast of football matters back home. But now satellite TV and text messaging have ensured that no matter where in the world you might be, Asia, Africa or mainland Europe, you stand a reasonable chance of being well informed of your teams progress back home. What of the US of A, though? Well now that's a different proposition altogether!

Of course they have satellite TV in Las Vegas, but then at this time of the year all those ridiculous casino sports bars insist on showing 'March Madness'... that's college basketball to you and me.

College basketball! Bloody Yanks, they are so full of parochial self importance when it comes to sporting matters. It's high time that somebody explained to them that basketball is a game played by men too tall and clumsy to play football.

As I began to make enquires about watching the match, the general reaction I got was one of incredulity that I'd had the audacity to even ask such a question in the midst of 'March Madness'.

Jetlagged, I sat with Zori in one of the myriad bars inside the MGM hotel nursing yet another bottle of Corona and listening with stony faced indifference as the barman, shaking his head at my request for information, quipped smugly that Vegas was a baseball town in a football country. I could have reacted but opted instead to shrug my shoulders and think to myself what I could have opined loudly.

Baseball! Only the Americans would take a simple game like rounders; change the rules slightly, rename it baseball, form a national league and with breathtaking arrogance call it the World Series!

Football! Just about everywhere else in the world football is recognised without question as being the number one sport. Whether using jumpers for goalposts on a dusty school playground, or playing in front of 120,000 people at the Nou Camp the enthusiasm that comes from participating in, or watching the game at any level is globally uniform.

In the United States, football is a seemingly bizarre combination of rugby and street fighting. It is played by motorcycle helmeted men, wearing Joan Collins style shoulder pads, following a set of rules devised by someone who had most probably overdosed on LSD. In the United States our beloved association football is known as soccer and played to a very high standard... by women!

I wanted to argue my point of view with the barman but I couldn't be bothered and anyhow Zori, whose patience was beginning to wear thin, indicated to me that if I wanted to avail myself of her very evident female charms... the original purpose of the trip... then I should call time on the evenings proceedings and escort her home.

I looked at the barman and then at my almost empty bottle of Corona before finally resting my eyes on Zori's 36 inch DD, $4000 treasure chest. As the song says, 'everybody needs a bosom for a pillow'. I smiled as the old Cornershop tune came into my head and, as I did so, my mood lightened.

It was a no brainer; my quest to find a venue screening the match would have to continue tomorrow. As I averted my gaze from Zori's chest back to the puzzled looking barman I started to laugh at the situation. It was absurd, funny and yet deadly serious; two countries which had the same culture and the same language were on different sporting planets.

* * *

Las Vegas is an oasis of life, energy and money, it is home to some one million people and, fortunately for me, one of them is a camp, bulbously corpulent, ex pat waiter from Liverpool called Jimmy. The night before the match Zori and I had gone for dinner at Morton's Steakhouse and despite Jimmy's best endeavours and a perfectly enunciated reading of 'todays specials' he just couldn't mask the flat nasal vowels that characterise the Scouse accent.

I've never met a Scouser who didn't have a love of the glorious game and I reckoned that despite his questionable sexual orientation, and evident Americanisation, Jimmy's footballing heritage might just shine through if I prompted him.

Jimmy had raised a distressed left eyebrow at me as I'd enquired not about the food, which turned out to be fantastic, but whether or not he was a red or a blue and, more importantly, if there was a football friendly drinker somewhere in the city that might be screening the match.

'The Crown and Anchor soft lad,' said Jimmy, who turned out to be a Tranmere Rovers fan, shaking his head, 'they show all the games there... it's out of town mind... East Tropicana... all the cab drivers know it. Now about the menu, would either of you care to choose an entrée?'

I nodded at Zori and suggested she order for both of us as I'd left my wallet in the car and obviously needed to retrieve it to pay for dinner. This of course was a lie; now it wasn't that I didn't trust Scouse Jimmy but in order to fully appreciate the Morton's dining experience I had to put my mind at rest and confirm that the information he'd given me was kosher.

I placed a call to the Crown and Anchor from a payphone in the restaurant foyer and spoke to a husky sounding woman called Jessica who confirmed the information that Scouse Jimmy had given me was correct.

Result! As I made my way back to the table I saw Scouse Jimmy stood by the bar waiting to collect a drinks order. He saw me and smiled as I gave him the thumbs up, he knew the score and I'm sure that he spent the generous tip I palmed him very wisely indeed.

*   *   *

The time difference of eight hours between Vegas and London meant that I found myself outside the Crown and Anchor at 11am the very next morning. It was relatively close to the office where Zori worked and she kindly dropped me off in the pub car park, promising to return in her lunch hour to have a drink and see how things were progressing.

The Crown and Anchor didn't look much like a pub from the outside, although its whitewashed walls and large ornate chimney set it apart from the drab low rise buildings that surrounded it. Although only a few miles away, it was a world apart from the monumental concrete and glass structures that formed the vulgarly ornate city styled resort hotels built along each side of the entire length of the fabled Las Vegas 'Strip'.

Given its appearance, the only clue to this particular drinkers location was the signage painted boldly in black on the chimney breast. Crown & Anchor... Pub... Restaurant... Video Poker. Despite it only being March it was already as warm as the hottest of English summer days and having paid the ubiquitous ten dollar cover charge to gain admission I was already looking forward to my first ice cold beer of the day.

*   *   *

With my head cleanly shaven and proudly wearing a retro-style Chelsea, circa 1974, replica away shirt, the white one with the green and red stripes down the centre, I couldn't contain my surprise when my entrance was greeted enthusiastically by a group of ten or so Chelsea shirted men stood by the bar.

'He's here, he's there, he's every fucking where Frank Lebouef, Frank Lebouef.'

The discordant and haunting chant, once reserved solely for the folically challenged French defender who wore the blue of Chelsea and now directed at me, reverberated around the cavernous wooden interior of the pub three times before being picked up by several younger lads who were watching proceedings from the galleried balcony above the bar.

The high raftered ceiling and quaint nautical décor gave the pub a distinctly English ambience. This, coupled with the motley looking assortment of displaced Chelsea supporters drinking from authentic looking pint pots, made me think momentarily that I had walked through some kind of matter transfer portal and was back in London SW6.

The chanting died away and, feeling slightly embarrassed, I applauded my fellow supporters before making my way to the bar.

'What can I get you?' asked the strikingly pretty barmaid, her dry American accent snapping me back to reality. It was Jessica the girl I'd spoken to on the telephone the previous evening.

'Er... La... Lager top please love,' was my hesitant reply.

Lager top is my unashamed drink of choice on match-days. Usually when abroad a request for a lager top is met with a blank stare. Lager isn't called Lager in many places outside Britain and, if it is, then the 'top' element is met with the disdainful question, 'Top! Vot ees thees top?'

Not in the Crown and Anchor though, here Jessica knew exactly what I meant.

'Fosters ok my love?' Jessica winked at me anticipating my positive answer.

'Fantastic!' I replied, winking back and reaching for my Marlboro Light's. This was better than I could ever have imagined. I nodded at her and turned my attention to my mobile phone which was vibrating in my pocket alerting me to the fact that I had a new text message:

HOWS THE PMT? HAVE YOU FOUND SOMEWHERE TO
WATCH THE MATCH?

The message was from Ugly John whom I knew would be with the rest of the Gate 17 boys knocking back a few Stella's in our pre-match drinker the One Bar.

PMT? ... pre match tension... I hadn't really thought about the match having been more preoccupied with finding somewhere to watch it rather than the game itself.

I texted my reply to Ugly John.

YES M8 AM IN PROPER DRINKER CANING OFF A LAGER
TOP WITH REAL CHELSEA FANS AND NOT A GOONER IN SIGHT

This wasn't strictly true; as I surveyed the bar, which was starting to get quite busy, I spotted four rather apprehensive looking young blokes wearing Arsenal shirts.

'Chelsea here, Chelsea there, Chelsea every fucking where la la la la, la la la la, la la.'

The chant started by the gallery boys gained momentum as the rest of the Chelsea fans in the main bar, myself included, joined in. The four Arsenal fans looked nervously at each other as they made their way away from the bar seeking out the anonymity of an alcove towards the back of the pub.

'Is that all you take away? ... Is that all? ... Is that all? ... Is that all you take away?'

The new chant, directed at the four Arsenal fans, broke up into raucous laughter and cheering as we watched them place their beers on the floor and applaud us; but they were never going to be allowed to get away with it that easily and the bar soon resounded to a new chant:

'Can you here the Arsenal sing? No... No... Can you here the Arsenal sing? No... No

... Can you here the Arsenal sing? I can't here a fucking thing... No... Oh Oh Shhhh.'

We all placed the index fingers of our right hands against our lips and waited for the Arsenal fans to come up with a response... but they didn't have one.

'Ahhhhhhhh... Ahhhhhhhh... Ahhhhhhh...'

Our mocking response to the Arsenal fans silence tailed off as the TV's in the bar flickered into life with a CNN news bulletin on the war in Iraq and the ongoing search for Saddam Hussein's weapons of mass destruction.

*   *   *

Jessica placed my lager top on the bar in front of me and I eyed it for a second, licking my lips with anticipation before putting the glass to my mouth and draining half the contents.

I don't know whether it's something that's unique to Chelsea, I'm sure it's not, but I couldn't stop myself from smiling as I placed my glass back on the bar and looked around the pub.

Resourceful or what? There was no way that all these Chelsea fans were U.S. citizens, members of some unheralded Nevada State supporters group. Where were they from then? How on earth had they come to find this unadvertised football outpost all the way out here in the wild wild west?

Well I'd found it hadn't I; so there in part lay the answer to my question. It was worth the effort... Chelsea were worth the effort... if you couldn't be there in person then seek out the next best thing. I rubbed my chin thoughtfully and picked up my glass again not realising that I was just about to be struck down by a severe bout of 'small world syndrome'.

I felt a tap on my shoulder and turned around to face a large barrel chested man whose tired eyes and rosy cheeked complexion led me to believe that the beer he was holding wasn't the first he'd had today.

'Hello mate... ere d'ya drink in the Stoneleigh?' Came the unexpected question.

'Yes mate... yes I do sometimes... but more often than not the Worcester or the Gamecock,' I replied, smiling and offering a handshake to the man who introduced himself as Vegas Dave.

Vegas Dave was in town for a stag weekend and since he and several of the other stags, including a straw haired lad with a maniacal grin called Bazza who'd also seen me in some of the local drinkers I frequented back at home, were Chelsea supporters it had been a priority for them to find somewhere to watch the game.

With pleasantries exchanged and the lager tops going down very well indeed I perched on a stool and focussed my attention on the large projector screen at the rear of the bar.

As the game kicked off the gallery boys started the chant *'One man went to mow...'* Everyone, with the exception of the four Arsenal fans, joined in and in time honoured fashion as the final *'Ten men went to mow...'* verse commenced we were all on our feet clapping our hands and braying at the top of our voices.

Our vociferous endeavours were in vain though; even if the Chelsea team had been able to hear us and raise their game in recognition of our distant and loyal support, they would still have been unable to cope with the sheer pace of an Arsenal team able to break from defence and cruelly expose any frailties in our five man midfield.

Viera and Wiltord were rampant and with just over half an hour gone, aided and abetted by the luckless John Terry, Arsenal were two goals to the good. Whilst this served to dampen our optimism it certainly didn't curb our desire to sing our hearts out.

The four Gooners and three bar staff were treated to the full Chelsea repertoire including a sparkling rendition of *'Blue is the colour'* initiated by my new best mates Vegas Dave and Bazza.

*   *   *

Zori arrived on cue at half time; her weapons of mass distraction which were concealed in the flimsiest of blouses proved to be the main talking point during the lemon break as opposed to anything Saddam might be hiding in one of his many palaces or the tactics Ranieri might employ to address the two goal interval deficit.

The tactics Ranieri chose to employ failed, and despite playing the final twenty odd minutes of the game against ten men and creating sufficient chances to pull the tie around, all we managed was one solitary goal ironically diverted into the Arsenal net by John Terry.

Terry's effort served to galvanise our vocal endeavours further; Bazza led a proud version of the Mick Greenaway terrace classic 'Zigger Zagger,' but it was all to no avail. With ten minutes left Lauren scored for Arsenal and put paid to any faint hopes we might have harboured that Chelsea might equalise.

The Arsenal curse had struck again; they'd won 3–1 having had only three shots on target. As the post mortem drinking session got underway, the main topic of conversation centred on the fact that this result would probably act as the catalyst for Chelsea's season going completely pear shaped. Pear shaped being defined as failing to qualify to qualify for the Champions League.

Vegas Dave remarked that given this was Chelsea, everything would probably boil down to the last game of the season... a game which everyone knew was against our main rivals for that coveted final qualification slot, Liverpool.

'Why are you all so disappointed?' asked Zori, a perplexed look forming across her finely honed features. 'It's only a game... maybe you'll beat them next time.'

I shook my head, there was no point trying to explain to Zori the disappointment that I felt. Next time? Why did it always have to be 'maybe next time' against Arsenal? Why couldn't it be now? This was neither glorious nor unpredictable and every time it happened it hurt like hell.

*   *   *

By the time I left the Nevada desert and returned home to leafy Surrey, Chelsea had just seven league games left. The penultimate of these resulted in a 1–0 defeat away at West Ham, and with Liverpool surprisingly losing their corresponding fixture at home to Man City this meant that Vegas Dave's prophecy, that it would all come down to the very last game, had become a reality.

The day of reckoning, Sunday May 11th, came around quickly enough. There was no more debate to be had about the depth of Chelsea's quality or the intensity of the competition for control of the midfield; by 5pm all the arguments would be settled once and for all.

In the days preceding the match the tabloids had been full of arrogantly expectant quotes from the Liverpool manager Gerard Houllier who proclaimed in no uncertain terms that it would be a footballing injustice were Chelsea to qualify for the Champions League ahead of Liverpool.

His claims that Liverpool had been the better team over the course of the season drew parallels with the sour grapes remarks Arsene Wenger had made when comparing his Arsenal team with Ferguson's championship winning Manchester United side.

All of this was a profound contrast to the manner in which Chelsea's Claudio Ranieri conducted himself. A man once ridiculed for his improbable use of the English language; he remained erudite, calm and collected maintaining his balance and dignity throughout the build up to the match.

Here was a man confident in his teams ability to go out and do a thoroughly professional job and this confidence permeated easily through my thick leathery skin. To put it simply... I believed!

Whilst that confidence remained even when Hyypia headed home to give Liverpool an early lead, it would be fair to say that the heightened tension caused by the goal was shared by the majority of the 41,911 fans witnessing proceedings first hand.

My frayed nerves were soon healed though, and the rest of the day belonged to Chelsea and to our enigmatic Danish winger Jesper Gronkjaer in particular. So often the target of the boo boys; 'Forrest Gump' ran the Liverpool defence ragged, first curling a wicked ball across the area for Desailly to head home the equaliser on 14 minutes, then latching onto a Melchiot pass, skinning the Liverpool defence and driving home a ferocious low ball which curved away from the flailing arms of goalkeeper Jersey Dudek and buried itself in the back of the net.

It was a sublime moment and it was savoured for the remainder of the afternoon as it became evidently clear that Liverpool lacked the guile and craft to pick their way through Chelsea's midfield and unlock an impressively solid defence.

The dismissal in the final minute of Gerrard for a second bookable offence, a wild challenge on the classy Le Saux, served notice on the Liverpool challenge. Long after the final whistle had gone and the red contingent departed, I had remained in the ground with the massed blue ranks of our support revelling in the glory of our achievement.

It had been a superlative performance by the players, ably assisted by the phenomenal atmosphere generated by the fans. With the seasons objective finally realised, and safe in the knowledge that there would be little for us Chelsea supporters to speculate about over the summer given the paucity of the clubs finances, all that remained for me to do that day was to get royally drunk with the rest of the Gate 17 boys and salute the ones, whom owing to geography, I wouldn't be seeing again until August.

* * *

What close season speculation there was about Chelsea surrounded the future of our greatest ever player; the diminutive, talismanic Sardinian Gianfranco Zola who was now out of contract.

Could Chelsea afford financially to keep him? Even if we could, would the lure for Franco of finishing his career playing for his home town club Cagliari prove too much?

In the end this drama was hurriedly transferred to a far smaller stage because unbeknown to all but a tiny minority the 'glorious unpredictability' factor, that normally entwined itself with the teams on field performances, was about to send a whiplash through the club that would be felt not just by Chelsea but by every team in the country... and beyond.

On July 2nd it was announced that Roman Abramovich, a Russian billionaire who at 36 years of age found himself billed as the 43rd richest man in the world, had purchased over 50% of the shares in Chelsea Village.

He was quoted as saying, "I don't look at this as a financial investment, I look at it as a hobby, as a sport rather than an investment. I'm looking at it as something to have fun with rather than having to realise a return".

The dawn of the Roman Empire was reported in exhaustive detail by tabloids and broadsheets alike. Who was Roman Abramovich? Why had he bought Chelsea? Was this the end of the Bates era? Was there a future for Claudio Ranieri?

In the meantime the rumour mill whirred at breakneck speed as everyone engaged themselves in an absorbing game of fantasy football. There was an immense amount of puerile pleasure derived from winding up Arsenal fans with bogus news stories proclaiming the departure to Stamford Bridge of Viera and Henry, to say nothing of the fun I had when I convinced my mate Chiller the Hammer that West Ham had signed a deal to become Chelsea's feeder club.

I had one date in my mind though, Friday July 25th, the date when the draw would be made for the third qualifying round of the Champions League; the stage at which Chelsea would enter the competition.

Fantasy football... what fantasy? This was reality... The Roman Empire was taking shape, true to his word Mr Abramovich was spending and spending big. The promising young legionnaire Johnson arrived from West Ham along with Geremi from Real Madrid, Bridge from Southampton and Duff from Blackburn, the latter for a club record fee of £17 million.

All in all almost £37 million had been spent in just 21 days by the time the team departed to compete in a pre season tournament in Malaysia. As we waited for news of the draw a new version of the *'Carefree'* chant was doing the rounds via text message and email.

'Debt free wherever we may be, we're gonna buy everyone we see... and we don't give a fuck about the transfer fee, cos we are the wealthy C.F.C.'

MSK ZILINA
UEFA Champions League
3rd Qualifying Round, 1st Leg
Stadion MSK, Zilina, Slovakia
Wednesday 13th August 2003

'Are you up for it Young Dave?'

'Does the pope shit in the woods Marco?'

'Don't you mean a bear Young Dave?'

'Yeah whatever son... I've almost cleared it with the missus, so count me in.'

I finished my conversation with Young Dave, clunked the telephone receiver back into its cradle and clapped my hands. The waiting was over, well almost; It was a little after 11am on Friday 25th July and my work schedule had been temporarily put on hold whilst I flicked around between the Chelsea official website and those of Sky Sports and the BBC looking for details of the draw for the 3rd qualifying round of the Champions League, the stage at which we would enter the competition. None of the sites seemed to be running any real-time coverage of the draw and so with increasing frustration I began to look elsewhere.

Just before midday I came across the official UEFA website which yielded the information I was looking for. Chelsea would play either Maccabi Tel Aviv of Israel or MSK Zilina of Slovakia, with the away leg being played first on August 13th.

I spent the afternoon researching travel options and finding out if anyone else was up for the trip. The first thing I established was that if Maccabi, the favourites on paper, won through then the venue for the away leg was subject to a UEFA ruling.

Chelsea had famously been eliminated from the UEFA cup two seasons earlier by Hapoel Tel Aviv. At the time the Middle East peace process was being tested to breaking point by a vicious cycle of terrorism and counter terrorism. In the week leading up to the away leg of the tie the Israeli minister for tourism had been assassinated prompting senior

15

club officials to lobby UEFA in an attempt to get the tie switched to a neutral venue.

Their endeavours failed; the match went ahead in Tel Aviv and, with six members of the first team squad refusing to travel, Chelsea were beaten 2-0. The media loved it, and for a time it became a divisive issue amongst our support particularly when a full strength side failed to over-turn the deficit in the return leg at Stamford Bridge.

With no end to the troubles in sight UEFA eventually ruled that Israeli teams must play their home fixtures at a neutral venue. This season Maccabi found themselves playing at 'home' in Budapest although in the week intervening the 1st and 2nd legs of their tie with Zilina, UEFA were scheduled to review this arrangement. The press latched onto the story immediately as did the chairman of Maccabi who labelled Chelsea 'cowards' for allegedly making a request to UEFA that the arrangement remain in place.

Against the odds MSK Zilina took a 1-0 1st leg lead to Budapest and, as they did so, UEFA ruled that should Maccabi win through on aggregate they would continue to play 'home' fixtures in Budapest.

From a time and money perspective a Maccabi victory was the preferred option. Budapest was well served by frequent, reasonably priced, scheduled flights and accommodation, if it were to be required, would be plentiful and cheap.

The internet is an invaluable tool to the travelling football fan. Inside a quarter of an hour I had established that Zilina was 200km to the north-west of the Slovakian capital city Bratislava, and that the cheapest return flights to the capital were showing up as being a budget breaking £588. I kept my fingers crossed for Maccabi Tel Aviv.

Match Result
Maccabi Tel-Aviv FC 1 v MSK Zilina 1
MSK Zilina win 2-1 on aggregate.
'Bloody typical!'

* * *

Young Dave was a family man who radiated morals and a particular kind of robust decency that the so called moral majority (non Chelsea supporting general public) might not necessarily associate with the followers of Chelsea Football Club.

The proprietor of a thriving restaurant business in Bath, a city I'd once had the pleasure of living in for a couple of years in the early 80s, Young Dave had embarked on a personal west country crusade down the years preaching the gospel of Chelsea to the heathen, carrot crunching, hordes who would otherwise have ended up following the likes of Manchester United, Liverpool or Arsenal.

Not quite fifty years old, Young Dave was not so young anymore but his passion for the club remained intact and his enthusiasm for, and knowledge of, the game of football verged on the encyclopaedic.

Young Dave had phoned to tell me that Mrs Young Dave was now onside and that he would definitely be up for the trip to Zilina if I could put together an itinerary which would see us complete the round trip in around 36 hours. I'd then added a further caveat; a budget of £250 per person all in.

Following Chelsea is a very expensive hobby, my season ticket for the Mathew Harding Upper Stand had increased to £715. If you factored in travel, food, the odd drink or six in the One Bar, and assorted sundry items, you could quite easily treble that figure over the course of a season.

European games weren't factored into the season ticket price and if Chelsea progressed to the group stage of the competition that would involve six matches, three at home and three away, all to be played before Christmas. Reaching the final would require Chelsea playing a further six matches with the final itself to be played in Gelsenkirchen, Germany. In total fifteen games... that would represent a serious financial investment!

Being single and not having kids to worry about made it easier for me to contemplate turning my dream about being an integral part of Chelsea's European odyssey into reality. For Young Dave this was payback time, he'd worked hard to build up a successful business, put his kids through school and give Mrs Young Dave a taste of the good life.

The rest of the Gate 17 boys, including Young Dave's son Hip Hop Dan, would, like the vast majority of Chelsea supporters, be cherry picking selected away trips and budgeting accordingly.

Apart from the craic, what were they missing through staying at home? Every game would be shown live on TV. Even this qualifier against Zilina had been picked up by the BBC for a paltry £50,000 and, given the surge in interest in Chelsea Football Club, was being screened live on BBC2.

The thing is it's more than just a craic... I could never quite put my finger on it, but there was something about following Chelsea over land and sea that was both beguiling and addictive.

*   *   *

The official Chelsea website gave details on ticketing arrangements for the game, the capacity of the Zilina ground was just over 6000 and Chelsea's allocation was 500 tickets. Tickets, at a cost of £20 each, would be issued in the form of vouchers to personal callers at the box office only with the strict proviso that passport, travel and accommodation details had to be supplied by way of a completed application form for each ticket required.

The official Chelsea website was up to date and informative, and the ticketing information precise... it had to be; there are however several independent websites which are of far greater use to supporters who are unable to call at the box office in person or who are seeking general information about travel and accommodation options for all away fixtures.

The best of these is the Chelsea Ticket Exchange which acts as an online notice board allowing Chelsea fans to buy / sell / exchange tickets with the minimum of fuss.

During my initial and hasty evaluation of the available travel options I had overlooked the fact that the Slovak Republic is located at the precise geographic centre of Europe. Slovakia borders five other countries: Austria, the Czech Republic, Hungary, Poland and Ukraine.

The European travel section on the Chelsea Ticket Exchange website had already been updated to provide several viable options for those wishing to travel to Zilina. Via Bratislava was one of them, the other two were via Vienna or Prague. Flying to Vienna and either hiring a car or taking the train looked like the best option. Vienna was just 60km from Bratislava whereas Prague was over 320km away.

Expedia have an excellent user friendly website which can be used not only to check out times, dates and prices but to book flights as well. Registration is quick, easy and free. Via Expedia I'd quickly ascertained that British Airways had a direct flight to Vienna which left at 07.25am arriving at 10.40am. With the match scheduled to kick off at 20.15pm, a timely arrival would allow us sufficient time, one way or another, to make the onward journey to Zilina.

The return flight options were slightly more restrictive. Unless we wanted to spend a whole day or more out in either Slovakia or Austria we would have to take the 07.40am flight back to London the following morning. The cost of the flights including taxes was a very reasonable £168. The margin for error though was negligible, there were a number of risks... getting to Heathrow on time... getting to Zilina on time... getting back to Vienna on time, although the latter would only be up for consideration after we'd seen the match. Getting to the game was the number one priority.

Young Dave also played a part in determining our final travel arrangements. He'd bought a map of central Europe, and as I confirmed the flight details to him over the phone he told me that it looked like the regional motorway network was efficient enough to make car hire, if we could organise it, a real alternative to relying on public transport.

Outside the UK you could generally guarantee that bus and rail services were cheap, timely and reliable, however given the tightness of our schedule we couldn't allow for any delays; hiring a car would be costly but it put our destiny firmly in our own hands.

I checked out the Hertz website and found out that to hire a small Ford Fiesta type car would cost around 160 Euros which was about £100. The only admonition on the rental agreement was the requirement that additional insurance be purchased as the car was being driven 'abroad'.

* * *

With the travel arrangements sorted, and given the fact that the capacity of the ground was tiny, I decided to take a drive up to Stamford Bridge on Sunday morning and sort out the match tickets.

I arrived just before the box office opened at 10am, I needn't have worried about having to queue... Chelsea Village was deserted.

'Chelsea Village... who'd 've thought it eh?' I nodded, and smiled inwardly. We live in a football world that creates and breeds envy, jealousy and arrogance... I used to be a jealous fan, but not anymore. I turned around and looked at the skilfully preserved Shed End wall, and as I did so a gleefully blasphemous chant came to mind.

'*Fuck 'em all, fuck 'em all... United, West Ham, Liverpool... cos we are the Chelsea and we are the best... We are the Chelsea so fuck all the rest...*'

Before the Taylor Report was implemented and the ground started to be redeveloped into an all seated stadium I'd spent season after season watching proceedings on the pitch from high up on the Shed terrace by the old tea bar. '*We are the Chelsea and we are the best...*' we'd sang whilst a biting December wind whipped up the rain and lashed it scornfully across our faces as we'd witnessed 'star studded' Wimbledon take our flat footed defence to pieces again.

Nothing more than propagandists that's what we were, having to bite our boastful tongues, doomed forever to remain in the shadows of the more illustrious teams we ridiculed in song.

Not now though, Chelsea were no longer banging on the door marked success we were threatening to kick it off its hinges. The recent cup triumphs were a statement of intent and up until three weeks ago the club, shouldering crippling debt and with no money to invest in new players, had relied on the tinkering of the brilliantly eccentric Claudio Ranieri to guide it to within two matches of the serious financial breathing space which qualification to the group stages of the Champions League represented.

But that was then... and this was now. Abramovich had taken away the heavy burden of uncertainty over the clubs future; until now none of us had fully understood the financial plight the club had been in or the dire consequences that failure on the pitch in that last game of last season against Liverpool would have represented.

"Abramovich has parked his tanks on our lawn and is firing £50 notes at us", was the profound observation made by a bemused David Dein, vice chairman of our North London rivals Arsenal.

Fantastic! I just couldn't wait. I purchased two 'tickets' for the Zilina game. Good old Batesy, you had to laugh; the 'tickets' were Chelsea tickets printed Stamford Bridge East Stand Lower!... Face value £20, which probably equated to several weeks wages in Slovakia!

I wondered how much of the £20 was going to Zilina and how much to Chelsea? Three days after we had beaten Liverpool on May 11th my ticket for the home leg of the Zilina tie, to be played over three months later on August 26th, turned up at my house; the cost, £30, debited from my account already... things must have been really tight indeed!

I asked if the 'tickets' I had just acquired would have to be exchanged for bona fide match tickets at Zilina's ground and was told that the legendary Eddie Barnett, Chelsea's affable Scouse box office supremo, would be on hand at the allocated Chelsea turnstile personally waiting to greet us and show us to our seats... now seeing that would be worth a significant portion of the admission money alone.

*   *   *

'Well it's brilliant innit... but what he hasn't bought yet is a mugger, y'know a real grappler, a spoiler an 'orrible guard dog like Roy Keane.' Young Dave finished pontificating about Chelsea's latest acquisitions and gulped down his first Guinness Extra Cold of the evening. He could profer endless blokeish chat about football and I for one was always a willing listener.

Young Dave had travelled over from Bath by train and we were sitting in my local drinker admiring the barmaids tattoos whilst discussing the matters at hand. It had been another blisteringly hot day in a month of blisteringly hot days and the Guinness was purposefully slaking my thirst.

'That Geremi looks hard though... played well for Boro last season, he can hold the ball up well,' I opined, nodding at the barmaid as I put my empty glass on the counter.

'Dunno about Veron though... never really did it for the scum did he... nah, Duff though he's quality what a pre-season he's had... he'll put some crosses in the box... we just need a world class striker to knock 'em in... Eidur's too fat and Jimmy's heart aint in it anymore if you ask me.'

This being pre-season the newspapers were busy promoting their 'fantasy football' competitions and in our 'fantasy' team we had Duff, Veron, Joe Cole, Geremi, Bridge and Johnson. The fantastic thing was though, this was no fantasy; for years Chelsea had struggled painfully to bridge the gulf between potential and accomplishment but now here we were, on the eve of our European adventure, speculating about which world class player we would buy next.

'Mutu he's class... top scorer in Serie A last season, he could do a job for us... or Vieri... Crespo ha ha Beckham... buuuuuuurp... now that would be something... '

Young Dave belched loudly and lengthily as he mentioned the England captains name, personally I was just glad that the wind was confined to one end, Guinness Extra Cold could be a real trouser browner if you were unfortunate enough to shart... sharting being the short code Gate 17 word for a fart with follow through.

'Yeah Becks... he'll be in a Chelsea shirt soon Young Dave I tell ya... have you seen him poncing around Madrid struggling with the language?... And that's before he's even started on the Spanish ha ha... Victoria's made no secret about wanting to live in London.'

*   *   *

Young Dave was stood on the low wall outside the front of my house; for 5am he looked tolerably alert, like one of those long nosed mastiffs that scavenge for bones around the tables in those faded pictures of renaissance banquets that hang on the greying walls of my local drinker the Gamecock.

His wiry physique was similar to that of a flyweight boxer, but a night on the Guinness had distended his stomach and right now he resembled a pencil that had swallowed a football.

We were travelling light, very light; our clothes were utilitarian and daywear focussed... no scarves or colours to attract the attention of officialdom either in this country or the two we were about to visit. I picked up my Stone Island denim jacket from the floor, stood up and winked at Young Dave as I pointed down the road at the dark grey Vauxhall Vectra that was making its way slowly towards us.

Clive the Gooner, Sex Case to his friends, was a highly engaging man whose appetite for life stood out like a beacon in a sea of griege. I'd often remarked that it was a shame he was a Gooner because his colourfully expressed opinions, brio and wit were obviously wasted on a crowd of supporters who in recent years seemed to have developed the charisma of a knitting pattern.

Sex Case owed me a couple of favours and, since he had to be in Sheffield by 9am, he'd kindly offered to give us a lift to Heathrow airport which at this time of the morning was a brisk 30 minute drive away. The talk on the journey was small; it was too early for ribald football banter, Young Dave and I were just beginning to develop hangover symptoms and Sex Case seemed more concerned with the large boil on the end of his nose than our little ruse that Chelsea's audacious £100 million bid for Henry, Pires, Vierra and Wiltord was likely to be accepted later in the day.

*   *   *

Terminal One was already very busy by the time we arrived, business commuters scurrying haphazardly from ticket counter to check in; a sea of faces all wearing the same anxious 'can't be late' expressions as they looked up at the monitors displaying the details of the mornings departures.

The beauty of electronic ticketing is the elimination of the need to check in. All you do is insert the credit card you booked the flight with into the e-ticket machine and seconds later it prints out your tickets with the seat numbers already allocated, it will even print out the tickets for the return flight if you request it to do so.

The flight, which was full, left on time and as it did so I nudged Young Dave and nodded at a group of four men sat four rows in front of us. They were all of similar ages to ourselves and similarly attired. They were Chelsea, had to be... not a brief case amongst them... and besides Stone Island casual wear and Union Jack lapel badges are a dead giveaway to the trained eye.

I eased my seat back and started to browse through the in-flight magazine but I was finding it increasingly hard to keep my trained eyes open. Within a few minutes of taking off the soporific drone of the planes engines had lullabyed me to leep.

The transit through Vienna airport was uneventful; there were two booths at the Hertz car rental desk, Young Dave stood at one filling out the required paperwork and the four blokes sat near to us on the plane were crowded around the other.

I looked at my watch it was just after 11.15am, perfect... everything was going to plan. As I waited for Young Dave I busied myself sending my customary 'The Eagle Has Landed' text message to the Gate 17 boys and to my 'Uncle' Robert who just happened to be in Zilina.

Our hire car for the day was a very modest little Volkswagen Polo without the luxury of air conditioning or electric windows. After several minutes Young Dave had mastered the vagaries of the vehicles controls and in particular a rather excitable gearbox and we were on our way.

* * *

The landscape was verdant and bathed in sunshine. Music would have made for a pleasant soundtrack to the journey but someone had stolen the car aerial rendering the radio redundant, however this was of little consequence to Young Dave and I who were more concerned with keeping cool as the temperature continued to rise.

With the exception of a couple of missed exits which lengthened the journey by some 10km, the first leg of the drive was uneventful and we arrived at the Austrian / Slovakian border checkpoint, which was unnervingly deserted, a little after midday.

Eastern European border checkpoints and their staff are, in reality, exactly identical to the way they are portrayed in the movies. Cold grey concrete boxes manned by surly, humourless, machine pistol toting guards whose sworn duty it was to intimidate and detain Westerners impertinent enough to disrespect them.

The officer who checked our passports at the Austrian exit checkpoint was friendly enough. A large, moustachioed man in an ill fitting uniform who looked more like a fluffer from a low budget porn film than someone tasked with the weighty responsibility of playing a part in upholding the national security of his country.

Porn Star rubbed his stubbly chin and nodded at Young Dave who dipped the Polo's clutch and eased the car forward to the Slovakian entry checkpoint. As Young Dave handed our passports over to be checked I couldn't help but notice the two uniformed border guards that were stood by the red and white entry barrier adjacent to the checkpoint office. One of them, clearly a woman, pointed at the registration plate of our car and as she did so she began to walk purposefully towards us.

I, like most men, love the idea of the female as a predator especially when she is dressed in a military uniform and carrying a gun. There's something about a woman in uniform, particularly an authoritative one, that distracts me to the point of fantasy. I'm a sucker for the sexual tick of the unexpected and the frisson that comes from imagining that underneath that uniform the woman might be wearing stockings suspenders and a lacey peephole bra.

My wandering mind was returned to reality by Young Dave who had fallen victim to 'pidgin English syndrome'... that strange affliction which affects all of us when we are abroad and faced with a decidedly difficult to negotiate language barrier.

'We are Chelsea... to see... Chelsea... football team of London, England...,' Young Dave mumbled, in an accent which could have placed him anywhere from Prestatyn to Pakistan. 'We come to watch our team play your worthy champions of Slovakia... Zil... er Zilee... Zilina,' he continued, before shrugging his shoulders and turning to me and asking for help.

'Marco... Marco you don't speak any Slovakian do you?'

'Not really mate, but Teddy taught me some Bulgarian... might be similar, you never know eh,' I replied, keeping my eyes trained on the rear view mirror and watching the female border guard as she looked quizzically at the back of our car.

'Go on then son... have a word with laughing boy here before he gets all serious on us with that shooter.' Young Dave leaned back and winked at the guard before pointing at me.

'Dobry den... ja som Anglican... prosim si chlieb e maslo.' I said confidently, biting my lip to prevent myself smiling.

I had no idea what the guard said in reply as he raised his previously furrowed eyebrows and pointed at the small be-flagged kiosk which was some 30 metres away adjacent to a small car park.

'Nasdravie.' I nodded, and gave him the thumbs up, prodding an increasingly wide eyed Young Dave in the ribs as I did so. The guard gave the OK symbol to his colleagues and raised the barrier; Young Dave engaged first gear, eased his foot off the clutch and kangarooed the Volkswagen Polo into Slovakia; as he did so I raised my hands and grimaced Mediterranean style at the female border guard who was trying hard to maintain the required level of decorum whilst witnessing our Pythonesque performance.

'Blimey Marco what did you say to that bloke?' Young Dave asked, as he parked the car in one of the bays by the kiosk. 'Whatever it was it did the trick... d'ya know anymore of the local lingo?'

'I said, hello we're English and we'd like some bread and butter,... but that's all mate, dunno anymore... at least we wont starve eh,' I replied, as we both got out of the car and surveyed the scene.

It was a very hot day but at least we were easily acclimatised, having just enjoyed the hottest weekend on record back in Blighty. I looked back across the border and then down the motorway, the haze serving to blur my vision. What I noticed was the difference in the quality of the road surface on either side of the border, obviously Austria had more money to invest in maintaining its infrastructure than its next door neighbour and this was something that was to become more evident as we continued our journey.

We had changed some Euros for Slovak Koruna whilst we were at the airport in Vienna. On hiring the car we'd been told that we would need to purchase a travel permit to enable us to drive on the motorways in Slovakia. The permit, which was valid for 15 days, cost 100 Sk (about £2) and was purchased from the kiosk along with a couple of litres of bottled water.

Young Dave, who had spent some time studying the map before we'd set off, was convinced it would take no more than a couple of hours to drive to Zilina. So, with time on our side, we decided that we would break up the journey and stop for some lunch at a town called Trencin which, according to the map, was some 30km south of our final destination.

The journey from the border to Trencin passed by without incident; the motorway which had very little traffic on it, seemed somehow out of place carving its way as it did through fields of bright yellow sunflowers which seemed to glow as they reflected the brilliant sunshine.

To the east the agrarian plains gave way to imposing conifer clad slopes whose green canvas was broken up by isolated castles and picturesque churches. Young Dave and I sat in silence as we sped along the motorway marvelling at a vista that was clearly made in heaven.

Slovakia, a nation of 5 million people, separated from Czechoslovakia in 1993. The 'Velvet Divorce' as it was called had been executed in a democratic and largely uneventful way; a marked contrast to the dictatorial way in which Czechoslovakia, on two occasions (1918 and 1945), and Slovakia, once (1939), had been created.

Czechoslovakia was no more a true nation state than say the USSR or Yugoslavia whose assemblages, masterminded by a ruling minority, had been glued together by force.

Slovakia has a rural tradition and there was little evidence of modern industry in or around the cities that we passed through on our way to Trencin. The motorway lacked the usual congestion associated with interchanges adjacent to major conurbations and the conurbations themselves, a mix of out of place high-rise tower blocks and low lying red roofed buildings, seemed lifeless for the time of day.

The city of Trencin, and the fortified castle that overlooked it, was clearly visible from the motorway. Without encountering too many navigational problems, Young Dave had been able to drive right into Peace Square in the centre of what was known as Old Town... in doing this he had however created a problem, because 'Old Town' was obviously a pedestrian area.

A mixture of pidgin English and sign language enabled us to find a legitimate place to park near Peace Square and, with a set time limit of one hour, we went in search of something to eat.

Trencin was evidently a city of some historical and cultural significance and as Young Dave and I made our way through Peace Square we noted two things. Firstly, there was a refreshing absence of the McDonalds-style commercialism that plagued the whole of Western Europe and secondly,... or should that be firstly... the women, all the women, seemed to exude a natural beauty and self possession that was unsullied by the wear of everyday life.

Peace Square was a potpourri of striking architecture dominated by a column erected in 1713 to commemorate the lives of those who had died during the plague epidemics. We could have done the tourist thing for slightly longer than the two minutes we spent scratching our stubbly chins in awe at the ornate elegance of the Piarist Church, but Young Dave's quest for food had gathered momentum and it wasn't long before a walk down one of the many narrow cobbled passageways that led off the square found us in a quiet courtyard standing opposite what looked like a very high class restaurant.

Like most Eastern European languages Slovakian in spoken format is impenetrable. Trying to make sense of what was written on the menu, even to a restaurateur of Young Dave's calibre, was like trying to understand ancient Egyptian hieroglyphics... impossible! Young Dave had one Slovakian word in his vocabulary though, a very important one... Pivo... beer!

'Yes... please we are sorry we no speak Slovakian... English from Chelsea football club, London... please Pivo... Pivo,' pleaded Young Dave, as his west country burr once again took on a mysterious Indian lilt. The waitress looked at me and then at Young Dave her face breaking out into an embarrassed grin as she finally made the connection.

Ordering food was obviously going to be a problem. This was no manky caff microwaving scrambled eggs and serving rehydrated burgers, this was a bonafide restaurant offering the finest in Slovakian haute cuisine... if only we could understand a single word on the menu.

Fortunately, help was at hand; when the waitress returned with our beers, she also produced another menu. This one had a section translated into English, although on closer inspection it became apparent that the translator was obviously a close relative of Young Dave's pidgin English teacher.

We both settled for a main course of 'Pork Like Your Grandmother' with side dishes of 'Wild Fired Potatoes' and 'Boils Greens'. It turned out to be a very good call; pan fried pork cutlets, chips and green beans was the dish of the day. I looked at the healthy portion on my plate and licked my cracked lips in anticipation catching my distorted reflection on the polished steel salver the waitress was holding as I did so.

It wasn't a flattering image; if anything my flaking, sunburnt scalp made me look like a diseased iguana... and if I looked that handsome I wondered what Young Dave's reflection might resemble?

Poor Young Dave; he was so old, legend had it that when he'd joined Friends Reunited Moses had got in touch. Aged he may have been, but his slow deliberate manner, salty humour, madcap jokes and blatant defiance of authority made him the most entertaining of travel companions.

Fortified by 'Pork Like Your Grandmother', and with our thirsts quenched by several flagons of the local pivo, we were ready for the final leg of the journey to Zilina. Our meal, drinks and a decent tip had cost roughly a fiver... *'Champions League... we're havin' a laugh... Champions League we're havin' a laugh,'* I hummed to myself as we made our way back to the car.

* * *

Sheltered by two mountain ranges, Zilina is situated near the Polish border at the confluence of the Rajcanca, Kysuca and Vah Rivers. A population of only 85,000 still made it the third largest city in Slovakia.

It took less than an hour to complete the final leg of the journey. Once we'd arrived in Zilina, Young Dave took it upon himself to complete three laps of the cities ring road citing that this would enable him to gain his bearings. Initially I thought that this 'gaining of bearings' was something he was doing to replace the marbles he had clearly lost, but then I began to understand his rationale.

On the first circuit we found the football ground and the railway station, on the second Budatin Castle, and when we passed the railway station for a third time Young Dave left the ring road and found a parking place in a side street which seemed clear of the restrictions we'd encountered in Trencin.

It was almost 4pm local time and still stiflingly hot. What was plainly apparent from our limited knowledge of Slovakian cities was that each seemed to have an 'Old Town' whose focal point of life was the main square. We set off walking away from the ring road, guessing that in a city so small it wouldn't take too long to find the centre.

'Uncle' Robert, whom I'd been in touch with as we'd driven into

Zilina, had sent me a text message telling me to listen up for the chanting and follow my ears. After a couple of minutes I stopped in my tracks and nudged Young Dave. 'Listen mate... can you hear em?' I said, cocking my head like a gun dog.

Young Dave nodded as the familiar strains of '*Carefree*', which could be clearly heard above the sound of the traffic, grew louder.

The first square that we found ourselves in was a modern affair. In one corner workmen were busy erecting a huge TV screen adjacent to a large open air bar. The opposite side of the square was dominated, somewhat bizarrely, by a huge branch of Tesco!

'Old Town' was reached by walking through the new square and then climbing up a series of fairly steep stone steps that eventually levelled out into a walled courtyard. Parched as we both were, we couldn't help but stop, look, and be tremendously impressed by everything that we saw.

Looking back down the hill we could see the football ground that, given our perspective, looked as if it had been hewn into the precipitous conifer clad hillside which formed a natural defence to the south of the city; behind us was the turreted Church of the Holy Trinity and the Burian Tower, an imposing belfry whose bells began to ring out loud and clear to mark the passing of the hour... it was now 4pm.

Every view was picture postcard perfect and, whilst the diversity of these views were momentarily breathtaking, the chiming of the bells quickly snapped us out of tourist mode and re-focussed our minds on why we were in Zilina.

The town square was surrounded by arcaded burgher houses, shops, restaurants and bars. On any other afternoon it would have been respectfully quiet, but today Chelsea were in town and its two main bars were bustling with life. Both of them similarly populated by a small congregation of flag waving blue shirted Chelsea fans singing in unison.

'*We are the famous... the famous Chelsea.*'

'*Zilina... Zilina... Zilina,*' chanted a harmless looking group of local youths, as they walked through the square bedecked in the Norwich Cityesque yellow and green of MSK Zilina.

'*Who are ya?... Who are ya?... Who are ya?*' The reply was predictable and lighthearted, there was no sign here of the bigotry and willingness to be violently contentious that had previously tarnished the reputation of our travelling support.

*   *   *

'Oi Marco... over here son.'

I recognised the gravelly voice immediately; it was that of my 'Uncle' Robert who was sat outside a bar on the opposite side of the square. 'Uncle' Robert wasn't my uncle really, but it felt like that. I'd known him since my formative years as a Chelsea fan; he was a terrace legend then, the butcher of the North Stand they used to call him... a man with a fearsome reputation whose girlfriend at the time just happened to live on our estate.

We walked over to his table and shook hands. 'Uncle' Robert must be in his fifties now but he'd kept himself in shape. Deeply suntanned, his craggy features, piercing blue eyes and full head of grey hair gave him the appearance of a matinee idol... my ex-wife thought he looked like Mel Gibson, but I couldn't see the resemblance myself.

'Uncle' Robert now lived in the Middle East state of Oman, I wasn't entirely sure why, or what it was exactly that he did out there. With some people its best not to pry, and this was the reason why I didn't ask too many questions about the people he was sat with; a youngish, freckle faced woman with a toothpaste ad smile called Charlie, and a ruddy cheeked, chain smoking, middle-aged man who went by the whimsical name of Tricky Dickie.

Young Dave and I sat down and 'Uncle' Robert ordered a round of drinks; the waitress who brought them over was tall, blonde and willowy with big blue eyes, a porcelain complexion and an elegant manner... a proverbial drink on a stick, who would grace any bar she worked in.

I made a mental note to remind Tara, the landlady of the One Bar, that she should place an advert in the Zilina Gazette next time she was looking for female bar staff.

When he went to the toilet, 'Uncle' Robert told us that Tricky Dickie had once been a Tottenham fan and that it was a condition of their business partnership, whatever that was, that he now supported Chelsea.

When 'Uncle' Robert went to the toilet, Tricky Dickie told us that this would probably be the only game they came to this season... but he didn't say why.

Unfortunately, Charlie didn't need to use the toilet whilst we were in her company so I didn't get to find out what the nature of her relationship was with either 'Uncle' Robert or Tricky Dickie.

We had a light hearted discussion about the old times, which was interspersed with observations from Tricky Dickie about the exquisiteness of the womenfolk of Zilina. Womenfolk who continued to attract a chorus of admiring wolf whistles and cries of 'she'd get it' as they walked on by through the square past the admiring eyes of the Chelsea boys.

'Uncle' Robert made a pledge to me that if I ever needed any help with tickets for future games in Europe, he'd 'sort it' for me as he had a few contacts inside the new organisation.

Fantastic! I thought, not knowing whether to believe him or not. I looked out across the square, at our lads drinking and chatting amongst themselves, at the locals going about their daily business and never once did I think about anything that might be going on back at home... following Chelsea in Europe was, without a doubt, the perfect antidote to real life.

*   *   *

We stayed at the bar for an hour or so before bidding farewell to 'Uncle' Robert, Tricky Dickie and Charlie and meandering unhurriedly back through the town to the car. On the way we came across a souvenir shop selling all manner of items related to the city of Zilina and its football team.

I bought a pennant and a couple of postcards. I had this schoolboy urge to collect the pennants of all the teams we played against in this seasons competition, harbouring the notion that if we won the tournament I'd put them all in a nice frame which would hang on a wall somewhere in my house.

'Yeah... season 2003–2004... the first time Chelsea won the European Champions League... I attended every game.' I could see myself now. A rheumy eyed, snuffly old man pointing at each of the pennants in turn and regaling nostalgic tales of past glories on foreign fields to a wide-eyed nephew or grandson just into their first full season worshipping at the temple that is Stamford Bridge.

'Oi Marco... look... look over there.' Young Dave snapped me out of my daydream as he prodded me in the ribs and pointed at a woman who was stood at the corner of the street where our car, in which we were now sat, was parked. She was chattering into her mobile phone, face partially hidden, lithe limbs tanned a golden brown, looking elegant in a slinky white skirt and black sweater... peerless.

'Your milk and two eh Marco heh heh?' Young Dave winked at me as he turned the key in the ignition.

'Not half Young Dave... n n n n not h h half m m mate,' I stuttered, as he jolted the car forward. 'She's just my cup of tea.'

As we drove past the girl, Young Dave tooted the Polo's horn. She looked up and smiled at us, a sweetly vacant smile that stayed with me for the ten minutes or so it took to drive to the ground.

*   *   *

The road leading up to the 'stadium' was uneven and potholed, its kerb-side overgrown with weeds. Harsh unintelligible graffiti was scrawled along the entire length of the high concrete wall that separated the road from the adjacent railway line.

The car park outside the ground was half full and we reasoned that given an expected crowd of 6000, it wouldn't take too long to retrieve the Polo after the match if we parked it here. Our final plan was to drive directly to Bratislava after the game and have a few beers there before crossing the Austrian border and heading back to Vienna airport.

Young Dave reverse parked the Polo into a space between a rusty Skoda and a battered old Trabant and cut the engine. As he did so, the unmistakable match day football ground aroma wafted in through the cars open windows.

'Smell that Young Dave... smells like onions fried in diesel,' I remarked, wrinkling my nose up and smiling. 'Same the world over, nothing quite like it eh mate,' I continued, unbuckling my seat belt and stretching out my arms.

Young Dave sat back in his seat and inhaled deeply, drawing the oddly perfumed air into his lungs as if it were a magical cure for some terrible respiratory ailment.

'Tell you what it smells of Marco... it smells... it smells of victory.' Young Dave patted his chest with both hands as he exhaled slowly.

With our bastardised version of the Robert Duval, Apocalypse Now, 'That's Napalm' soliloquy at an end we wound up the windows and got out of the car checking to make sure that anything of any importance was out of sight or locked in the boot.

On every single trip abroad there always seems to be at least one person I encounter whose appearance and mannerisms remain etched in my memory ready to be recalled at some point in the future when fireside stories are being told on a cold winters evening in the Gamecock

Zilina was to prove no different. We had walked only a few metres from the car when we were confronted by a gyroscopically unstable giant of a man whose mullet haircut, gravestone teeth, and body contours would have given him the opportunity to eke out a comfortable living playing the villain to anyone of Stallone's or Schwarzenegger's Hollywood superheroes.

The only problem was, this wasn't a film set and the child frighteningly hideous monster confronting us now hadn't spent several hours in make up... he was for real. The giant pointed a gnarled hand at our car and spoke with a huge booming voice that resonated like a rumbling thunderclap.

'There is a problem with the car?' Young Dave looked up at the giant and removed his yellow baseball cap, scratching his head Stan Laurel style as he did so. 'We are from England... Chelsea FC London... yes to see them play your mighty green and yellows of Zilina,' he continued, in his default second language.

The thought crossed my mind that the giant could be nominating on behalf of some hitherto unseen gang of psychotically violent, xenophobic MSK Zilina fans in which case Young Dave's wilfully stupid admission of our nationality would be tantamount to signing both our death warrants.

I looked around the car park, nobody was paying any attention to the giant; all the Zilina supporters were making their way to the bars at what was clearly their 'end' of the stadium. Well at least that was encouraging; I looked at Young Dave who was still scratching his head, and then at the giant who was now on his knees pointing at the Polo's number plate.

'Wien... Wien... meine schwester wohnt in Wien und ich will dass du dorthin fahrst um sie zu ficken.'

The giant was grinning now and roaring with laughter as I began to nod my head giving him the OK symbol and pointing at Young Dave as I did so. Realising that we didn't speak Slovakian, and thinking we were Austrian, he was trying to communicate with us in something resembling the level of German I could understand and recall from my time at school.

'Ja Ja,' I replied in my best Anglo German, my accent perfected from watching too many episodes of Colditz when I was a kid. I nodded at the giant who was now back on his feet and towering over me.

'Mein freund vill ficken your schwester venn vee get back to Wien after ze game ja,' I continued confidently, biting my tongue when I'd finished speaking and trying to remain poker faced.

The giant continued to bellow with laughter as he gave us the thumbs up sign and waved us on our way with a huge sweeping gesture of the type normally reserved for visiting foreign dignitaries.

*   *   *

The stadium, or stadion as it was known locally, was dual purpose; the section we had entered was in fact an ice hockey rink complete with two teams of school kids playing with enthusiastic zeal in front of a hundred or so friends and relatives.

Young Dave went off to the bar and returned with a couple of extra large beers and a packet of cigarettes and we sat down in the refreshingly cool atmosphere of the ice rink and relaxed.

'Marco... er... so what was the giant... er going on about?' Young Dave paused as he asked the inevitable question to draw deeply on the Marlboro he had just lit. 'What the fuck did you tell him, you weren't offering him some bread and butter were you?'

'Nah mate... better than that,' I replied, sparking up a welcome cigarette myself before continuing. 'The giant was interested in our car because it's got Austrian plates and his sister lives in Wien which is what we call Vienna. He wanted to know if we would go and visit her when we got back to Vienna and give her a good fucking... so I told him that you would be only too happy to sort her out.'

'Bloody hell Marco... whaddya say that for? I couldn't ever be unfaithful to Mrs Young Dave and besides imagine what his sister must look like... ugh, it's too 'orrible to even think about.' Young Dave grimaced as he considered his fate, shrugging his shoulders and shivering as he did so.

It was too cool in the ice hockey rink, in fact it was positively Baltic so we finished our drinks back in the bar and then walked out into the car park.

The sun had just started to dip behind the hills but if anything it had become warmer, the atmosphere felt muggy and I nodded as Young Dave pointed at the large black clouds gathering on the horizon. It was going to rain at some point, 'that would make matters on the pitch more interesting than they were already,' I thought to myself, as we walked out of the car park and joined a group of thirty or so Chelsea fans noisily making their way down the road which ran alongside the ground.

The security presence at the entrance gate designated for Chelsea supporters was nothing more than functional and there, waiting to check our tickets as promised, was a slightly harassed looking Eddie Barnett.

'All right lads? Safe trip eh? Ha ha... come on in... come on in.' Eddie chirruped in his ever cheerful sing song Scouse accent. 'The seats are up there and the bars through there and they've got all the facilities... very nice soft toilet paper as well if you need to go,' he continued merrily.

The enthusiasm with which he shared this last piece of information led me to believe that poor Eddie's backside might have had a grazing encounter on more than one occasion with the more coarse grained variety of bog roll that was the bane of many supporters lives when they'd found themselves caught short and having to use the often primitive facilities in some of the less well appointed stadia on planet football.

Eddie Barnett had managed the box office at Stamford Bridge for as long as I could remember. He was one of those blokes who could be suited in Armani and still look scruffy, and this evening was no different.

Poor Eddie was sweating profusely; the blue shirt he was wearing bore ample evidence of that and to make matters worse his regulation club tie was knotted so tightly around his neck it made his eyes bulge unnaturally. If it wasn't for the fact that he seemed liked he was genuinely enjoying himself you'd have thought he was in the middle of having fatal heart attack!

I followed Young Dave as he eagerly bounded up the broad concrete steps into the section of the stand we were in that was reserved for Chelsea supporters. MSK Zilina may well have been the Slovakian champions but my first impression of their ground was that it reminded me of the efforts English non league clubs go to when they entertain league opposition in the FA Cup.

Both 'ends' were uncovered and the open terracing had given way to temporary plastic bucket seating. The main stand opposite us, in which 'Uncle' Robert told me he would be sitting, ran alongside the length of the pitch; it looked slightly dilapidated but functional enough.

To our left was a small paddock which was already full of Zilina supporters peering curiously at us through a wire mesh fence. To our right, a smaller rickety looking stand, again fenced off from our visitors area. The view of the pitch was more than adequate though and fortunately there was no perimeter fencing to spoil it.

The pitch itself looked like it hadn't seen rain for weeks; but just as Young Dave and I were discussing how this might prove to be a leveller, and how the press back home... not to mention the rapidly growing and resentful band of Chelsea haters, would love it if we screwed things up, the heavens opened.

This was rain, real rain, huge great stir rods of the stuff that came pelting out of the leaden clouds bouncing of the ground as it hit and collecting in rapidly forming puddles on the narrow asphalt track between the pitch and the stands.

A bolt of lightning arced across the sky and buried itself in the forested hillside visible at the far end of the tiny stadium, the crack of thunder that accompanied it seemed to physically shake the very ground we were stood on. I hoped that it wasn't a sign from the great god of football that something ominous was about to happen.

*   *   *

With three quarters of an hour to go before kick off we decided to repair to the bar and, with this being a Champions League fixture, avail ourselves of some Slovakian low alcohol lager that had an almost immediate bowel loosening effect on my constitution which gave me an immediate, albeit unplanned, opportunity to verify or refute Eddie Barnett's lofty claims about the stadiums toilet facilities.

Eddie was right, the khazi was immaculate, not even a single word of graffiti to attempt to understand while I waited for nature to take its course. I pulled out the program I'd bought and began to flick through the few pages it contained; adverts mainly; one for a restaurant, I think; one for a courier, I think; one for a company called Colspedia and finally one that covered the programs back page which was for a company called Tento.

Toaletny papier XXL it proclaimed, the rest of the unintelligible blurb was accompanied by pictures of toilet rolls which evidently came in Butterfly or Standard quality. I reached over to the toilet roll holder and tore off a sheet of the paper it contained, rubbing it between my thumb and forefinger as I did so. 'Definitely Butterfly quality that my son,' I said to myself confidently, as if I was participating in the bog roll equivalent of the Pepsi challenge.

Despite being very light on content the programme was huge on entertainment, containing as it did English transcripts of the articles on both clubs histories which were written in Slovakian. The transcripts could well have been written by Young Dave's pidgin English teacher, I sat there laughing my head off as I read about the 'History of Chelsea FC London.'

In the nineties Chelsea became a pioneer of changes in traditional English style play. The club under the leading of a president Ken Bates pushed an expansionary source policy and a few great names of world football removed annually to London. Chelsea is the first English Club which in a league match played with the base squad, which was all-composite from legionaries. A blue dress with a lion on a chest put on: Ruud Gullit, Gianlucca Vialli (both worked later in a function played coach, btw. as coaches), Brian Laudrup, George Weah, Didier Deschamps, Dan Petrescu, Tore Andre Flo, Frank Leboeuf and another. The favourite of London audience became Gianfranco Zola, but after the passed season he decided to return to Italy and he will play in Cagliari. The key change, during the summer pause, was the coming of the Russian petroleum magnate Roman Abramovich, who bought the major deal of the club and he has great planes in football business.

Outstanding, what a read and what a shame there wasn't much more of it. I finished my business with the aid of a few sheets of Tento's finest Butterfly quality toilet paper and made my way back out into the ground where I found Young Dave, who had taken up position four rows up from the front in the middle of our little pen, busy taking photographs of the Chelsea players who were going through their customary warm up routine under the watchful eye of Claudio Ranieri.

*   *   *

Thankfully the rain storm had lasted no more than ten minutes. As the air cleared an eerie mist began to rise from the pitch, and as it did so the celebrated Chelsea fan known as Spangle exercised his vocal chords and led the chanting for the first of many times that evening.

'*You are my Chelsea... my only Chelsea... you make me happy when skies are grey; You'll never notice how much I miss you... until you take my Chelsea away... la la la.*'

The Zilina fans in the meantime were being cajoled into singing by a couple of mullet haired rockers who were cavorting around the pitch wielding electric guitars and miming to a heavy metal rendition of the club song.

'*Loads and loads of money,*' was our response, as we waved the contents of our wallets at them.

The heavy metal sound of Zilina contrasted beautifully with the melody for our next two chants that according to my mother originated from an operatic piece composed by Guiseppe Verdi entitled 'La donna e mobile', the mobile bit being pronounced mo- beel-eh.

'*West Ham's our feeder club... West Hams our feeder club.*'

'*Roman Abramovich... Roman Abramovich.*'

There couldn't have been more than 350 of us present, the official figure from Chelsea was 268, but we made ourselves heard and when the players finally came out for the start of the match every single one of us picked up the chant which finally acknowledged the respect the supporters had for the manager.

'*Ranieri's blue and white army... Ranieri's blue and white army.*'

They were here, we were here: all the usual suspects, a magnificently undiluted cross section of Chelsea supporters bound together by a common hope which served to swamp the less attractive tendencies that some might bring to the party.

At times like this the passion for Chelsea was tribal; every tribe had its factions and the kinship came from unifying as one seemingly against the odds to spur the team onto victory.

Marco, Young Dave and a few empty seats ... Zilina ... August 2003

'*Chelsea... Chelsea... Chelsea... Chelsea...*'

Our continuous chant drew applause to a man from the Chelsea players lining up for the kick off in the stunning new white away kit. With Claudio giving debuts to Glen Johnson, Wayne Bridge, Juan Sebastian Veron, Geremi and Damien Duff it was a much changed line up from the team that started the final match of last season against Liverpool.

In fact only four members of that starting line up were on the pitch as the referee blew his whistle to commence proceedings here in Zilina; Cudicini, Desailly, Lampard and Gudjohnsen: The two players making up the team were John Terry and Mikael Forssell.

The home supporters did their best to get behind their team with the unimaginative '*Zilina... Zilina*' chant and several attempts at a Mexican wave which predictably broke down when it reached our section.

For the first few minutes we looked positively vibrant. Every one of the debutants participated in the type of crisp, intelligent passing football which had become the trademark of Ranieri's Chelsea.

Forssell went close with a shot that was deflected for a corner that was subsequently wasted and left our defence exposed to a counter attack.

Their number ten, who looked like a very lively customer, hit an inch perfect pass for number five, but Zilina were unable to make the most of the opportunity and Desailly, 'The Rock', was there to sweep things up.

Young Dave, observant as ever, drew my attention to the name of the sponsor emblazoned across the yellow shirts of MSK Zilina; Tento, the toilet paper manufacturer. Quality!

A few of the lads broke into the Loyalist chant *'No Surrender'*, but not everyone joined in. Whilst race, colour and creed had become largely immaterial to the 21st century Chelsea supporter, patriotism however, remained an emotive issue. For some it was a fervent, flag waving display of love for your country, for others it was fragmented bizarrely by sectarianism which, for Chelsea, was a legacy of it's allegiances with the predominantly protestant supporters of Glasgow Rangers from Scotland and Linfield from Belfast, Northern Ireland.

Tonight here in Zilina a couple of hundred Chelsea diehards were witnessing the start of a new chapter in the clubs history. Personally, I couldn't give a flying fuck about the pedigree of our support, religion never equalled coolness in my book. What mattered was that we all had the blue blood of Chelsea coursing through our veins... if it kicked off we would stand firm, and we would stand together.

Chelsea's future had been secured by a Russian billionaire, who happened to be Jewish. How tolerant would the club remain of the traditional, blatantly anti-Semitic chants used to bait Spurs fans?

It was exciting, breathtaking almost, to think that in the next couple of years John Terry could be captaining the side to the Premiership title and that would be just the start. European glory by way of winning the Champions League was no longer a dream, it was a real possibility. If being a part of all that meant some old habits had to die then so be it, I for one wouldn't lose too much sleep at the prospect of not being able to participate in certain chants for fear of being 'banned from the club for life', and besides there was always the One Bar where we could sing what we liked, as loud as we liked, and as often as we liked as long as things remained orderly and we paid for our drinks.

'Loads and loads of money... loads and loads of money,' and, for the umpteenth time, *'West Ham's our feeder club... West Ham's our feeder club.'*

The new chants had started already. It was great that we could still wind our rival supporters up as they watched the game at home on TV praying that Zilina would upset the odds.

The malevolently vitriolic chanting of the past was as much a reflection of Chelsea's lack of success on the pitch as it was genuine in it's loathsome put downs of the so called 'big four' clubs of my youth.

It was only a matter of time before all that hatred would be repaid in spades as the Man U's, Arsenal's, Spurs and Liverpool's of this world focused their jealous attentions on the goings on in London SW6.

John Terry was having a magnificent game and one of the Chelsea Up Norf boys in front of us was vocal in his praise, constantly leading the chant, '*Terry for England... Terry for England.*'

It was the youngster Johnson that caught my eye, what a real bargain he could turn out to be and Veron, ' Oh what a ball,' exclaimed everyone, applauding the Argentinean as he hit a free kick a full fifty yards across the pitch; the ball was chested down by Duff who skinned a couple of Zilina defenders before passing the ball to Forssell who toed the ball fractionally over the bar.

Chelsea were clearly on top and, with ten minutes or so to go to half time, just as we were beginning to become impatient, Duff, who had mesmerised the Zilina defence at every given opportunity, played a neat one-two with Forssell and knocked the ball across the box where 'fat boy' Gudjohnsen, who looked like he'd avoided the burgers over the summer break, slid in at the far post. GOAL!

'*Eidur Gudjohnsen... Eidur Gudjohnsen.*'

The home support was silenced and the remainder of the half played itself out to the incessant chant of '*Chelsea... Chelsea... Chelsea.*'

*   *   *

'Marco, check these out.' Young Dave smiled as he handed me several magazines that he had been perusing in the company of a couple of strangely attired youths.

'These lads are from Poland, they follow a team called Wid... er Wid...' Young Dave's attempts at pronunciation were interrupted by both his new acquaintances.

'Widzew Lodz!' They cried out proudly, one of them baring his right forearm to proudly display a self inflicted tattoo which displayed the clubs initials.

'We are here to learn from the true masters of hooliganism the famous Chelsea FC of London... but why no fighting?... We learn nothing... all that is happening is the singing of songs where are your famous hunters of heads?' Dodgy Tattoo was clearly upset that he had come all this way with his friend hoping to witness an orgy of violence and destruction and instead was party to nothing more sinister than a spot of good natured Chelsea terrace karaoke.

The magazines were disturbing, depicting page after page of violent clashes between rival sets of supporters and the police.

'This happens every week at your games?' I enquired, handing the magazines back to Dodgy Tattoo.

'Every week, my friend... it is our religion... we learn much from the TV... where we come from we fight all the time,' came the equally disquieting reply.

'Well fuck me,' I said, turning to Young Dave and smiling, 'I'm glad we didn't draw Dodgy Tattoo's outfit at this stage of the competition... looking at our numbers we might have been re-enacting the siege of the Alamo.'

'Charge of the Light Brigade son,' replied Young Dave, nodding in agreement as we turned our attention to the pitch. The players had re-emerged from the tunnel and taken up their positions in readiness for the start of the second half.

*   *   *

In European competition, teams are allowed to field any three from seven substitutes and therefore it came as a bit of a surprise when Mr Ranieri, the self styled 'Tinkerman', recommenced proceedings with his original starting eleven.

It didnt take long for him to effect a few changes though. First Gronkjaer replaced Forssell, and then with twenty minutes left Duff was replaced by Joe Cole whose arrival on the pitch was met with rapturous applause from our little posse. Oh how those West Ham supporters watching back at home must have been clenching their fists and biting their bottom lips as they were treated to a couple of sweet Chelsea moves involving Johnson, Lampard and Cole.

It was Cole who produced a clever little back heel for Gudjohnsen which resulted in Chelsea's winning goal as Zilina's number 28 spectacularly chipped his own keeper from the edge of the box. As a contest the game was over, and by way of a celebration we treated the Zilina supporters to a magnificent rendition of 'One man went to mow'.

At the final whistle the Chelsea players came over to the section we were in and applauded our support which has been loud and sustained throughout. And in what was a very nice touch, John Terry removed his shirt and gave it to Knife, the big northern bloke who had been encouraging him throughout the match.

Disregarding the fact that the shirt was soaking wet with Terry's sweat, the lucky recipient proudly donned it over his own blue, Terry 26, shirt and turned around to receive a rousing round of applause from the rest of us.

'I bet he doesn't take that off for a month,' chortled Young Dave to no-one in particular, 'It aint on sale until the 10th of September, I've checked already, can't wait to get one myself... it's pukka,' he continued, as we gave our heroes a standing ovation before they left the pitch.

Match Result

Mestsky Sportovy Klub Zilina 0 : Chelsea FC 2

* * *

It was 10pm and we'd been politely told over the tannoy that we would be kept in the ground for 15 minutes whilst the home crowd dispersed. Around thirty or so interestingly attired security personnel had been deployed to ensure there was no disorder. They took up positions on the track in front of the low perimeter wall which ran the length of the stand we were in, and from which the familiar assortment of Chelseafied Union Jack and St George flags were now being removed by their proud owners.

'Bleedin 'ell... look at 'em, they look like a bunch of faggots off a George Michael video or someink,' someone behind us remarked loudly. Everyone started to laugh, even the security guards, although what they were laughing at was anyone's guess.

The bloke had a point though. The security guards were garbed in tight fitting black trousers, black blouson jackets and shiny black boots. Each of them carried a long black truncheon which looked real enough and several of them were wearing 'aviator' style mirror shades. Young Dave made the point that they looked like they had turned up to audition for the Chippendales, but I thought they just looked very wrong.

'Do you reckon the giant will be waiting for us in the car park with directions to his sisters flat in Vienna?' I asked Young Dave, trying to keep a straight face while I sparked up another Marlboro.

'Shit, I forgot about him ha... lets hope the motors still there though eh Marco... even though the train stations just over there, I don't fancy chancing it on the chuff chuff and besides I fancy a couple of slurps in Bratislava.'

'Fair point Young Dave... fair point my son,' I replied, patting Young Dave on the back, 'You want me to do the driving on the way back mate?' I asked, knowing what the reply would be.

Young Dave always drove... even if it was just a lousy VW Polo... Young Dave would always insist on doing the driving, which was fine by me.

Before Young Dave had the chance to reply we all began to cheer as the security guards opened the gates and we began to shuffle out of the ground and into the dimly lit street which led back to the car park.

If either of us had harboured any doubt about the security of our little Polo, which we hadn't, we needn't have worried. There she was bathed in the yellow glow of a streetlamp, a welcoming sight, waiting for us like a forlorn friend; even in a comparatively poor country like Slovakia a VW Polo clearly had little currency with the car thieves we had been warned about by the Hertz official at Vienna airport.

*   *   *

The journey to Bratislava was run of the mill; the road out of Zilina which led to the motorway was still greasy from the earlier downpour, so we sat in silence whilst Young Dave concentrated on his driving and I busied myself texting the part timers back at home.

By 1.30 am we were sat outside a bar called Coco Loco nursing a couple of very welcome bottles of pivo and engaging in the ritual post mortem discussion of the days events. We'd come across the bar purely by chance whilst driving through the city centre looking for, amongst other things, a post box. As it happened the bar was on the opposite side of the street from what appeared to be the main post office.

Tradition dictated that on every football trip abroad I always sent two postcards, one to my Godson Joshua who was already indoctrinated in the blue religion, and the other to my dear mother. My mum was an interesting soul. As mad as a box of frogs, and probably the most fanatical armchair Chelsea supporter on the planet... her neighbours had long since desisted dialling 999 when they heard shrieks coming from her house as she rode the big blue rollercoaster from the comfort of her living room.

The bar was really busy and our discourse was frequently interjected with the phrase 'show us yer monkey...' a blunt anatomical reference to the incredibly horny, wide-eyed, loose limbed waitresses who busied themselves at the tables which seemed to be mainly occupied by middle aged businessmen.

Young Dave decided to share with me his passion for collecting art!

'What, Art Garfunkel?' I said, trying to make light of Young Dave's cultural hobby. In all the time I'd known Young Dave I never knew he collected works of art.

I wondered if he was pulling my leg and was actually referring to some vast collection of pornographic magazines that he probably kept well hidden from Mrs Young Dave in his garage, but he was being serious. The only works of art that I was familiar with were normally suspended from poles in the seedy lap dancing clubs that I frequented from time to time back in London.

'One mans art, is another mans hard-on,' I mumbled by way of self justification, glancing at my watch and yawning... it was now 3am.

'Right son, you've had enough for one night,' said Young Dave with an air of fatherly authority. 'Time to Foxtrot Oscar,' he continued, getting to his feet and rummaging in his pockets for the car keys.

The streets of Bratislava were deserted so it didn't take too long for Young Dave to find his way back onto the motorway. We were all talked out, so I tried the car radio again figuring that despite the lack of aerial it might be more receptive at night and sure enough this time it worked. I turned the dial trying to find something decent to listen but only managed to find the one station that it was tuned to when I'd switched it on.

'Leo fucking Sayer... bloody hell!' I exclaimed, shaking my head and tutting as I listened to Young Dave singing along word for word with the seventies hit 'You make me feel like dancing'.

It got worse as well; after two more Leo tunes, which left me wondering if he had either died or achieved celebrity status in Slovakia in the same way that Norman Wisdom had in Albania, we were treated to the full ten minutes of Lynyrd Skynrd's 'Freebird'.

The worrying thing about 'Freebird' is the lengthy guitar solo in the middle which, in the same way as the heavy metal riff in Queen's 'Bohemian Rhapsody', always induces involuntary head-banging in all but the most reserved of listeners.

Young Dave was going some, shaking his head and playing one handed air guitar. At least he had his other hand on the steering wheel most of the time, which was a relief as the road signs were now indicating we were nearing the border checkpoint.

The Slovakian guards checked our passports and waved us through. Their Austrian counterparts however instructed us to get out of the car whilst they looked inside... this gave Young Dave another fabulous opportunity to practice his pidgin English.

'We come back to your country... Yes... having watched our Chelsea FC London play football in that country back there... we go to Wien to the airport and fly home now... our home is in England... we are Englanders.'

I was glad that Young Dave had been chewing on a few tabs of Wrigleys, thereby giving himself a minty fresh breath, because if he hadn't I strongly suspect that the border guard might have breathalysed him and the consequences of that could have been very dire for us poor Englanders.

Young Dave though was a master of his craft and within minutes the border guard, having looked in Polo's empty boot, was satisfied that we weren't international drug traffickers and allowed us back into Austria.

* * *

'Well done son, you played a blinder there mate,' I said, as I patted Young Dave on the back. We were sat in the departure lounge at Vienna airport. It was 5am and we had just a couple of hours left to kill before the flight home. We'd been on the go for a full 24 hours now, and being substance free both of us soon descended into the maddening world of the zombie rubbernecker.

Thankfully the flight was on time and soon we were in the air and on our way home. Two hours kip on the plane was enough to restore our batteries sufficiently to deal with a 9am arrival at Heathrow. The airport was teeming with people but I was past caring, I knew that I'd be home by mid morning.

For Young Dave it was a different matter, he still had to get to Paddington Station and then endure the train journey back to Bath. If he'd played his cards right before he left, Mrs Young Dave would be there waiting for him. The only trouble was Young Dave was too tired to remember how he'd played his cards, or if in fact he'd even played them at all.

We shook hands in the main concourse of the terminal and bade each other farewell. Young Dave headed off to catch the Heathrow Express and I made my way down to the underground station. For me it would be the Piccadilly Line to Earls Court, the District Line to Wimbledon and then a train to Worcester Park.

'Did you watch Chelsea last night?' said the portly middle aged man in the blue pinstripe suit to the equally portly bespectacled man sat next to him.

The two men were sat opposite me on the tube and I eaves dropped their evolving discussion as I waited for the train to depart.

'Yes I did George,' came the reply. 'We played pretty well... mind you we should do given all that money we've spent.'

Pinstripe pointed at an article in the newspaper that was neatly folded on his lap.

'It says here they only had a few hundred supporters out there with them, made a proper racket by all accounts, imagine if you'd been one of them Charlie... witnessing the dawn of the Roman empire... it would've been pretty special eh, something to tell young Sammy about when he's old enough to understand.'

'Pretty special,' I thought to myself, 'yeah it had been pretty special all right.' I smiled and closed my eyes as the train left the station and began to pick up speed, and as it did so I began to hum and drum my fingers on my thighs in time with the metronome clicketty click of its wheels.

'*We are the famous... the famous Chelsea.*'

AC SPARTA PRAHA
UEFA Champions League
Group G
Letna Stadion, Prague, Czech Republic
Tuesday 16th September 2003

There had been the usual flurry of emails modifying and rescheduling the plans for the trip to Prague. Chelsea had comfortably seen off MSK Zilina in the second leg of the qualifier and a reasonable draw saw the newly dubbed Chelski pitched in Champions League Group G against AC Sparta Praha from Prague, SS Lazio from Rome and Turkey's oldest football club, Besiktas JK from Istanbul.

Four of Gate 17's finest were heading out to the Czech Republic; Young Dave, myself, Ossie and the legend that was Ugly John. Ugly John worked in the travel business and harboured ambitions to become the next Martha Lane Fox... a sobering prospect even for the most gifted of cosmetic surgeons.

All joking apart he had the contacts and the industry know how to ensure that we could get decent flights and great accommodation at a very reasonable price and this trip was to prove no exception, the only minor inconvenience was that we would be flying from Stansted Airport.

Getting from leafy Surrey to deepest, darkest Essex bandit country where 'London' Stansted is located is a chore at the best of times. The choices are simple; drive and take a chance on the road to hell, the M25; or let the train take the strain. Either way I would be looking at a journey time of at least a couple of hours... more than the flight time from Stansted to Prague!

The train from Worcester Park to Waterloo was virtually empty, it was just after 2pm on a Monday afternoon and even with all the kids back in their classrooms after the summer break, the carriages were dirty and littered with newspapers left by the mornings commuters. For mid September it was unseasonably hot and, as I made my way through to the front carriage of the train, I began to think about my first beer of the day and the more I though about it, the more I fancied a change from my usual lager top.

Guinness again... the extra cold variety... that ought to do it; yeah, if my memory served me well enough then I'd be downing one or two of those in an hour or so when I got to the Last and First bar at Liverpool Street Station where I'd arranged to meet Young Dave, Ugly John and Ossie.

I opened all the windows in the carriage, picked up a copy of the Standard from the floor, and sat down in a slovenly fashion putting my feet up on the seat in front of me. Even now I still found it unfathomable how many column inches of news print were still being devoted to Chelsea Football Club.

Statistics, statistics and more statistics; I gave up on the article I'd started reading about the minutiae of Chelsea's finances and sat back in my seat. I closed my eyes and began to figure it all out for myself.

In the thirty odd days since Young Dave and I had heralded the dawn of the new Roman Chelski empire on a balmy evening in Zilina, plenty had happened both on and off the pitch. By the time the transfer window had been slammed firmly shut at 5pm on September 1st Mr Abramovich had spent a total of £109.1 million on new players, an investment which represented almost half the value of all transfer business done in Europe over the summer.

Since the Zilina match several significant additions had been made to the squad; from Parma the highly regarded young Romania striker Adrian Mutu, from Inter Milan the Argentina goal poacher Hernan Crespo and finally, and perhaps most importantly, Real Madrid's France international midfielder Claude Makalele.

Here was a player with the tenacity, steel and guile in the middle of the park that could make us serious contenders at home and abroad. Contenders we were all right, winning 2–1 at Anfield on the opening day of the Barclaycard Premiership season had hammered a huge stake of intent in the ground and sent out a clear message to Manchester United, Arsenal and the small clutch of clubs hoping to challenge for honours that the all new Chelsea were armed and above all ready.

Chelsea's starting eleven in that Liverpool game featured just five of the players who began the final game of last season against the same club; Cudicini, Desailly, Gronkjaer, Lampard and Gudjohnsen.

Despite the optimistic start to the season it was evident from some of the performances that the team would need time to gel. No matter how much Ranieri loved to tinker, eventually he would need to settle on his first eleven.

Even with young talents like Carlton Cole and Mikael Forssell allowed to go out on loan there was still an embarrassment of expensive talent available for selection. Some players were going to be disappointed, and the press as usual wasted no time in raking over the hot coals in the Stamford Bridge fire trying to stir up some dressing room angst with the apparently dissatisfied Hasselbaink the focus of attention

The away victory over Liverpool had been followed by four consecutive home matches; An unconvincing 2-1 win over Leicester City, a 3-0 2nd Leg canter against the lacklustre MSK Zilina, a frustrating 2-2 draw against a very well organised Blackburn Rovers side and the past weekend's predictable 4-2 cuffing of Tottenham Hotspur.

In just six games Claudio Ranieri had already featured eighteen different players in his starting line ups and, with Claude Makalele and Hernan Crespo set to make their full debuts tomorrow night in Prague, it was clear that the Tinkerman was still in experimental mode.

* * *

'I hope he plays Crespo from the start,' trilled Ugly John, wiping the Guinness froth moustache from his wrinkled face. 'He didn't look match fit when he came on for Mutu in the Blackburn game but he must be up for it now,' he continued earnestly, smiling as Young Dave, Ossie and I nodded our heads in agreement.

In a world of mates Ugly John was one of the best. In a world of dogs, if Young Dave was a long nosed Mastiff then Ugly John with his crew cut mousey blonde hair, lined face and fat neck was a Sharpei. Away from the football Ugly John was known to one and all as The Edge, not because he bore any resemblance to the U2 guitar hero, but because of the way he seemed to embrace all the stressful aspects of modern life... quite simply, he lived life on the edge.

The sobriquet 'Ugly' had been bestowed on John by Ossie, a genuinely courteous and amiable man with an engaging line in self deprecating humour. Ossie Osgood, like his Chelsea legend namesake, had the look and the manners that endeared him to the ladies. Even though grey had long since crept into his stubble, his hairline had receded no further in all the years I'd known him.

'Crespo looked more like a gunslinger from a Western film than a star striker when they paraded him at half time in the Zilina match the other week,' remarked Young Dave, pointing at the clock on the wall as he did so.

'He looks like a fucking hippy if you ask me,' I said, necking the rest of

Young Dave and Ossie model the latest headgear ... Prague ... September 2003

my pint and standing up, 'needs a decent haircut... knoworrimean... right
come on time to board the Stansted Express we don't wanna miss the
flight now do we?'

'Fucking hippy... everyone looks like a fucking hippy to you... you
bald git, your just jealous.' Ugly John seized the opportunity to dig me out
with some of the playful verbal small arms fire that more often than not
rat a tat tatted away in his general direction.

Everyone that travelled away with Chelsea in Europe seemed to adopt
an endearing, carefree, sense of humour and stubbornness which was
more often than not fuelled by self propagated hype and enthusiastic
drinking; Ugly John was no exception to the rule. It was this, coupled with
a tradition of expectation rather than achievement that separated us from
the homogenised, vacuum packed, red hordes that followed Manchester
United and Arsenal.

* * *

'Carefree wherever we may be... we are the famous CFC... and we don't give a fuck whoever you may be 'cos we are the famous CFC.'

As if to echo my thoughts, an instantly recognisable chant became clearly audible above the general clamour of chattering passengers and tannoyed announcements as we took our seats on the Stansted Express. It articulated perfectly our mood, a mood of expectant anticipation not only for the football match we would witness tomorrow night but also for the attractions the city of Prague itself had to offer.

We'd all visited the city several times before and so from a slightly un-cultured perspective a very simple itinerary for the evening had been drawn up. Our schedule once we had checked in to our hotel and rapidly turned out again would reflect two very important facets of Czech popular culture.

Firstly, drinking; the Czechs per capita, drink more beer than anyone else in the world so it's no surprise then that they also brew the best lager in the world... Staropramen, although Ossie liked to argue the case for Pilsner Urquell.

Secondly or should this be firstly? dancing girls; Prague is home to the world renown lap dancing club, Goldfingers... enough said for now.

* * *

Young Dave looked down from his paper a broad smile cracking across his face as he spoke. 'It says in the Standard they reckon on a couple of thou Chels being out for the match... should be a triffic atmosphere... listen to that lot down the other end of the carriage, they must be pissing a few people off ha ha.'

'Ahh you bastard... now you've spoilt it,' I tutted, shaking my head in mock dismay.

'Spoilt what?' retorted Young Dave, Ossie and Ugly John in unison.

'I was having a Goldfingers moment... that's what... y'know, just thinking about all that perfectly choreographed female flesh parading itself in front of my disbelieving eyes.'

'So you'll be enjoying a few private dances will you Marco?' Ossie asked me rhetorically, nodding his head as he did so in a slow deliberate manner.

'A few... more than a few all right,' interjected Ugly John, 'he's been saving up especially for this trip haven't you? Dirty little sod.

'Listen to you lot... yer all just jealous, so what if maybe I have saved up... nothing wrong with that then is there eh?' I reached under my seat for my holdall, picked it up and placed it carefully on the table unfastening the zip in freeze frame slow motion.

The compartment we were sat in was full and at this very moment it seemed as if everybody had their eyes trained on the bag waiting, with a noticeable element of unremitting unease, for it's contents to be revealed.

The middle aged woman in the seat adjacent to mine across the aisle looked nervously at the bag and then at the Stone Island button down logo on the upper part of the left sleeve of my shirt. The thought occurred to me that she might think we were the eccentric cell of some secret terrorist organization about to draw weapons and hold the train to ransom.

But she needn't have worried; I pushed the bag across the table to Ugly John motioning him to look inside. 'Go on son, show 'em what we've got... show em.'

Ugly John reached into the bag and pulled out £2000 worth of Gate 17 'big money' and waved it in front of everyone.

'Look at that eh... LOADS A MONEY... ha ha... we've got LOADS A MONEY,' he bellowed, in the style of the famous Harry Enfield character. 'That'll get Marco a few private dances down at Goldfingers later... even if he has got no hair.'

The tense mood in the carriage eased as the impromptu audience began to laugh and applaud loudly. 'Big money' was the invention of one Tim Connery a native of Slough and probably one of the funniest men never to grace the stage. Tim had scanned the full range of banknotes into his computer and enlarged them by 300%. All you needed then was a decent colour printer (like the one at work), a pair of scissors, some patience and a little imagination.

Since it's invention, 'big money', had been deployed in a variety of situations ranging from chatting up women, to a bungled attempt to defraud the bureau de change in Times Square New York out of several thousand dollars.

'Cor blimey love 'av you won the lottery or just robbed a bank?' The woman in the adjacent seat to me peered through her bifocals at the huge wedge of cash that Ugly John was proudly brandishing.

'No love we are Chelsea, we've got loads a money... now here you are darling, get yourself back up west and buy yourself a new frock and have a drink on us.' Ugly John carefully picked out two 'big money' £50 notes from the stash and handed them to the woman who gratefully accepted them, holding first one and then the other up to the light to check their provenance.

'Cooh... I ain't never seen money this big before... and it's only printed on one side,' she sighed cheerily. 'You Chelsea boys are so generous... my 'usbands a Spurs fan and when he goes to the bar to buy a lager he only ever buys one for himself.'

We all began to cackle whilst the woman looked on perplexed as Young Dave stood up, winked at us and acknowledged the group of men at the far end of the carriage, one of whom like himself, was wearing the new white Chelsea away shirt.

'Sounds like a cue for a song lads that does... ready boys?' Young Dave spoke in a reverential manner, and as he did so a hushed silence descended in the carriage as everyone waited for him to lead the not so reverential chant.

*   *   *

The airport, when we finally arrived was very busy; flights to Spain were being delayed and as a result of this the departure lounge was full of irate parents and frustrated children squabbling amongst themselves.

In amongst the melee we spotted a group of Celtic supporters whom we assumed were heading out to Germany for their teams fixture with Bayern Munich which wasn't until Wednesday evening. Maybe I was being a bit hasty in moaning about having to travel to Stansted from Surrey, imagine having to travel down from Glasgow what a nightmare.

The Czech Airlines Boeing 737 left on time and landed in Prague bang on schedule. The flight was full and, on disembarkation, as we made our way through passport control, it was apparent that the majority of passengers on board were en route to the match.

Prague Ruzyne airport is to the northwest of the city centre, Ugly John had booked us into the Corinthian Hotel which was to the south, meaning we had a slightly longer taxi journey than we'd anticipated. It was worth it though, the hotel was very well appointed and on checking in we agreed to meet in the lobby in half an hour ready for the eagerly anticipated sortie into the centre.

Rooming with Ugly John on away trips was something I'd become accustomed to over the years. He was tidier than me, didn't snore, which apparently I did, and didn't have that annoying habit of switching on the TV and flicking aimlessly around the channels for minutes on end until it was time to go out.

He did however spend an inordinate amount of time in the bathroom, something I often quizzed him about wondering what it was he was doing in there. "Fuck off I'm getting ready", would be the normal reply and tonight was no different.

Whilst Ugly John endeavoured to give himself a beautifying makeover, I cracked open a can of beer from the well stocked mini bar and looked out of the window of our room which, being on the fourteenth floor, afforded me a splendid night time view of the city of Prague. It was pure coincidence that following that last away trip to Slovakia, we would find ourselves in the neighbouring Czech Republic for the very next game.

Prague is a city with a rich history and culture which, very quickly after the 1993 separation of Czechoslovakia into the Czech and Slovak republics, established itself as one of the top tourist destinations in the world.

Its continued affordability to tourists coupled with a solid industrial base, had resulted in a marked increase in its prosperity particularly when compared to the economy of the rest of the country.

When I first visited the city in 1994, Sterling went a hell of a long way against the Czech Koruna particularly in the drinking stakes. The last time I was here in 2000 things were noticeably that much more expensive; the bar owners of Prague, recognising that the city had become a mecca for those stag and hen parties that now descended on them for long weekends of high speed vertical drinking, reflected this in their tariffs.

With the Czech Republic imminently due to become a part of the EU it would be just a matter of time before the currency lost its national identity. Once it had joined the Eurozone, parity of prices with other member countries would soon follow... potentially forcing all the stags and hens to find other low cost Eastern European drinking havens.

My concerned thoughts about the potential impact that this loss of custom might have on Prague's tourist economy were cut short by the text message alert bleeping from my mobile phone. The message was from Young Dave;

COME ON YOU TWO FAGGOTS STOP PONCING AROUND
IN FRONT OF THE MIRROR AND GET DOWN HERE NOW
ITS BEER O CLOCK

One thing was certain; if the part of the Czech economy that was index linked to beer consumption had a less than rosy future, for now it was pretty secure especially since there were 2000 thirsty Chelsea supporters in town.

* * *

'Four more Staropramen please love... go on son... go on YESSS... ha ha four nil... goin down they are lads... goin down.' Young Dave finished his beer and handed his glass to the waitress shouting up the next round as he did so.

We had decided to commence the evening's proceedings in the Sports Bar which was at the top end of one of the livelier 'bar' streets that spoked off Wenceslas Square. Depending on which way you viewed things the trouble with Prague was that pretty much everyone spoke a very good standard of English, indeed a lot of the bars were staffed by English or Irish gap year students. The downside for me was the fact that Young Dave would have limited opportunity to utilise his pidgin English.

The Sports Bar was no different. To complement its Anglicisation the huge projection TV was screening Sky's live Monday night football match. Besides Young Dave, the only other person in the bar paying much attention to the fact that Leicester City had just gone 4-0 up against Leeds United was an elderly bespectacled man wearing a tatty blue football shirt with the name Lineker and a large number 9 on the back.

As good as the beer in the Sports Bar was, the place was virtually empty. The local time was almost 11pm and we had a small challenge on our hands; finding somewhere lively, with a bit of atmosphere on a Monday night.

Ossie was all for going straight to Goldfingers, but there was still plenty of time for that so we elected to try a couple of bars at the other end of Wenceslas Square.

'It's named after King Wenceslas this square you know... he's the patron saint of the Czech Republic and was responsible for making Christianity the state religion of Bohemia.' Ugly John spoke earnestly with the comfortable manner of a travel guide; normally his observations would go unchallenged, being met simply by appreciative nods from those around him who were happy to be informed; but not this time!

'Yeah, he last looked out on the feast of Stephen didn't he,' remarked Ossie drolly, winking at me as he did so.

'That's right Ossie... and I do believe the snow lay round about and was deep and crisp and even that night if I'm not mistaken,' I added, trying to keep a straight face and wondering if Young Dave might be able to take things a step further... which if course he did.

'Spot on Marco,' crowed Young Dave, 'and I heard that on that night the moon shone very brightly but the frost was a bit cruel and some old bloke came out gathering winter fuel.'

'Arghh you wankers... very funny,' said Ugly John, slapping me across my back with some force. It had taken about thirty seconds for the penny to drop before he realised we were reciting the verses of the Christmas carol Good King Wenceslas.

* * *

'Are you lot sure you don't wanna go in now... it looks inviting doesn't it?'

We were stood outside the Hotel Ambassador which was located at the far end of Wenceslas Square. The Ambassador's basement played host to Goldfingers seven days a week and Ossie was making a play for an early entrance.

'Nah Ossie,' I said, 'lets go down to Double Trouble, it's only ten minutes walk from here... if it's crap we can come straight back, and besides they aint gonna let us in with those two stuffing their faces with mustard covered spicy sausages ha look at 'em.'

I laughed as I pointed at Young Dave and Ugly John who had propped themselves up on the counter of the take away food kiosk nearby. Both of them were concentrating on trying to eat their sausages without smearing mustard all over themselves and both of them had so far succeeded.

Ossie and I waited for them to finish before we all ambled across the pedestrianised crossroads at the bottom of Wenceslas Square. It was getting cold now, well at least it was to me... the others laughed as I pulled the collar of my jacket up against the stiffening breeze and thrust my hands into my pockets. I didn't do the cold very well, so I was grateful that the designers of the casual clobber I liked to wear catered for my lily livered constitution.

'Jeeeesus Christ look at the state of him.' Ossie pointed at what looked like a bundle of rags lying in the doorway of the toy shop across the road from Double Trouble.

'Blimey what a stench... what is it?' Young Dave took a couple of strides closer to the doorway before recoiling in horror and staggering back across the pavement.

'It's only a bloody tramp innit... poor bastard look at him... here you go mate, go and buy yourself a new suit,' said Ugly John, tossing a handful of coins into the doorway and stepping quickly back as the bundle of rags moved.

The tramp looked days away from death; his face was all but hidden by a mane of unkempt matted hair, and a huge bushy beard that gave him the appearance of the mad Russian monk Rasputin. He reached out a filthy hand festooned with open sores. Grime beneath long, jagged, nicotine stained fingernails was clearly visible as he scrabbled for the coins that Ugly John had thrown on the ground.

The tramp looked at each of us in turn, fixing his stare with narrow dark piercing eyes which seemed to burn with a malevolent intensity that sent a shudder through my body when he caught my gaze.

'Right... come on... come on now... I need a drink.' Ossie had seen enough and was clearly as shaken as the rest of us had been by the vision of decaying humanity that he later christened The Stench From The Trench.

The rest of us needed no encouragement, crossing the road quickly and heading for the welcoming entrance to the Double Trouble music bar.

'Whatever you do... don't look back... just don't look back.' I looked directly at Ugly John keeping a poker face as I made the remark and nudging Young Dave as we opened the door to the bar.

'Why... eh... why not? I gave the poor bloke some money... it's more than any of you lot did innit.' Ugly John's indignant reply was tempered with disquiet.

'Because my son... because he is... he is the dee eee vee eye el... the Devil ha ha... seeking new souls to steal HA HA HA.' I cackled loudly and jumped on Ugly John's back, the impetus of my action sending both of us clattering down the wide stone stairs which we had begun to descend.

'Bloody hell Marco... you've killed him.' Young Dave was stood over the crumpled, motionless figure of Ugly John, 'Ere Ossie have a look... call for an ambulance... Marco's murdered Ugly John.'

I picked myself up and crawled on my hands and knees over to where Ugly John was lying and, as I did so, Ossie walked over to the prone body, got down on bended knee and rubbed his chin thoughtfully.

'Hold on let me see if he's breathing,' he said confidently, 'I've seen it on Casualty... I know what to do.' Ossie put two fingers against the side of Ugly Johns throat and kept them there for a few seconds whilst Young Dave looked at his watch.

'Nah he's a goner mate... brown bread... you've killed him you daft sod.' Ossie raised his eyebrows and frowned as he stood up and put his hands on his hips.

'Bollocks... he can't be dead... he only fell a couple of feet and besides I'm still alive aint I... let me see.' I took closer order and as I leant over Ugly John's prostrate form to check on his welfare I was embraced in a sudden bear hug which made me scream out like a frightened kid playing his first game of murder in the dark.

'Arghhh... arghhh... you fucking bastard... you're alive, thank fuck for that.' There was relief in my voice as I wrestled Ugly John away from me and we both pulled ourselves to our feet laughing.

'Of course I'm alive you bald git... and thank fuck I am, I thought you were gonna give me the kiss of life for one minute... I figured you might have been watching Casualty with Ossie and picked up the technique... didn't fancy that all, I'd rather kiss your grandmother... how old is she now? 86... yeah she'd get it... ha ha.' Ugly John slapped me across the back in his own inimitable way and I laughed as I saw Young Dave shaking his head in incredulity at the puerile behaviour of his juvenile travelling companions.

*   *   *

Double Trouble was a labyrinth of linked cellars. The largest cellar had its own bar and dance-floor which tonight was a heaving mass of gyrating bodies all kissing and groping to the pounding beat of European house music. Cocktail fuelled teenage girls were flirting and flitting amongst a group of men oddly attired in pink shirts; the atmosphere was electric with the desire of those men as they locked eyes and tried to feel with their hands what they wanted with their minds.

The smaller cellar, with its impressive sit up bar, was playing host to several groups of familiar looking characters. Knowing glances, nods and thumbs up were exchanged as we made our way to the bar and Ossie ordered up four Pilsner Urquell's.

'Blimey!' said Ugly John, 'look, it's like a Stone Island fashion parade, I bet they've got absolutely no idea that the main market for their clobber is with well attired football casuals.' He looked around the bar, shrugged his shoulders and then fingered the small enamel badge on my jacket which featured the Stone Island motif and the wording Chelsea On Tour. 'Their brand police wouldn't be too impressed about that eh, now would they?' he said, in a pseudo vexed manner which made me smile.

'I dunno son... they wanna sell clothes don't they,' I said purposefully, taking a slug from my beer bottle before continuing, 'it's not as if it's just us Chelsea boys that patronise the label, if you go on E Bay you can get these things for just about every football club in the land, I bought this one off Billy the badge who always comes in the One Bar on match days... only two quid... and as for the clobber, it's nice and expensive... well designed and well put together, I'd still wear it even if it had no ties to the football... anyway cheers lads.' I raised my beer and the four of us chinked glasses before continuing our discourse about football fashion.

'Seriously, I dunno if Stone Island would be that happy, look at the company that owns the Burberry brand they want to get shot of it because of its association with football hooligans; that clobber was everywhere you looked from Euro 2000 onwards, same with Hackett.' Ossie spoke matter of factly, knowing that Young Dave and Ugly John were more interested in lager than fashion.

'Well its an Italian outfit, CP Company, that own the brand for a start,' I said, pausing to take a deep drag on the Marlboro Light I'd just lit. 'They launched the Stone Island label in 1981 with the aim of establishing an innovative sportswear collection. You wanna get yourself down to their flagship store in Soho. It's as near as you can get to a religious experience if you take your casual wear seriously... the manager knows that it's mainly football fans that buy the gear and he doesn't have a problem with it, he's a fan himself.'

Ugly John was shaking his head at me as I spoke but I continued unde-terred.

'It's all about visible labels, fundamental basics and tribalism... but for me the bottom line is the clothes look fucking great and the winter clobber keeps you as warm as toast, and I'm happy to pay for that cos I really... really... hate the fucking cold.'

'Bollocks.' Young Dave offered, he'd been pretty quiet so far but it was only going to be a matter of time before he volunteered his opinion. 'Are we here for a football match or for some mincers clothes convention?'

'Fair point Young Dave... I'm with you on this one.' Ugly John nodded at Young Dave before turning to the bar to order the next round although he kept glancing round to keep an ear on the conversation.

Ossie looked offended, 'Oh yeah and look at you two... who picked your clothes out this evening Stevie Wonder? Honestly... I've seen wounds better dressed than that.' The phrases seemed to drop unpremeditated from his lips and, having uttered them, Ossie rocked back on his heels like a fly fisherman whom having cast his bait into the river was now waiting for a fish to bite.

Just as the verbal small arms fire looked as if it was going to get out of hand everyone's attention in the bar became focussed on a brawl that had broken out in the main cellar.

It wasn't so much of a brawl as a stand off... a stand off between a large mullet haired man, not too dissimilar to the Giant of Zilina and the group of pink shirted lads we had seen earlier.

Mullet Man removed his shirt and raised his clenched fists above his head, his naked torso was a riot of tattoos and pasty fat... an obvious state-ment on its owners behalf that he wasn't going to be taken down easily.

The music was still pounding away although the dance-floor had cleared. The teenage temptresses, sensing that a gusset moistening fight was about to kick off, were now stood on the chairs around its edge jostling each other in an attempt to secure the best view.

Mullet Man pointed at the tallest of the pink shirted brigade and then jabbed himself in the chest in a scene reminiscent of the wrestling show-downs on TV. As he did so the smallest pink shirted man stepped forward and, with a perfectly aimed right upper cut, caught Mullet Man on the point of his chin with his fist.

Mullet Man collapsed to the floor, the music stopped and everyone, ourselves included, began to cheer.

'Got your number 118,' shouted Young Dave at the top of his voice. Everyone that was English and watching proceedings roared their approval. The advert for the new directory enquiries service featuring the two mullet haired athletes had caught the publics imagination and its slogan was currently being bandied about at will.

The bars security staff walked across the floor and dragged the still unconscious Mullet Man out through the fire escape at the rear of the cellar.

Within a matter of minutes, with order restored, everything was back to normal; the lads in pink shirts returned to their peacock like courtship rituals with the teenage girls, and we continued our discussion about the merits and demerits of fashion in football.

*   *   *

'Blimey... what you been doin in there,' Ugly John asked Young Dave, as he finally returned from the toilet. 'We've been waitin ages... c'mon it's Goldfinger time.'

'Yeah yeah... I'm here son,' said Young Dave, unapologetically. 'I bumped into one of the pink shirted geezers in the khazi and I was havin a little chat with 'im... you'll never guess what though?' Young Dave tapped his fingers on his hips, raised his eyebrows and pursed his lips like a camp game show host.

'Go on what?' came the reply from all of us.

'The geezers in the pink shirts... no wonder that little guy took out Mullet Man in the way he did, they are part of the Swiss army boxing team... been coming out here for a holiday every year since 1993 when they were stationed just outside Prague as part of the NATO peacekeeping force overseeing the separation of Czechoslovakia.' Young Dave raised the index finger of his right hand in a 'knowledge is power' manner and turned to head up the stairs.

'Bollocks,' I countered confidently, ' the Swiss don't have an army... they never go to war.'

'Course they do donut... what about all those pen knives with the red enamel finish and silver cross... what are they called then?' Young Dave had a valid point, why would you call a penknife a Swiss army knife if it wasn't named after an army?

'Who cares anyway... come on... come on now, Goldfingers awaits our custom.' Ossie clapped his hands impatiently and ushered us along the street in a schoolmasterly fashion his mind already drawn to the waiting pleasures that lay ahead.

* * *

I loved everything about Goldfingers; I loved the cut glass Venetian chandeliers that hung from the ornately decorated ceiling, I loved the heavy bronze statuettes and figurines that stood sentinel like on the Italian marble floor in the foyer, and I loved the mauve coloured rich velour upholstery of the well appointed seats we had taken up at a table which was perfectly positioned at the end of the catwalk which snaked out from the stage.

There was a decadent grandeur about the place which never failed to impress even the most ethical of clientele, although ethics tended to be left at the entrance door to be collected several hours later at the time of departure.

For me though if I was put on the spot and asked, "what is it that you love most about Goldfingers Marco?" Well it would be a very simple straight forward answer. 'The dancing girls.'

Each one was a miracle of human engineering able to display a range of perfectly choreographed gymnastic skills on the pole which would have challenged the legend that was Olga Korbut. Their proud aquiline features were etched by the penumbral lighting which flashed in time with the soft RnB music to which they danced in turns. In short, if you wanted to see the best looking women in the world disrobing for your pleasure then this was the place to visit.

Goldfingers was a world away from the grotty pubs of my youth, where talentless slappers with greasy hair and naked flesh the colour of old powdered milk paraded their bodies for a bucket of loose change. Of course the world had moved on since then, with the likes of Stringfellows and the Spearmint Rhino chain creating a more luxurious environment for the discerning voyeur.

We sat and watched in silence, applauding occasionally like well disciplined theatre goers. Soon though our silence became increasingly punctuated by sharp intakes of breath accompanied by 'look at the money box on that' type observations as we marvelled at the wonders of the female forms displayed before us.

The equally beautiful waitresses had a beguiling candour and their eyes seemed to twinkle seductively at me as they walked past our table compelling me to finish my drink and order another. It was all part of the game, and the game basically involved the girls getting us punters to part with our money as frequently as possible.

Of course the other great thing about Goldfingers was the comparative cost. Yes it was expensive when compared to any other night out that Prague could offer, but compared to similar racy establishments back in London it was an absolute bargain.

If Ossie, Young Dave and Ugly John arose from their drunken slumbers the next day with slightly troubled consciences, concerned that their wives or girlfriends might be less than impressed that their men-folks loins had been stirred by such visions of female gorgeousness then I knew I would not.

In the amoral world that I inhabited, the only thing that I was concerned about was ensuring that I maximised my enjoyment of the whole Goldfingers experience. 'Maximising' being defined has having a private dance in one of the partitioned booths which sat behind the frosted glass panel at the rear of the seating area.

The procedure was simple. Once each girl had completed her solo slot on stage she would don a slinky cat-suit and walk from table to table offering to dance in private for anyone willing to invest 1500 Czech Koruna (about £35) for the privilege. With so much mouth watering eye candy to choose from in this particular sweetshop it was difficult to know where to start.

The oily, gold toothed, perfidious mafia types sat at the next table were launching themselves indiscriminately on the girls as they walked by. Their lascivious leers were greeted with coquettish smiles as deals were struck and one by one they would venture to a booth with the girl of their choice returning ten minutes or so later ready for the next selection. It was an addictive business and like most addictions it could prove to be very expensive if it wasn't kept in check.

We were discussing the actions of the mafia gang on the next table when I first saw her... there she was, the perfect girl for me. She danced with effortless ease and perfect timing. Her raven black hair was pinned up above eyebrows that looked like they had a life of their own, and her breasts seemed to crave fame more than any other part of her body.

Her skin was deeply tanned and flawless except for two words tattooed across her stomach in antique style writing. The first word was

Fred, the second I couldn't quite make out although Ossie was convinced it said Perry. I couldn't imagine for one minute that a Czech stripper would have Fred Perry tattooed across her stomach and if she did then there would have to be a very good reason for it. With my curiosity and libido sufficiently aroused, there was only going to be one way to find out.

As I ran my hands down the perfectly sculpted curves that formed her hips she looked at me with her chocolate coloured slightly melancholic eyes and told me her name was Patricia. The dance was slow and seductive but this was as far as the sexual fantasy would ever go... there would be no realization, no frantic coupling and no happy ever after... Goldfinger's ever vigilant security staff would see to that.

I asked her about the tattoo, which on very close inspection spelt the name Fred Egil. It was the name of her boyfriend, a Norwegian snowboarder whom she had met several years ago. She told me that they fought a lot because he didn't appreciate her working as a dancing girl. I asked her if she regretted the tattoo and she said no because if they split up then she would have laser treatment to have it removed.

She told me that she was only going to 'dance' for another year or so and then she was going to buy a house in the country and work as a school teacher, and while she told me all of this I traced the tip of my tongue from her belly button to her throat drawing my hands across her breasts as I did so.

I paid Patricia an additional 500 Koruna for an 'extended play' which was over all too soon, and then she was gone, leaving me to regain my composure before returning to the table and the enquiring questions of my friends.

We stayed until 4am, by which time the club was ready to close and we were all staggeringly drunk. I remember little about the cab ride home or how I managed to get myself undressed and into bed. But as I lay there in the muddy stream of semi-consciousness my thoughts drifted back to Goldfingers and in particular to Patricia... Had my conduct been worthy of moral condemnation?... Bollocks, who cares!

* * *

Not withstanding the fact that the four of us had spectacular hangovers and that crowds of tourists were swarming all over the place, we still couldn't fail to be impressed by the architectural drama that greeted us on every street corner as we made our way through the maze of alleys that led to Prague's 'Old Town' square.

It was just before 1pm and the squares perimeter cafes were spilling customers, many in the blue and the white shirts of Chelsea, out onto the pavements as they struggled to accommodate the demand for liquid refreshment brought on, as much as anything, by the blazing midday sunshine which had sent the temperature soaring into the 80's.

'Tell you what we should do... a boat trip, be nice that... you get a nice bit of air on those boats.' Ossie had been pretty subdued for the last couple of hours and took me by surprise with his suggestion which was a timely alternative to the aimless sightseeing we were currently engaged in.

I looked up at the brooding art nouveau sculpture of the Czech martyr Jan Hus which dominated the square and shrugged my shoulders.

'Good enough for me,' I replied enthusiastically, 'I'm knackered, don't wanna be tired for the game tonight, it's a long day innit.'

To tell the truth I'm a lazy sod. I could appreciate culture and beauty, but if it involved walking aimlessly for hours on end then it was nice to have a few other options.

We walked slowly across the square to join Ugly John and Young Dave and watch the famous old Astronomical Clock strike 1pm. Mechanically the clock was somewhat of a marvel having survived heavy damage during World War 2. We all watched with some amusement as Ugly John wrestled with his camera and a crowd of Japanese tourists as he endeavoured to get a snap of the clock as it struck the hour. This was no ordinary clock though; not only did it serve to mark the hours, but symbols of the zodiac also charted the course of the heavens. As the bell tolled the windows in the clock tower snapped open impressively and a procession of mechanical apostles, skeletons and sinners began their ritualistic dance of destiny.

'You know the story about the geezer that built the clock don't you?' Ugly John didn't wait for our response as we made our way back past the Old Town hall, through the Royal Way and across the cobbled street that ran along the banks of the River Vlatava.

'Town officials were so worried that he'd duplicate his masterpiece that they had him blinded... in revenge he managed to climb the clock tower and stop the clock and it remained silent for over fifty years.'

We were so wrapped up in the Ugly John 'Prague, city of culture' lecture, that to a man we all failed to see the tram that was speeding its way along the road towards us. Had it not been for the piercing shrill of a nearby policeman's whistle which alerted us to the oncoming danger there was a fair chance that we would have been spending some time in the local infirmary... at best!

*   *   *

The Charles Bridge is one of Prague's key attractions and today it was alive with tourists crossing the River Vlatava from Old Town to visit the city's famous castle. Buskers, performing dogs, souvenir hawkers and caricaturists competed with each other for peoples attention along with the monuments and statues that provided a dramatic frame for vistas up and down the river.

Ossie was leading the way and we followed him to the top of a wide stairwell that led down from the main walkway of the bridge to the riverbank.

'Look, it's Nobby Enfield,' whispered Ossie out of the corner of his mouth, as he spotted the Chelsea TV presenter and his crew at the foot of the steps.

Personally I didn't have much time for the man. His reports to me seemed one dimensional given the level of access he had to the players and officials at the club. I'd also long since tired of the obsequious manner in which he paraded ex players in front of the crowd at home games. At halftime, the announcement over the tannoy that it was 'time to go pitchside with Nobby', was my cue to curse and go and empty my bladder.

Despite all of this, Ossie was keen to find out what Nobby Enfield knew about Chelsea's backroom activities and in particular a certain rumour that had been troubling everyone for the past few weeks.

After allowing Nobby to conduct a short 'interview' with us for Chelsea TV, during which a stage-fright enveloped Ugly John informed the viewers back at home he'd enjoyed watching Chelsea play 'Inter' Milan in the San Siro and that it was his humble opinion that 'William' Bogarde [sic] had been a less than wise investment, Ossie seized the opportunity to probe the mans knowledge of what was being plotted in Chelsea's boardroom.

'All right Nobby, what's the craic with Eriksson?' Ossie's question was both pertinent and direct.

'Well of course you know that Eriksson was Roman's second major signing... it's a done deal,' quipped Enfield smugly, the matter of fact manner in which he replied forcing me to bite my tongue to prevent myself from verbally abusing him.

'If it's true then that's bad news,' replied Ossie, voicing our sentiments. 'Everyone loves Ranieri, look at what he did last season without money to spend... he's a Chelsea man... he gave players like John Terry their chance in the first team and he has their respect.

Enfield wasn't having it, but Ossie hadn't finished yet. 'Eriksson's a mercenary,' he continued, 'he's hardly achieved much since he's been in England, beating the Kraut's 5–1 in their own back yard, I'll give him that... but what else? Unless you count getting into that Swedish weather girls knickers... which aint exactly hard now is it?'

Ossie wasn't happy, and neither was I... particularly when Nobby Enfield made the observation that Eriksson would be able to communicate with the players properly. Enough was enough. Since the discussion wasn't really going anywhere, and I could see that Ugly John's normally taciturn features had been replaced with a menacing glare that had Enfield shuffling nervously from one foot to the other like a nervous meerkat surveying the high plains and espying a hungry pride of lions advancing towards him, I decided to call time on proceedings by pointing at my watch and then at the pleasure boat moored on the nearby river-bank.

*   *   *

Finally we boarded the Blue Heaven, a less than seaworthy looking vessel crewed by an enterprising bunch of trouser enthusiasts who plied us with Pilsner Urquel and herbal cigarettes. The cruise was pleasant enough; we sat up on Blue Heaven's deck basking in the warm afternoon sunshine reliving Ugly John's inspired interview and pondering who Roman's first signing might have been if Eriksson truly was his second.

Young Dave was of the opinion that it may have been Beckham; a secret deal done with the England captain to ensure that when he was through at Madrid the next club he would play for would be Chelsea. The general consensus however was that it most likely related to the recently announced departure of the clubs highly regarded chief executive Trevor Birch.

Birch's replacement would be Manchester United's CEO Peter Kenyon; yet another Abramovich 'finger in the eye' to those who continued to believe that he wasn't serious about Chelsea and that it was just an expensive toy for him to play with until he got bored.

Kenyon had been given most of the credit for building United into a global brand and brokering the sponsorship deals with Nike and Vodafone as well as retaining the managerial services of Fergie when he was an alleged target for Chelsea back in the summer.

So if it was true that Abramovich had made him his first signing, then it was now clear to all of us that right from the off he'd had a vision and a strategy to make the football club that he'd purchased, and rumours had it that he'd looked at Rottenham Dropspur, Leeds and Man U first, number one across the globe.

'Look out Young Dave!' shouted Ossie, as the Blue Heaven cruised under the Charles Bridge distracting a flock of pigeons roosting on its cornices. But it was too late for Young Dave, he wasn't as quick as he used to be and he couldn't avoid the shower of pigeon shit that rained down from above and splattered itself across the back of his pristine white new Chelsea away shirt.

'Don't worry... it's a sign from God,' said Young Dave, grinning as he took a swig from the beer bottle he was holding before carefully removing the shirt.

'What sign is that then?' burbled Ossie. 'A sign that the Chels are going to get shat on tonight?' he continued, his voice trembling with laughter.

'No my friends,' replied Young Dave in a scholastic manner, 'in the Czech Republic when a pigeon shits on your shirt it's God's way of telling you that all your hopes and wishes for the day will come true.'

'Bollocks!' retorted Ossie, his face crimson with mirth, eyes watering as he watched Young Dave try and wipe the rapidly drying pigeon shit from his shirt. 'It's God's way of telling you you're a homosexual.'

'I'm telling you... it's the truth. When we got on the boat... the skipper was wiping pigeon shit off his hat... and he told me it was good luck.' Young Dave wasn't going to concede the argument, but then neither was Ossie.

'Yeah!... But look at him, he's a right mincer,' he replied, 'I'm telling you... if a pigeon shits on you, it means that you're a faggot... and in your case Young Dave, an old faggot ha ha.'

'Enough girls... enough!' Ugly John banged his empty bottle of Pilsner Urquel on the floor to draw attention to himself and draw to an end the verbal spat between Ossie and Young Dave. 'Look, as far as I'm concerned you're both faggots now stop digging each other out and shout up some more beer... let's get back to the world of football do you agree with me Marco?'

I sat there shaking my head in mock disbelief at our immaturity. 'Yeah come on Ossie you tart leave the old boy alone... he's got some laundry to do. Now sort out the blobs and tell us what you know about the new Roman Empire.'

Whilst Young Dave busied himself with his cleaning duties, Ugly John went to the toilet and Ossie shouted up the beers. I sat back in my seat and turned my face up to the sun stretching and yawning as I did so, grateful that my hangover was finally wearing off.

Ossie, who had gleaned from various sources a fairly detailed knowledge of the workings of Chelski explained how Abramovich, who was not a director of the club, had installed three key power brokers, Eugene

Tenenbaum, Richard Creitzman and Bruce Buck, on the board of a new company which was now known as Chelsea Limited.

Respected by the City, this financial and legal muscle had been hired to work alongside the now 'non-executive' chairman Ken Bates and, up until the last weekend anyway, incumbent chief executive Trevor Birch.

In addition to these people Ossie explained that Abramovich also used a cabal of advisers, most notably Eriksson's mate Pini Zahavi and Eugene Shvidler to keep him updated on football matters both inside and outside the club.

I sat there and thought about it all as Ossie was unravelling things. The more I thought about it, the more I realised that Abramovich, for a man of so few years, was a shrewd, commercial genius who maybe really did have a long term plan for Chelsea.

He had after all bought up every single last share in the club and taken it private again, a deal which had netted old Batesy, the original saviour of Stamford Bridge, a cool £17 million. In doing so he'd said, "I am sure people will focus on me for three or four days, then it will pass. They will forget who I am".

If he'd bought a club in any other country in the world then maybe this would have been the case, but not in England. The media were doing their best to disentangle his business dealings and every day the papers were full of anecdotal stories about the origins of his wealth and his motives for buying an English football club, our football club.

The best of these anecdotes was the one Young Dave loved to tell about when Roman was flying back to Heathrow in his private helicopter after unsuccessful takeover talks with Spurs. Legend had it that as the chopper banked over West London on it's approach to the airport, Abramovich looked out of the window and saw Chelsea Village. He asked the pilot, who was a Chelsea supporter, what he was looking at... and the rest as they say, was history.

*   *   *

'Nearly as ugly as you eh, that gargoyle son,' I said to Ugly John, as we looked up in awe at the magnificent Gothic edifice of St Vitius Cathedral which formed part of the grounds of Prague Castle, the largest ancient castle in the world.

'I'm not ugly,' replied Ugly John, as he began to stroll at a leisurely pace down the steeply inclined path which led down from the castle.

'Seriously son, you are... isn't he lads?' I looked to Young Dave and Ossie for support and they duly nodded their agreement.

Ugly John stopped in his tracks and turned to face us speaking sardon-
ically in pronouncements beyond contradiction.

'I tell you now... I'm not ugly... that Nobby Enfield, look at him... now
he's really ugly... didn't you think that when you saw him just now? What
an ugly bloke eh.'

It was a fair point, Nobby wasn't particularly handsome... but Ugly
Nobby didn't sound right, and anyway he wasn't one of us so what did it
matter? Ugly John was Ugly John, not Handsome John or Striking John or
even Gorgeous John. As we continued our walk down the hill I wondered
if Nobby Enfield was aware of the fact that he had a Marmite effect on
people... you either loved him or you didn't.

Maybe if he wasn't so full of his own self importance, then Chelsea
fans like us might be slightly more tolerant. The trouble with Nobby
Enfield was, that he really believed he was an elegant opinionated provo-
cateur... one cut above the rest of us... which, given the fact that we were
meant to be his audience, was a big mistake.

We eventually ended up in the Jewish Quarter, an area that had
suffered serious damage during the floods which ravaged the city in
August 2002. Following weeks of torrential rain the River Vltava had
burst its banks and in the ensuing debacle sixteen people died and thousands more had been forced to evacuate their homes.

I remembered watching on TV the desperate attempts to rescue the
elephant trapped by rising water in the city zoo and wondering at the
time if it would be possible to repair all the damage that was being done
to Prague's numerous cultural and tourist attractions?

Well the evidence was here for all to see. If you put your mind to it...
anything was possible. Everything had been painstakingly restored.
Plaster and brickwork perfectly rendered, paint colour matched, and
wood varnished... the attention to detail was nothing short of magnificent.

* * *

'Got your number 118... got your number 118... got your number 118.' The three
Chelsea shirted lads walking just in front of us were pointing out each
Sparta fan they spotted sporting a fine mullet hairdo and milking the gag
to its limit.

They had it just about right though, the road leading up to the Letna
Stadion was busy enough with groups of Puffa jacketed '118's' congregating in the gathering gloom around the ubiquitous hot dog and beer
stalls viewing our progress with a mixture of befuddlement and suspicion.

Another group of Chelsea fans walking just behind us began

chorusing the 118 jingle from the TV advert which simply involved chanting 118 over the Rocky theme music; this was the cue for all of us to join in the sing song.

'118... 118... 118... 118... 118... 118... 118...118... 118... 118... 118...118.'

'Sparta... Sparta... Sparta,' came the half hearted reply.

Outside the stadium the police presence was low key but unlike their counterparts across the border in Slovakia this lot looked the part, dressed head to foot in full Darth Vader style riot gear, wielding menacing looking batons.

'Zees von von ate... von von ate... vot eet means please?' The question was asked of me by a thickly moustachioed, mullet haired man who was stood in front of me in the queue I'd joined outside the Sparta club shop.

I thought about my answer for a split second before replying.

'It's a traditional English greeting for people with long hair,' I offered, looking around at the puzzled faces of the other Sparta fans in the queue who were trying to understand what I was talking about. 'Er it comes from the time when our King Charles was on the throne leading his Cavalier's into battle with Oliver Cromwell's Roundhead's... the Cavaliers had long hair and 118 was the code by which they identified each other.'

I wasn't exactly sure what had prompted that utterance of complete bollocks but my answer was graciously accepted by this particular '118' who then proceeded to translate into his native tongue the misinformation I had just given him to the remainder of the people in the queue.

I watched with interest as each of the Sparta fans in front of me made their way to the counter and made exactly the same purchase; a small bag of what looked liked balloons that required inflating.

The man in front of me who'd asked about the meaning of 118 stuffed the bag of balloons he'd just bought into the inside pocket of his crimson puffa jacket and then pointed at my shaven head, smirking and shaking his head as he said, 'You not von von ate... no hair... you Oliver Cromwell.'

*   *   *

The Letna Stadion although relatively new, lacked any kind of character at all. Quite simply it looked as if it has been symmetrically moulded from one huge slab of drab grey concrete.

On gaining admission through the turnstiles the first thing we noticed was the smell; this was no stench from the trench, no familiar football ground smell of hot dogs and burgers, this was the smell of... chickens!

'Look at that,' exclaimed Ossie, pointing at row after row of rotisserie chickens turning slowly on their spits in a specially customised trailer that was parked in the stadium concourse. 'There must be thousands of 'em in there... Jesus that can't be good for ya,' he continued, scratching his head as we watched a steady stream of Chelsea fans, clearly oblivious to the potential health risks, queue up and part with their cash for an entire roast chicken that was presented to them wrapped in kitchen roll.

'Ranieri's blue and white army.'

The chant was loud and clear and it rung in our ears as we ascended the steps and walked out into the Chelsea section of the upper tier of the stadium. We were in a corner section of the ground forming that was adequately partitioned off from the home supporters whose most vociferous element was to be found behind the goal away to our right. A huge net, suspended in a similar fashion to the safety nets you see in circus tents, was positioned in such a way that any objects thrown in the direction of the pitch from our section would land on it rather than the heads of the home supporters in the stand below.

Claudio was once again going through his pre-match ritual, scrutinising the players feet as they performed the now customary sprints in front of him.

The team was announced amid some groans. No John Terry or Lampard. Cudicini was in goal. Bill Gallas, making his first start of the season, partnered Johnson, Bridge and Desailly in defence and Makalele and Crespo were being given their full debuts. The remainder of the starting line up comprised of Geremi, Petit, Veron and Mutu.

'Hernan Crespo... Hernan Crespo... hello, hello Hernan Crespo.'

Hernan acknowledged his name being chanted, clapping his hands 'footballer style' above his head. As I watched and listened I wondered if he might ask one of the other players what the name of the tune was whose melody had been hijacked for this purpose.

If he did ask, then how would he react to the news that the anthemic melody belonged to a song called 'Good to be back' which had been taken to the top of the charts by a convicted paedophile called Gary Glitter?

* * *

The stadium looked pretty full. The official attendance was later given as 18,997 of which 1230 were quoted as being Chelsea fans. I assumed that 1230 was the number of tickets that had been sold by the club directly to Chelsea supporters. This number would not take into account the fans who had bought tickets from touts in Prague and had then blagged their way into the Chelsea pen.

I put our number nearer to 2000. Everyone was represented. The

Battersea mob, the Bromley contingent, Chelsea Youth, Chelsea Up Norf, the usual cross section of Stone Island casuals, Burberry boys, scarfers and of course Chelsea Gate 17.

I couldn't see the old school Chelsea Headhunters; Spangle, Stanley, Fuck Off Colin, Freddy Fingers, Ronny Cutlass and the like, but I knew they'd all be here just as they were in Zilina.

The game kicked off with Chelsea attacking our end and within a couple of minutes Mutu headed a great looking cross from Johnson just wide of the far post.

'*Миииии Тиииии... Миииии Тиииии,*' was the chant every-time the Romania striker touched the ball. 'First name on the team sheet,' Ossie had said earlier, when we were analysing the strength and depth of the current Chelsea squad.

The first half of the game was a scrappy affair littered with fouls, offsides, missed tackles and passes that failed to find their man. For Sparta, the original '118' himself, Poborsky looked as impressive as he had in his early days at Manchester United.

For Chelsea, Veron showed the occasional flash of brilliance and Makalele worked tigerishly in midfield but it was Crespo, who'd hit a crisp volley early on which the Sparta keeper did well to save, who'd come the nearest to breaking the deadlock; an effort which had us all chanting his name again.

Mutu and Petit were substituted at half time, replaced by Frank Lampard and the welcome sight of Damien Duff. With the change, Chelsea's shape improved markedly, both Bridge and Johnson began to get forward more often to threaten Sparta down the flanks.

'*If she don't come I'll tickle her bum with a lump of celery... celery... celery.*'

This was another chant for Crespo and the Sparta fans to ponder, as a hail of oversize celery sticks accompanied by a healthy portion of chicken bones were thrown repeatedly into the air eventually finding their way onto the safety net in front of us

The Sparta fans didn't seem to go much beyond chanting the name of their team although I finally figured out the purpose of the balloons that the home support had bought in large numbers from the club shop. The crowd gathered behind the far goal had inflated them and, from where we were sat, seemed to be jumping up and down and hitting each other over the head with them until they burst... and we thought we were mad!

We looked on with increasing frustration and gathering impatience as Seba Veron twice knocked inch perfect balls through to his fellow Argentinean Crespo only for the latter to fire wide on both occasions.

'Don't tell me he's gonna be another Robert Fleck?' remarked Ugly

John, casting our minds back to the profligate performances of the little Scotsman who'd retained the affection of the Shed faithful despite scoring more goals in opposition colours at the Bridge than he ever did for Chelsea.

'Give him a chance Ugly,' retorted Young Dave, a man who always staunchly defended Chelsea's newest recruits in the face of the sternest criticism.

But even Young Dave couldn't help himself from joining in the chant that had undoubtedly been started by an individual whose thoughts were in tune with those of Ugly John.

'And number one is Robert Fleck, and number two is Robert Fleck...'

The chant, sung to the melody of The Beatles 'Yellow Submarine', finished with the rousing chorus of *'We all live in a Robert Fleck world a Robert Fleck world a Robert Fleck world...'* and we applauded each other at its conclusion. It was one of those transcendent Chelsea terrace moments that are hard to convey to neutrals and as the applause died away, in what was a bizarre feat of timing, Ranieri substituted Hasselbaink for Crespo.

'Chelsea... Chelsea... Chelsea...'

The chanting gained momentum and served to inspire our team to continue to press forward. The goal, when it eventually came six minutes from time, was a scrappy affair with Bill Gallas of all people getting ahead of West Ham reject Vladimir Labant to sweep Jimmy's flicked header into the back of the net.

Cue the Gary Glitter classic with a different set of words this time.

'Chelsea are back... Chelsea are back, hello hello... Chelsea are back.'

The remaining time was played out with the minimum of fuss and at the final whistle the Chelsea players came over to applaud our support and everyone stayed in their places to cheer them from the pitch. Ugly but effective football had won the day.

Match Result
Athletic Club Sparta Prague 0 : Chelsea FC 1

* * *

We were detained in the stadium for a quarter of an hour or so but nobody was too concerned; news filtered through that Lazio had beaten Besiktas 2-0 in Istanbul, a result which confirmed the pundits predictions that Chelsea and Lazio would be the likely qualifiers from Group G... so far, so good.

The police escort from the ground was well coordinated but unnecessary. There had been no hint of trouble either before or during the game and there were no groups of '118's' loitering with intent as we made our way back down the main road that led away from the stadium.

The faces I'd looked for, but hadn't seen in the ground were here now; at the head of the escort was Spangle, hips swaying, chest puffed out, he had the bravado and the swagger of a military general and an air of confidence about him that suggested he could pull any girl in town... without paying for the privilege.

We stayed with the escort until the police lines thinned out and then crossed the road; Young Dave hailed one of the numerous taxi's that were cruising slowly past and within minutes we were speeding back across one of the River Vltava's many bridges heading for the Double Trouble bar where we'd had such a craic the previous evening.

*   *   *

Young Dave was perched on the edge of his bar stool, beer in hand grinning from ear to ear. This was his time now, he loved it... he was in the zone, dissecting Chelsea's performance while it was still fresh in his mind and sharing his opinions on the match with anyone who cared to listen.

Ugly John was entertaining himself by counting the number of people wearing Stone Island clobber and then trying to prove if there was a statistical correlation between this and being bald. His theory was based on the fact that I was wearing a Stone Island shirt and was, as he often reminded me... a slaphead.

Ossie and I were embroiled in a conversation about the benefits of having a much younger girlfriend. Well it wasn't much of a conversation, it was an opportunity for Ossie to justify his love for a woman half his age and for me to conclude that I needed to sort my life out.

Young Dave and Ugly John were family men, and like most family men they loved to have a moan about the missus... and if it's not about the missus then it's about the kids and if it's not about the kids then it's something else... but they love it really.

Ossie, well he seemed to have it all worked out on the female front... a proper strategy and an end game with a lot of tangible benefits, fair play to him.

As for me; well things hadn't worked out with Zori. After my visit to Vegas she'd come over to England and immediately started picking holes in my lifestyle and my mates; no matter how large her breasts were the relationship was never going to flower on such uncompromising ground.

I couldn't be bothered with one of those 'right for now relationships' where love was guessed at and not expressed, where mealtime conversations ended up being restricted to 'pass the salt'. No, that wasn't for me... trouble was, I wasn't really sure what was.

Of course the one benefit of bachelorhood was that I never had to wrestle with my conscience when it came to matters of the flesh, which was why I was now trying to canvass support for another excursion to Goldfingers!

Unfortunately there was to be no reprise that evening. A new virus was spreading through the Gate 17 camp like the latest computer worm, it was called guilt.

'There's nothing to feel guilty about,' I said, trying to hide the disappointment in my voice. 'We're only looking... it's no different to visiting an art gallery or a museum really is it?'

Young Dave slugged back the last dregs of his beer and wiped his forearm across his mouth before beckoning us all in close so we could listen to what he had to say.

'Marco... it's nothing to do with feeling guilty, not like that anyway... you all know that Mrs Young Dave is the only woman I've ever slept with; no for me it's more to do with the fact that... mmm well... places like Goldfingers well... er well...'

'Well what Young Dave?' I looked at him impatiently, nodding at the others as I did so. This ought to be good I thought to myself.

'Well they degrade women and create an imbalance in the local economy.' Young Dave sat back up on his bar stool and waited for a reaction.

If it wasn't for the fact that the music was so loud, for a split second you could have heard that proverbial pin drop.

'You hypocrite,' we bellowed simultaneously, in a mock purgatory of umbrage that drew the unwanted attention of the oversize '118' who was ordering a drink at the bar.

It was Mullet Man from the previous evening.

'Heee Po Creeeeete... Heee Po Creeeeete... ha ha ha,' roared Mullet Man, turning to us and raising a large glass which was filled brimful with an emerald green liquid that looked like it could inflict damage. 'Heee Po Creeeeete... Good,' he said once more, in the manner of a master of ceremonies proposing a toast at a wedding.

We looked on in amazement as Mullet Man made the sign of the cross and then downed the contents of his glass in one before pirouetting like a prima ballerina and collapsing unceremoniously in a heap on the floor in front of us,

'Kin 'ell... what is that stuff?' asked Ossie, the furrows between his eyebrows deepening as he grimaced at the sight of poor Mullet Man who, for the second night running, was being bundled out of the bar by a couple of burly security men.

'Absinthe mate,' said Ugly John, without hesitation. 'Invented by a French physician called Doctor Ordinaire,' he continued expertly, 'it's made from wormwood soaked in ethanol and was originally administered to the French troops fighting in the Algerian wars as a malaria preventative.'

Ugly John amazed me sometimes with his depth of trivial knowledge. Once he was into his stride there was no stopping him as he went onto explain how the drink had been banned just about everywhere for the best part of half a century before an enterprising Czech distiller called Radomil Hill began legally producing it again.

'Sounds great UJ,' I said, studying the row of Absinthe bottles on the top shelf behind the barman who was stood, hands on hips, waiting patiently for me to order the next round of drinks.

'Right then... four Absinthe please mate.' I raised four fingers of my left hand and then pointed at the bottle of Hills Absinthe which had a distinctive green fairy on its label.

The barman smiled at me. 'You drink it the proper way... yes?' he said, putting the bottle on the bar along with four glasses, a spoon, a bowl of sugar and a bottle of mineral water.

'Yes mate... the proper way,' I replied, nodding and giving the thumbs up to Ossie who was looking on nervously.

The barman filled four glasses with Absinthe and then heaped some sugar on the spoon. He asked me to pick up one of the glasses and then dipped the spoon into it taking great care not to spill any sugar. Young Dave was asked to spark up his lighter and the barman held the spoon over the flame until the sugar started to melt at which point he dripped it slowly into the glass which I was still holding until the Absinthe caught fire.

'I put some water in now to put out the fire yes... then you drink it all in one... then the same for your friends,' said the barman, dousing the flames with a small measure of water

As I drank the liquid it seemed to explode on my tongue and vaporise through my nostrils, I could feel the heat of it coursing down my throat and burning its way into my stomach. I felt my eyes begin to water as I placed the empty glass back on the bar; the dry yet bitter aniseedy aftertaste left in my mouth rendered me uncharacteristically speechless.

'The Russian's call wormwood Chernobyl,' Ugly John said sagely, patting me on the back as we watched the barman prepare a glass for Ossie. 'It grows throughout central Europe along what is said to be the path the exiled serpent took from Eden.'

'Urgh... there's nothing good about that... nothing good about that at all,' spluttered Ossie, when he drained the contents of the glass which he was now holding up to the light.

'70% proof this gear Absolut vodkas only 40%,' continued Ugly John, a man who was clearly enjoying the spectacle as Young Dave prepared himself for the inevitable. 'They banned it because it causes hallucinations, brain damage, epilepsy and degenerate behaviour.'

We all laughed as Young Dave cursed the effects of the Absinthe.

For me it felt as if I'd injected the stuff rather than drank it. I felt an internal glow that reminded me of the time when I'd experimented with intravenous hard drugs as a teenager.

'Come on then Ugly... let's 'av it then my son.' Ossie, composure regained, was as keen as the rest of us to see Ugly John, professor of Absinthology at Double Trouble University, imbibe the medicine about which he knew so much.

'Arghhhh... YES!' Ugly John clenched his right fist and brought it down hard on the bar as he swallowed the contents of the glass he was holding in his left hand. He staggered backwards clutching his stomach and fell to the floor laughing.

'Fucking hell... your right Ossie, there's definitely nothing good about that,' he said, staggering back to his feet and ordering another four drinks.

* * *

I was struggling to keep my eyes open as I sat on the train at Waterloo station waiting for it to depart. We'd gone our separate ways at Liverpool Street and so I was on my own now, well not quite I also had three days stubble and a heinous bout of indigestion for company.

I looked and felt like shit. I'd looked like shit when I'd woken up this morning with a hangover that would have terrified the likes of George Best and I'd looked even worse when I'd admired myself in the toilet mirror on the flight back from Prague just prior to throwing up the entire Absinthe soaked contents of my stomach.

The severe looking woman who came and sat opposite me viewed me with suspicion through narrowed eyes. I imagined what she might be thinking as she surveyed my dishevelled state and I smirked as she wrinkled her nose at the pungent smell of the fart I had just let go silently.

I looked at her and scowled, picking up my copy of the Evening Standard from whose back page beamed the genial face of Claudio Ranieri. Claudio interviews never failed to make me smile and this one was no different.

"We are like a baby," he'd said after the game, "we have learnt to crawl but although we are trying to get on our feet we have not been able to do it".

'Brilliant, the mans absolutely brilliant,' I muttered, watching with contempt as the severe woman shook her head at me, collected her belongings and stood up. When she left the carriage she slammed the door so loudly behind her I thought it would come off its mountings.

'Yeah fuck you too love,' I exclaimed, for no-ones benefit other than my own before burying my head back in the Ranieri article. "We are like a baby". What a great analogy, I thought, and thank fuck then that Bill Gallas had been able to stand on his feet momentarily and score the winner last night.

The train moved off and as it did so my mobile rang, it was Sex Case calling to get the low-down on Goldfingers from whence I'd sent him numerous texts on Monday evening. During the course of our conversation he informed me that his beloved Arsenal were 3-0 down at home to Inter Milan and it wasn't yet half time.

'Fuck me son... that's terrible,' I said with mock sincerity, kicking off my shoes and putting my feet up on the seat in front of me... happy days!

SS LAZIO
UEFA Champions League
Group G
Stadio Olimpico, Rome, Italy
Tuesday 4th November 2003

Sometimes trying to coordinate European away trips can seem more arduous than the task politicians have trying to negotiate peace in the Middle East. The trip to Rome for the Lazio match was always going to be 'the' fixture for those fans looking to cherry pick just one of Chelsea's Group G fixtures. With more and more supporters opting to make their own travel arrangements you needed to be quick off the mark as flights were being booked up within hours of the draw being made.

Initially just Ugly John and myself were confirmed to travel; Ugly had come up with a great deal flying with BA from Heathrow on the morning of the game. The package comprised of the return flight and one nights accommodation in a four star hotel... the cost, £160 all in... well played Ugly John.

Young Dave originally hadn't put his name forward for the trip as Mrs Young Dave had been prevaricating about his level of commitment to their restaurant. Having been to Rome the last time we played Lazio there he wanted to show willing in order to replenish the number of brownie points he had, which would need to be at their maximum level, to permit a visit to Turkey for the Besiktas match in December.

Young Dave however had a cunning plan; He'd wooed Mrs Young Dave with a flowery yarn about how the word romantic had first been used to describe the wealthy Italian noblemen who used to take their consorts to Rome for lavish weekends of passion. He'd also described the hotel that Ugly John had booked us into as an 'oasis of tranquillity immersed in an intricate labyrinth of colourful and vivacious narrow streets'.

What he hadn't done was tell her that just about every room in the 'oasis of tranquillity' had been booked up by Chelsea supporters who would be among the 4000 strong contingent of travelling fans drinking in the bars and cafes that populated those 'vivacious narrow streets'. Mrs Young Dave perceived the proposed visit to the Eternal City as a sweeping romantic gesture from her old man, she even wanted to go to the match itself which had taken him completely by surprise.

By the time Young Dave had confirmed their attendance, any available seats on our BA flight had long since gone. Fortunately, Ugly managed to get them on an Alitalia flight which arrived in Rome at roughly the same time as ours, thereby allowing us all to make the onward journey into the city together.

A far sterner examination of Ugly John's skills as a travel agent came when Lemon and Geordie Jase finally decided that they too also wanted to come on the trip. Match tickets and accommodation were not the problem, it was getting them to Rome that was proving difficult.

Any nagging doubts that we had as to whether or not Ugly John could deliver the goods were banished when an email arrived in my inbox with the subject heading *Lemon and Geordie Jase SORTED!*

They were sorted all right. £80 for a return flight from London to Rome with Czech Airlines; not only that, the flight departed from Heathrow... the only potential fly in the ointment was the fact they had to fly via Prague! Despite the detour, they were still scheduled to arrive in Rome at 2pm just three hours after the rest of us; Ugly John had done a good job and was once again applauded for his efforts.

*   *   *

'Tell you what mate it's mad innit... you know like the lead of Premiership, it's changed hands more times than a bottle of cider at youth club disco... between us, the Mancs... and the Arse... great though eh.'

Ugly John pointed at the league table printed on the inside of the back page of the Daily Mail he'd just been given by the matronly looking air hostess who was attending to our welfare on the flight this morning. I nodded my agreement to his statement and glanced back down the aisle as I did so, wondering to myself if it was something peculiar just to BA that the air hostesses on these short haul trips looked liked they needed to pay a flying visit to Inch Loss Island.

'Yes mate... and if it wasn't for the fact that Arsenal begins with an A and Chelsea with a C, we would right now be at the top of both the Premiership and Champions League Group G... good enough.'

Good enough?... Not half, in the six weeks since our victory in Prague we had been top of the domestic league on no less than three occasions.

The highlight of our league form had been a 5-0 away demolition of Wolverhampton Wanderers; a match which had seen Hernan Crespo silence the early doubters, myself included, with a well taken brace of goals.

The lowlight had to be the predictable reversal of fortune at Arsenal. 2-1 was the narrow margin of defeat, a loss made all the more frustrating because the winning goal had resulted from an uncharacteristically dreadful error by Carlo Cudicini... the devilish 'gloriously unpredictable' factor had entered the fray again.

That day I'd thought to myself about how and when I'd next like Chelsea to buck the trend in our matches against the Arse. How about if we met in the Champions League? Now that would be one hell of a day... or two... or maybe even three.

If the loss at Arsenal had not been unexpected, the loss at home to Besiktas in our second Group G game had been nothing short of disastrous. 0-2 in the driving rain playing against ten men. Oh yeah, that had been 'gloriously unpredictable' and bloody expensive as far as I was concerned.

Nobodies perfect, least of all me. I count gambling amongst my vices and like many gamblers I thought I'd hit upon an infallible system. In a nutshell this involved backing against, or 'laying off' to use the correct vernacular, a strongly un-fancied team in a football match.

I'd built up a very healthy pot of money laying off teams that were playing away at the likes of Man U, Arsenal, Celtic and Rangers. The good thing about 'laying' the outcome of a match was the fact that if the fancied side won or drew, you won the bet. The bad thing however, was that if the un-fancied team upset the form book and won... you were, to put not to fine a point on it, fucked!

Any gambler worth his salt will tell you, 'don't place sentimental bets'. In my case this would mean not betting on matches involving Chelsea... 'but it makes it more exciting doesn't it?' I'd thought to myself, having profited from placing bets on every single game Chelsea had been involved in this season with the exception of the matches against Liverpool and Arsenal which I'd left alone.

On the morning of the Besiktas game I'd actually thought about laying off Sparta Prague who were playing away at Lazio. The odds were the same as laying the Turkish side, but there was no way that the Chels were going to lose... so I placed my sentimental bet.

At half time, even though we were 0-2 down I still believed we could at least come back and snatch a draw. The half time score from Rome was 0-2 to Sparta and so I still felt vindicated in my decision.

There was no comeback. 'Gloriously unpredictable?' Fucking rubbish, more like. In the words of Ossie, there was 'nothing good about that'... nothing good about that at all. To rub salt in my festering wounds, Lazio came back to level the tie in Rome; if I'd gone with my initial gut instinct I wouldn't have been a monkey out of pocket.

Several weeks later I laid Australia in their rugby world cup semi-final match against 'red hot' favourites New Zealand. I don't know much about 'egg chasing' but this seemed like a dead cert according to the press. Australia won the match and I lost all my money, I don't gamble any more now.

*   *   *

Fiumicino airport, which serves Rome, is some 25km to the southwest of the city; we had already decided to take the train from the airport rather than a taxi since our hotel was close to Stazione Termini and Roman taxi drivers had an unscrupulous reputation for taking tourists to their destinations via the scenic route. In a city like Rome, where there was plenty of scenery, this could result in a hefty fare.

Vegas Dave and Bazza, the lads I'd first met in the States and subsequently bumped into with uncanny regularity in all manner of places including our usual pre-match watering hole the One Bar, were also booked into our hotel. Arriving the previous evening, they'd unsuspectingly taken a cab directly from the airport to the hotel; the language barrier had tipped the scales in the cab drivers favour and two hours later the boys had found themselves stiffed with a fare of 150 Euros (£100).

Travelling to Italy was always a pleasure for me now. My dear Chelsea worshipping mother was a native and luckily for me she'd taught me how to speak the language when I was kid. I hadn't always felt that way about it though, when I was a young I'd hated the fact that I was different and that my mum had a 'funny' accent.

As a leery teenager I all but denounced my Italian heritage; however, as with most things, the older you get, the wiser you become. Suddenly all things Italian became very cool; suddenly my ability to speak the lingo became a secret weapon in my armoury which could be called upon for a variety of purposes... ranging from getting us out of a few scrapes at Italia 90, to very occasionally charming the knickers off an impressionable disco dolly; suddenly the very heart of the team I loved had an Italian beat to it.

The most successful manager in the clubs history, Gianluca Vialli, was Italian; the most revered player in the clubs history, Gianfranco Zola, was Italian. The fastest and most memorable goal in the entire history of the

FA Cup had been scored by Chelsea's Roberto Di Matteo, an Italian... and of course then there was Claudio Ranieri, the man from Rome who was rapidly becoming a Chelsea cult hero.

* * *

'Bloody hell it's warm... how much further is it do you reckon?' Young Dave had broken into a sweat as he struggled to cope with the weight of Mrs Young Dave's suitcase which he'd offered to carry for her in a foolish act of chivalry.

'Should be just up here on the right,' replied Ugly John, squinting at the map he was holding. 'Blimey,' he continued, looking round at Young Dave, 'we're only here for a night what has the missus got in there, the kitchen sink?'

'Dunno mate,' replied Young Dave, stopping to wipe the perspiration from his brow. 'All I've got in there is my toothbrush and a change of underpants... I'm bloody knackered... and no wonder, you said it was just up here on the right ten minutes ago.'

Young Dave called after his wife who was walking some twenty odd meters in front of us. 'Oi Mrs Young Dave... wait... wait for us darling, come on.'

Mrs Young Dave eventually paused outside a delicatessen and looked back down the road towards us; she could have said something but she didn't have to, the look of contempt on her face said it all. It wasn't so much the walk that she didn't find agreeable, more so the environment we were walking through.

The area around the Stazione Termini was no different to the areas around major city railway stations the world over; it was a magnet for beggars and thieves, for addicts and their pushers, for prostitutes and their pimps. This profusion of drabness and futility always held a morbid fascination for Young Dave wherever he went; unfortunately for him however, this fascination was not mirrored by his wife.

'Tell you what why don't I ask those old dears over there where it is eh?' I offered. Without waiting for an answer I walked over to two ancient looking women swathed in black shawls who were sat outside a café on the other side of the road watching us with detached amusement.

'Mi scusi signore, va bene per l'Hotel Torino?' I asked, pointing up the street and then at Young Dave who had picked up Mrs Young Dave's suitcase and was now walking laboriously towards his wife.

'Dritto, sempre dritto,' rasped the older of the two women, a smile cracking across her wizened features. 'In fondo alla strada,' her friend continued helpfully, explaining that the Hotel Torino was straight on at the bottom of the street.

'Grazie mille,' I said graciously, thanking the women and turning to walk away.

As I did so one of the women called after me, I turned around and saw the elder of the two pointing at Young Dave who had taken off his jacket to reveal the white Chelsea 'away' shirt which, after the pigeon shit episode in Prague, was considered to be lucky and to be worn at all future away European fixtures... for the foreseeable future anyway!

The woman asked me which football team played in the shirt that the porter struggling with our lady-friends suitcase was wearing. After I'd stopped laughing, I explained the nature of Young Dave's relationship with our 'lady-friend' and told them the story about the shirt and obviously why we were visiting the Eternal City.

Both women sniggered and chinked their wine glasses, each taking a sip; the eldest lady cleared her throat and complemented me on my linguistic ability whilst her slightly younger companion wished me, my friends and Chelsea Football Club the best of luck for this evenings game.

It turned out that the old dears were fans of Lazio's bitter enemies Roma. Both sides were scheduled to meet in 'il derby' this coming Sunday, so if we gave Lazio a hard match tonight it would do Roma a big favour at the weekend.

'Biancocelesti... Merda! heh heh heh... Laziali vafanculo! heh heh heh.' The women were cackling with laughter like two old crones. I couldn't quite believe what they had said, which translated as 'Skyblue and whites (Lazio's nickname)... Shit!... Lazio supporters go and fuck yourselves.' Fantastic! I love this country... a country where even saintly looking old women have an irreverently partisan opinion when it comes to matters related to football.

*   *   *

Rome is a sprawling conurbation that straddles the banks of the River Tiber about halfway down Italy's Mediterranean coast and some 20km inland from the sea. The historical centre is shoehorned into a comparatively small geographic area and was well within walking distance of our hotel, but with so much to see and so little time available we decided that after we'd checked in, we would have a lazy lunch and then pay a visit to the Colosseum; from there we would be able walk across to, and through, the Forum.

By the time we had done that, Geordie Jase and Lemon, who were now on the Prague / Rome leg of their flight, would be in town. Together, we'd be able to get in a couple of hours drinking before it would be time to head off to the Stadio Olimpico for the match.

We found ourselves sitting outside a trattoria in a lively piazza within sight of the Colosseum. It was Peroni's and pizzas all round and an opportunity to chill out and observe; there's nothing serene about Rome. Despite the baroque magnificence of its churches, temples, bell towers and basilicas, it's a busy place with its natives bustling past tourists on crowded pavements accompanied by a cacophonous soundtrack of revving engines and braying car horns.

'You could draw some interesting parallels between SS Lazio and the Chels... very interesting indeed... could bode well for the future.' Young Dave paused to take another hearty slug of beer before giving an unimpressed looking Mrs Young Dave a peck on the cheek and expanding on his theory.

'Lazio right... massive under achievers from the capital city, won the league title once, flitted about between Serie A and B, flirted with financial disaster before being rescued by a wealthy industrialist... bought a few star players... won a few cups before finally winning the league title... again in their centenary year... sound familiar?'

Ugly John and I nodded whilst Mrs Young Dave looked up from her copy of Hello magazine and pointed at her empty glass.

'I'll have a glass of Pinot Grigio my dear... if it's not too much trouble,' said Mrs Young Dave, sighing and shaking her head. She'd seen it all before and knew that she was resigned to an afternoon of football talk; her compensation package came in the form of the agreeable surroundings she found herself in and the attentive looks of the impossibly handsome head waiter.

'Now the really strange thing is that when Lazio won the league for the second time in their centenary year it was under the guidance of non other than Sven... and it's our centenary season next year.' Young Dave sat back in his chair and casually lit up a cigarette; as a deeply superstitious man, he was a firm believer in coincidences and this one, after Nobby Enfield's revelation in Prague, seemed a real possibility.

'Fuck me... Mystic Meg would be proud of you my son,' quipped Ugly John, rubbing his chin thoughtfully. 'Be nice if we could win it under Claudio though eh.'

'Yeah and here's something else,' I said, my mind whirring over the possibilities. 'Chelsea won the title in 1955, which was fifty years after the club was formed. If we win it next year it'll be another fifty years on from then... spooky innit.'

Young Dave, Ugly John and myself would have been quite happy to while away the entire afternoon slowly getting drunk and trying to think of more and more elaborate football coincidences but Mrs Young Dave was growing restless, she wanted to go and visit the Colosseum.

I began to get the feeling that two thousand odd years ago if Mrs Young Dave had been a member of the Roman senate, the three Christian Chelsea fans she was sat with would have been thrown to the lions.

*   *   *

We strolled at a very leisurely pace along the broad strada that led to the Colosseum. Geordie Jase and Lemon had been in touch to let us know that they had landed at the airport and we arranged to meet them at sixish in an Irish pub called the Druids Rock. The Rock was just around the corner from the hotel and would be easy enough for them to find once they had checked in and sorted themselves out.

'Awesome that innit,' marvelled Young Dave, 'the photos don't do it justice although they did a bloody good job recreating it for the film Gladiator... come on Mrs Young Dave get a snap of me and the lads eh.'

We stood, hands on hips, looking up at the structure for a few minutes and then Mrs Young Dave got us to pose for a team photo in front of the pillars. There was no admission after 4.30pm which was disappointing for Ugly John and I; Mr and Mrs Young Dave weren't too bothered, they would have the opportunity to return the next day if they so desired since their flight didn't leave until the early evening.

As it happened, Young Dave had a full tourist agenda lined up which included a visit to the Vatican where he hoped he'd be able to find out what the Pope really did say to the 'famous' Tottenham Hotspur when they came to Rome to see him.

There were quite a few Chelsea shirts in evidence being worn by families as well as the usual brigades of youths and older men. Outside the Colusseum enterprising Romans dressed as Gladiators were doing a brisk trade with tourists willing to pay 10 Euros to pose for a photo with them.

'Imagine if they'd had battles between rival firms of hooligans in there... that would've been something wouldn't it eh?'said Ugly John, picking up a flat pebble and sending it skimming across the grass verge behind us.

'Interesting thought UJ,' replied Young Dave, craning his neck and straining his eyes so he could get a better view of an argument that had broken out between three Chelsea shirted youths and a Roman gladiator. 'I can see it now, the different cages each hosting a different crew;

Headhunters, ICF, BBC, Soul Crew, Bushwhackers, 6.57, Naughty Forty...
out they'd come, their arrival heralded by a fanfare...'

'Yeah,' interrupted Ugly John enthusiastically, 'and instead of using
swords, lances and those mace things... they'd be able to choose between
Stanley knives, broken bottles and baseball bats.'

'Boys look ha ha... now that is fucking funny.' I stood up and pointed
at the Benny Hillesque sketch that was unfolding in front of our eyes.

The Roman gladiator; cigarette in one hand, plastic sword in the other,
was chasing after one of the lads who had obviously short-changed him;
his two mates, overcome with hysterics were rolling around on the floor
laughing. Everyone in the vicinity stopped to watch and applaud the
action. The pursuit continued for several minutes before proceedings were
brought to an end when the Chelsea lad, who'd momentarily looked
behind him to see where the gladiator was, careered headlong into one of
those old fashioned tricycles that doubled as an ice cream kiosk.

Onlookers held their collective breaths as the tricycle reared up on its
back wheels like a startled horse with the force of the impact; a volcano like
shower of ice cream flew through the air, its trajectory widened as a result of
being caught in the gentle breeze which had stiffened in the last hour or so.

The ice cream vendor; a tall lithe octogenarian, who possessed reflexes
that belied his age, moved swiftly to rebalance his bike thereby preventing
what would have been certain catastrophe, not only for the remainder of
his stock, but also for the Chelsea lad.

Poor bloke, not only did he have an irate gladiator and a vexed ice
cream man to contend with, but also the unwanted attention of small dog
that was barking at him vehemently as he lay sprawled on the floor spat-
tered in raspberry ripple.

The ice cream man began gesticulating to the gathered crowd in a
wildly animated Italian way before turning his attentions to, and remon-
strating with, the gladiator who had arrived on the scene to a chorus of
boos. In the meantime our man in blue was still slithering and sliding
around on the floor. A series of unsuccessful attempts to get to his feet
culminated in the ever attentive dog cocking its leg and urinating over
him before it scampered away. I half expected a film director to appear
from somewhere and yell 'cut', but this was all very real.

'*Champions League... we're having a laugh*,' chanted a contingent of
Chelsea supporters stood nearby. Not half, I thought to myself... not half.

* * *

Like the Colosseum, the Forum seemed to have the ability to transport me back in time; It was as if I could see the centurions, the slaves, the senators and the priests going about their lives in what had been the commercial, religious and political centre of ancient Rome.

I reasoned that this was because down the years, without realising it until now, I'd probably seen more films that had been set in Rome than just about anywhere else. It was a fine testimony to the people that created film sets so unerringly accurate. As we walked through the valley floor between the Capitoline and Palatine hills, amongst crumbling columns rising from grassy knolls, over repositioned pediments and past spectacular arches and temples I had the most incredible feeling of déjà vu.

'Oi Marco... are you with us son?'

I shook my head and looked around to see Ugly John, camera in hand, smiling at me as he fired off another picture.

'Yes mate... yeah... just taking it all in my son, impressive innit,' I replied , rubbing my hands together and blowing on them. The sun had almost sunk from view leaving a golden red halo over the buildings at the far end of the valley. The shadows from the columns were lengthening rapidly and an eerie silence had replaced the incessant twittering of the small birds that had previously been flying amongst the ivy and agapanthus covered ruins.

This sepulchral calm, enhanced by the cold damp mist that had descended in accompaniment to the setting of the sun, enveloped me like an invisible shawl causing me to shiver in the manner you associate with the saying 'someone has walked on my grave.'

'Come on lets get back,' I said, shrugging my shoulders and thrusting my hands into the pockets of my jeans. 'It's getting cold and I need a drink.'

*   *   *

Geordie Jase was an interesting character with a background shrouded in mystery; the story goes that he'd turned up at Young Dave's restaurant one day looking for work, his only possessions being the dodgy looking shell suit and trainers he was wearing and a youthful, expectantly arrogant, look on his face.

A few years later, with his haughty juvenility channelled into a deeply competitive determination, Geordie Jase had firstly set up his own bar and then become involved in the lucrative business of developing property.

It was a true to life and heart-warming, real Dick Whittington, rags to riches story, and Geordie Jase was happy to recant it particularly when he had a pint of Guinness in his hand.

As far as the great walk of life went, Geordie Jase had taken several jaunty steps down a variety of paths before following the yellow brick road south from his northeast homestead. As a lad he'd had trials with the legendary 'monkey hangers', Hartlepool United. When that hadn't worked out he'd auditioned to join a now famous boy band... the only trouble was Geordie couldn't sing.

If you couldn't make it as a footballer or a popstar their was another route open to fame and fortune... boxing. Young Geordie Jase joined the army and under the careful tutelage of the iconic Nigel Benn became a pugilist specialist.

Sadly though, what could have been a very promising career as a middleweight boxer was curtailed by a life threatening injury which resulted in a frustrated Geordie Jase having to return to civvy street, Newcastle upon Tyne. With nothing to look forward to apart from joining the back of an ever lengthening dole queue, Geordie Jase decided to find out which town or city in the country had the lowest rate of unemployment and go and try his luck there.

At the time the answer was Milton Keynes, but Geordie Jase thought the place name sounded a bit noncey. Second was Basingstoke, but a bloke he'd known in the army came from Basingstoke and he'd said it was a shit hole so that too was out. Third on the list was Bath, no one he knew had a bad word to say about the place... sorted!

The next day, Geordie Jase bought a one way ticket to the historical old Roman spa town and, upon his arrival, made his way straight to the local job centre... several hours later he found himself doing the washing up at Young Dave's restaurant.

*   *   *

Despite having a characteristic, boxers nose, Geordie Jase had retained his boyish good looks which, along with a keen sense of casual style and a winning smile, enabled him to attract the attention of the ever busy barmaids struggling to cope with the thirsty demands of a pub full of Chelsea legionnaires. It was one of the unwritten rules in the Gate 17 code of conduct that if you wanted to get served quickly in a bar, you got Geordie Jase to shout up the round.

The Druids Rock in Piazza del'Esquilino was an Irish pub, no different to any Irish pub that you might find in any city, in any country in the world. Irish pubs have a McDonalds like quality to them; it doesn't matter where you are they look exactly the same, all darkly polished oak, wooden beer kegs and Sky TV.

'The famous Tottenham Hotspur went to Rome to see the pope... the famous Tottenham Hotspur went to Rome to see the pope...'

There were some thirty Chelsea supporters in the bar and it didn't take long for one of our most famous chants to get a raucous airing. The various conversations that were taking place amongst groups of fans were momentarily put on hold as everyone joined in...

'the famous Tottenham Hotspur went to Rome to see the pope and this is what he said ...FUCK OFF... whose that team they call the Chelsea...'

The chant continued into its second verse and upon completion was applauded to a man, even the barmaids looked impressed!

'Won't be the last time we sing that tonight eh... lets hope we play as well tonight as we did in the second half of the home leg... cheers lads.' Young Dave raised his glass and, with Geordie Jase at the bar getting the next round in, the rest of us joined in the toast... 'CHELSEA!'

*   *   *

Young Dave looked calm and relaxed, Mrs Young Dave had returned to the hotel for a late siesta and he was making the most of the opportunity to engage in one of his favourite pastimes... football exorcism.

Becoming a football exorcist involved many years of training and required a high degree of skill and patience. Young Dave was a grand master in the field and over the years had exorcised the red devil from many a hapless soul who had fallen foul of the common belief that if you didn't come from Manchester, and you didn't already have team to support, then you automatically followed United.

In the late seventies and early eighties it was the reds at the other end of the East Lancs Road that had been responsible for football fallow areas spawning ubiquitous Liverpool fans who rode on the coat tails of the most successful team of that era.

One such individual hatched in this way was a slight, dark haired boy called Lemon whose mercurial football skills had been brought to the attention of Young Dave. In his spare time Young Dave, himself no mean player, coached the kids side at crack local amateur outfit Athletico Dunkerton.

All the kids who played for Atletico Dunkerton had one thing in common, they all supported Chelsea. If they didn't support Chelsea then they didn't play for Athletico Dunkerton, it was that simple. Occasionally Young Dave had found himself on the wrong side of a verbal lashing from an odd irate parent who'd spent a pretty penny kitting his son out in the red of Liverpool, Arsenal or Manchester United. Young Dave remained unfazed by this, if money was a problem then he'd refund it if he had to... the rules had to be adhered to, other wise what was the point in having them.

"It's ok sonny... don't cry", Young Dave had said as he'd handed his handkerchief to Lemon motioning him to dry his eyes. "You'll get over it, and one day you'll realise that this was the most important day of your life... you played well in the trial, but as I explained to your mum we only follow one team here... now lets have that Liverpool shirt eh, and try this on for size".

Young Dave had then handed Lemon the navy blue Athletico Dunkerton home shirt he was holding and smiled to himself as he'd watched the boy begrudgingly accept it, shrug his shoulders and begin to walk away.

"You're in the first team on Sunday son, you'll be playing upfront, just off the fat kid... you know the one they call Big Chris... now don't be late do you hear?"

Lemon had stopped in his tracks and turned around.

"Course I won't be late Mr Young Dave... thanks", he'd beamed, clutching his new shirt to his chest. "I won't let the side down, I promise".

"I know you won't... I know... and tell me son before you go home for your tea, who is it that you support?"

Lemon had looked up at Young Dave and held out the shirt.

"Why Athletico Dunkerton... and... and Chelsea of course".

In time Lemon became a fully paid up Chelsea season ticket holder and although he never made the grade as a professional footballer, he still retained the all-time Athletico Dunkerton record for the number of goals scored in a season, 58.

*　*　*

'I reckon I'll get him this season Marco... I'll get him to turn.' Young Dave tapped his nose and pointed at Geordie Jase who was now having a game of pool with Lemon.

'I reckon you could be right Young Dave,' I replied, looking over at Geordie Jase and nodding. 'He loves all this shit, he's even wearing the clobber now... with his Stone Island top and everything... a proper Chelsea boy innit... is he coming to the Bridge this Sunday?'

'Course he is,' answered Young Dave, 'and if we give the Magpies a good cuffing that could well be the straw that breaks the camels back.'

'Yeah,' interjected Ugly John, 'he's just gotta treat it like he's a player whose been transferred, I mean take Lamps for example... West Ham born and bred, his Dad before him a claret and blue legend... have you seen him now when he scores? He kisses the club crest on his shirt... he loves Chelsea now... and I reckon Geordie Jase will too.'

Young Dave and I nodded in agreement. Ugly John's analogy was spot on, just a few more results, a few more away trips enjoying a laugh and a joke and it would happen. Jase would either celebrate wildly when Chelsea scored a goal, or subconsciously join in a chant. Just now he'd bit his bottom lip when we were all cheering, one day though I could imagine him saying in his ever softening Geordie accent, "why aye man... I'm Chelsea now yae know".

*   *   *

The Italian taxi driver was larger than life. Yet another Roma fan with wild black hair, big eyes, and a never ending stream of enthusiastic commentary only matched by a tangible passion for cursing at the events going on outside on the road ahead.

Mrs Young Dave had sensibly organised a minibus taxi from the hotel and after one false start when we'd had to return because Lemon had forgotten his match ticket, we were on our way to the Stadio Olimpico.

Situated at the foot of Monte Mario, the stadium is on the northern outskirts of the city. In normal traffic the journey would have taken thirty odd minutes, tonight it was nearer to an hour. It would have been even longer had it not been for the taxi drivers ability to use a dodgem style approach to his driving which often involved mounting the kerb to make the most of any opportunity that arose to overtake the vehicle in front.

This, combined with threats of physical violence and a ferocious appetite for using the horn, ensured that we arrived at our destination in plenty of time for the big kick off.

'Laziali froci!' shouted the taxi driver, waving his fist at a group of Lazio supporters festooned in the sky blue and white colours of their team. The Lazio boys responded with middle finger gestures and a hail of spittle which failed to reach its intended target as the taxi driver had already managed a deft three point turn and manoeuvred his cab to the other side of the road.

'Laziali lo prende in culo!' bellowed the cabby as he accelerated away, tyres squealing in protest.

'Fuck me Marco... I'm glad we were out of that cab before he pulled that stunt,' said Ugly John, rubbing at the bristles on his chin. 'What the fuck did he say to those Lazio fans anyway?'

'He told them that they were queers and that they all took it up the arse,' I replied, with a cheesy grin on my face. 'Maybe he's the son of one of those old dears we saw earlier eh... they weren't Lazio's biggest fans either were they.

*   *   *

'*We are the famous... the famous Chelsea...*'

Chelsea's support, officially numbering 4,343, ensured that the chant was impressively deafening; its constant repetition won the respect and applause of the Laziale contingent closest to the six metre high toughened perspex partition that separated the two sets of supporters.

Through the narrowest gaps in the 'fence' fans were exchanging scarves and shirts under the watchful eyes of police and stewards. The Laziale unfurled a banner on which was written one word... WELCOME. We reciprocated this with a solid round of applause. It was a nice touch and with twenty minutes still to go to kick off it set the mood... a mood of relaxed, good natured optimism.

Rome's Stadio Olimpico had an elegant symmetry about it which fascinated me. I loved symmetrical architectural designs; when they were simple and uncluttered they conveyed a comforting sense of order that was easy to comprehend.

The same could be said for the symmetrical design of the motif that graced the jacket I was wearing; two circles centred by a four pointed star that created quadrants in which the words Stone Island were embroidered... I loved that as well.

I looked back up the segment of the curve in which we were penned and I could see that there were a considerable number of people whom, judging by their attire, appreciated this symmetry too.

'*One man went to mow, went to mow a meadow... one man and his dog... Spot, went to mow a meadow... two men went to mow... went to mow a meadow, two men, one man and his dog... Spot, went to mow a meadow...*'

Everyone was stood on their seats and chanting, everyone apart from Mrs Young Dave and Geordie Jase who were sharing a sandwich and admiring the Roman candles and flares which were being ignited and held aloft in the packed 'curve' at the opposite end of the stadium.

'*Three men went to mow, went to mow a meadow... three men, two men, one man and his dog... Spot, went to mow a meadow... Four men went to mow... went to mow a meadow, four men, three men, two men, one man and his dog... Spot, went to mow a meadow...*'

The Laziali adjacent to us had unfurled a huge blue and white banner emblazoned with the SS Lazio club crest, a golden eagle. It was fabled that the founders of the club stole the colours from the sky in honour of Greece, the cradle of western civilization and founders of the Olympic games. The golden eagle was the symbol of Rome, its claws dug deep into the culture and historic tradition of the Eternal City.

'*Five men went to mow, went to mow a meadow... five men, four men, three men, two men, one man and his dog... Spot, went to mow a meadow... Six men went to mow... went to mow a meadow, six men, five men, four men, three men, two men, one man and his dog... Spot, went to mow a meadow...*'

The players were out on the pitch going through their final warm up routines. The team had been announced; it had a settled feel about it with Claudio once again opting for a midfield diamond formation in a starting line up of Cudicini, Johnson, Bill Gallas, Terry the captain, Bridge, Makalele, Lampard, Veron, Duff and Mutu with Crespo taking over from Gudjohnsen who was on the bench alongside Hasselbaink, Joe Cole (who was displayed on the scoreboard as his namesake Carlton!), Geremi, Huth, Gronkjaer and reserve keeper Ambrosio who had been less than convincing in his full debut against Notts. County in the League Cup last week.

'*Seven men went to mow... went to mow a meadow, seven men, six men, five men, four men, three men, two men, one man and his dog... Spot, went to mow a meadow... Eight men went to mow... went to mow a meadow, seven men, six men, five men, four men, three men, two men, one man and his dog... Spot, went to mow a meadow...*'

I gave the thumbs up to the omnipresent Vegas Dave and Bazza. Looking around I could see plenty of familiar faces and a few more terrace legends to boot; Balham Alan, Freddie 'fingers' Laidlaw, Fuck Off Colin, Belfast Billy and Del Goss to name but five. Serious geezers from the archetypal school of hard knocks whose reputations were nurtured on the terraces in an age when disputes were settled with ferocious immediacy.

Everyone crouched down, including Mrs Young Dave and Geordie Jase.

'*Nine men went to mow... went to mow a meadow, nine men, eight men, seven men, six men, five men, four men, three men, two men, one man and his dog... Spot, went to mow a meadow...*'

All and sundry sprang to their feet, our singing had drowned out the Laziale's efforts and they looked on with shock and awe as the mantra reached its deafening crescendo.

'*Ten men went to mow... went to mow a meadow, ten men, nine men, eight men, seven men, six men, five men, four men, three men, two men, one man and his dog... Spot, went to mow a meadow... Chelsea... Chelsea... Chelsea.*'

* * *

Chelsea's attitude and commitment from the first whistle paralleled that displayed in the second half of our game with Lazio at Stamford Bridge. Dazzling attacking prowess was matched by gutsy, ball winning tackling in midfield and sturdy, typically English, defending.

Veron, spurred on by playing against his old team whose supporters had treated him like a prodigal returned, was on fire and almost scored from a Bridge cross which had beaten the nervous looking reserve goal-keeper Sereni.

Young Dave remarked on the strange coincidence that Sereni had played in goal for Ipswich Town against Chelsea in a Premiership game at Stamford Bridge on exactly the same date as today, two years ago... the result that day was a 2–1 victory for Chelsea.

We unanimously agreed that we'd settle for the same score here tonight and I wondered how Young Dave managed to retain and recall such detailed information. As I wondered about this, the hitherto subdued Lemon piped up to inform us that in that very same game Mark 'sniffer' Bosnich had been the Chelsea custodian.

I tried to think of some quirky statistics but couldn't; I thought about making some up but couldn't be bothered, what was happening on the pitch was all that mattered now.

'Миии Тиии... Миии Тиии,' we chanted, as the Romanian was bundled to the floor unceremoniously by Liverani after chasing down a defence splitting pass from the imperious Veron.

'Go on Seba... go on my son...' Lemon, like the rest of us, was stood on his seat; fists clenched, eyebrows deeply furrowed, the biting of the lower lip all the more nervous as he waited to see what magic Veron could conjure up from the resultant free kick.

The ball curled wickedly as it was lashed across the box; at the near post Sereni flailed and flapped and patted it out as far as Hernan Crespo from whose face it rebounded back into the net.

'Goal!'

To call it a header would have been a lie, but the Argentinean was in the right place at the right time and we had a 1-0 lead with less than fifteen minutes gone.

'Hernan Crespo... Hernan Crespo... hello hello... Hernan Crespo.'

Our cheers for the hero of the minute replaced the jeers from the home supporters that had greeted his every touch of the ball, the legacy of his season in Italy with Lazio's bitter rivals from the north, Internationale.

For the next ten minutes it was all Chelsea with Lampard oozing class in midfield and the precociously talented Johnson remaining confident in defence. Another goal now would have killed the tie off well before half time, and it was Crespo again who went closest when a spectacular overhead volley whistled just past the post.

* * *

In football the dividing line between success and failure, cool and naff, war and peace is wafer thin. The previously hospitable atmosphere in the stadium was on the turn and reflected the frustrations being harboured by Lazio's players, and the gypsyesque Mihajlovic and Inzaghi in particular.

Inzaghi had dived blatantly in front of John Terry and the dubious free kick he'd won off Gallas had almost been converted by Albertini, whose stinging shot had been blocked by Mutu of all people.

'Someone's gonna go... someone's gonna go,' exclaimed Ugly John, as the tackles started flying in and the battle for midfield supremacy became more intense. Lazio had played themselves back into the game and were threatening to score every time they pressed forward.

'Booooo you dirty pikey bastard.' Geordie Jase, the slightly biased neutral was disgusted by Mihajlovic who had responded to an innocuously loose Mutu elbow by spitting in his ear, an act the referee failed to see.

Off the pitch, a couple of Lazio scarves which had been exchanged earlier went flying back over the perspex dividing wall; friendly waves between opposing supporters were now replaced by raised middle fingers and masturbation orientated hand signals.

On the pitch a Stankovic shot and Corradi header could have turned the tie back in Lazio's favour had it not been for two pieces of colossal defending by John Terry. Mutu, who was finding it difficult to maintain his composure, was finally booked for a wild challenge on Liverani. He responded positively though and provided a great cross for Crespo whose shot was brilliantly saved by Sereni in injury time.

'*Champions League... we're having a laugh... champions league we're having a laugh,*' was the cry from the Chelsea 4000 as the players headed down the tunnel at the breather.

* * *

The second half started at a frenetic pace.

'No... fucking hell!... Go on... you'll never beat the Spider... Carlo... Carlo... Carlo... Carlo... Fuck!' Lemon momentarily lost his balance as he reacted to a miraculously acrobatic Cudicini double save.

Mihajlovic, who should have been sent off in the first half for spitting at the recently substituted Mutu, finally received his marching orders less than ten minutes into the second half when he hacked Duff down twice in successive passages of play.

This seemed to momentarily galvanise Lazio's efforts as they continued to press forward looking for an equalizer. The goalkeeping mastery of Cudicini was put to the test once again as he spectacularly tipped a Corradi thunderbolt over the bar. The Lazio players hung their heads in frustration as it became clear to them that whatever they might do they were not going to put the ball past Cudicini this evening.

'Eidur Gudjohnson... Eidur Gudjohnsen.'

The popular Icelander was sent on by Claudio to replace a tired looking Hernan Crespo and his first act was to tap the ball into the Lazio net after a fierce Lampard drive was only parried by Sereni. 2-0 to Chelsea, come on!

'You're not very good... you're not very good... you're not very, you're not very, you're not very good.'

'Go on Duffy... Go on son skin em.' Ugly John's eyes were widening as we watched the livewire Duff waltz past three defenders before rifling the ball past the demoralised Sereni.

'Are you Tottenham... are you Tottenham... are you Tottenham in disguise... are you Tottenham in disguise?'

No-one could quite believe what was happening, particularly the Laziali who were beginning to leave the stadium in their droves. The gate for the game was a fraction under 50,000, a capacity crowd would have been 82,000. By the time Lazio restarted at 0-3 down, the ground seemed less than a quarter full. The fireworks had stopped, the banners were being folded away and the only chant to be heard now was the familiar repetitive one of *'Chelsea... Chelsea.'*

Joe Cole came on for Seba Veron and played a major part in Chelsea's fourth goal in what was becoming an unforgettable evening. His snap shot was deflected to Eidur whose unleashed a rocket like effort which was only parried by Sereni and the ball fellat the feet of Frankie Lampard... 0-4.

'Ranieri's blue and white army... Ranieri's blue and white army... Ranieri's blue and white army.'

By the time Glen Johnsen was sent off for a petulant piece of indiscipline deep into injury time, I estimated that there were less than 15,000 people left in the stadium. At the final whistle the Chelsea players celebrated as wildly as we did. The way I felt reminded me of the time we

Lazio's Stadio Olimpico scoreboard says it all ... Rome ....November 2003

beat Middlesboro in the 97 cup final... complete elation. As the players left the pitch everyone present knew they'd witnessed something special... Fantastic!

Match Result
Societa Sportiva Lazio 0 : Chelsea FC 4

*   *   *

'Look fuck me its JT... what's he doing? Looks like he's nicked someone!' Young Dave drew our attention to John Terry. Terry had re-emerged from the tunnel at the half way line man handling a smaller, brown corduroy clad, individual towards us along the running track which encircled the pitch.

'*Gianfranco Zola... la la la la la la... Gianfranco Zola... la la la la la la...*'

The original and best terrace version of the timeless Andy Williams classic 'I love you baby' got a raucous airing as John Terry brought the diminutive Sardinian hero to the front of our section. It was just a short flight from Cagliari to Rome and Franco hadn't missed out on the opportunity to cheer on his former Chelsea team mates to one of the clubs most famous victories.

'Roman Abramovich... Roman Abramovich... Roman Abramovich.'

In a display of solidarity with the followers of his club who had now been locked in the stadium for thirty minutes following the final whistle Mr Abramovich, flanked by six burly looking minders, made his way over to applaud our support. It was a great gesture and further verification that the man had genuinely fallen in love with the team he'd purchased some five months earlier.

'Let us out... you fucking eyetie wankers...' A young lad, stripped to the waist, his voice pregnant with outrage and self pity was voicing his discontent at a group of policemen dressed in riot gear who were blocking the exit nearest to where we were stood.

'Come on then you cunts!' he roared, hands beckoning and chin jerking forward, 'We'll have ya.'

Two policemen moved forward wielding riot sticks and the youth, who had over-stepped the mark by spitting at them, was clubbed several times about the head and torso. Spangle and Ronny Cutlass, who had been keeping a close eye on proceedings, stepped in and pulled him to safety.

In the modern era Chelsea's travelling support policed itself. Those from within who provoke unplanned trouble, especially with the police, can expect a stern lecture at best from the terrace elder statesmen.

Fortunately, despite this altercation, everyone remained in high spirits and a situation which could have gone ugly early diffused itself as the police, realising what was going on, backed off.

I walked down to the front of the terracing and asked one of the stewards why we were being kept in for such a long period of time. The reason given was that they were waiting for the coaches that were being used to ferry the day-trippers back to the airport to arrive.

It was midnight before we were allowed out of the stadium. It was bastard cold and any lingering sense of euphoria we might have had dissipated as it became clear that the only way to get back to the city centre was going to be on foot.

* * *

With the exception of several thousand Chelsea supporters, the streets outside the stadium were deserted. We watched as the day tripper coaches, flanked by an unnecessarily large police escort comprising of motorcycle outriders, cars and armoured vehicles complete with water cannons, all with blue lights flashing and sirens wailing, sped past us.

I looked at Young Dave, Ugly John and Lemon and shrugged my shoulders. There was no point saying anything, if we saw a taxi or a bus then we might save ourselves a long walk, if we didn't... mmm well I could see that Young Dave might have a few problems with Mrs Young Dave.

Geordie Jase was noticeably quiet. Perhaps he was contemplating coming out of the Chelsea closet, perhaps he was nervous about the fact that Chelsea were due to play Newcastle United at home this coming Sunday and if they played like they had tonight then his beloved Magpies would be taken to Sketchleys.

'Look... look over there, across the road... there, you see it?' Lemon's hawk like eyes had spotted something. We'd been walking for forty minutes or so; every bar we'd passed was either closed or closing, the bus services had clearly finished for the evening... and we hadn't even seen a taxi.

Young Dave, Marco, Lemon and Geordie Jase celebrate the 4–0 victory over Lazio with a few glasses of Red Erik ... Sgt. Peppers Bar ... Rome

We had broken away from the two main groups of Chelsea supporters who had been walking either side of the main road that led away from the stadium; our theory was that if we walked down one of the smaller roads we might find something open where we could stay for a while before calling a cab.

One of the main groups of supporters wasn't that far away and the bleating sound of 'baaa... baaa... baaa' could be heard as they pretended to be sheep following the rest of the flock back to the city centre. I wondered what the locals must be thinking as they lay in their beds, their sleep disturbed, awakening to think they have been spirited away to the countryside. I hoped for their sakes that they might be Roma fans, who would enter into the spirit of things knowing that the following day at work they would have a golden opportunity to taunt the Laziali.

*   *   *

'Nice one Lem, well spotted son.' Geordie Jase was happy again, waving a fistful of Euros at the doe eyed barmaid and doing his best to try and make sense of the selection of beers on draught.

Lemon was milking the praise, and rightly so since his razor sharp eyesight had brought us to this place... Sgt Peppers... where we were now happily enjoying a few glasses of Red Erik and awaiting the arrival of a variety of burgers, relishes and good old fashioned English chips. Mrs Young Dave had a smile on her face again and Young Dave looked relieved.

Red Erik? We didn't have much choice on the alcohol front. It was either Red Erik or Orangina, the bar had run out of everything else and was on the verge of closing before we'd turned up.

Sgt Pepper's owner, an effeminate looking individual who bore a striking resemblance to Freddie Mercury, explained that the bar was a popular haunt for Roma supporters and that they had gone large on the regular lagers as they celebrated the demise of their fierce rivals.

Red Erik was Freddie Mercury's favourite hooch, it tasted like Stella but had a syrupy consistency. Freddie assured me that we'd soon be rocking after a few glasses and I wasn't going to argue with him.

The bar was festooned with Beatles memorabilia; occasionally the jukebox, when fed by Young Dave, would crackle into life with what he would refer to as a timeless classic.

'Paperback writer... writer... writer... wri... OUCH!' Young Dave's falsetto vocals were met with applause from everyone in the bar apart from Mrs Young Dave who kicked him under the table causing him to yelp in pain.

'I bet you bought that when it first came out eh didn't you Young Dave?' Lemon, bravado fuelled by several glasses of the potent Red Erik, was in the mood for digging people out now but Young Dave didn't care as he opened Mrs Young Dave's purse looking for more coins to prolong the nostalgia.

Freddie Mercury told me that he had called a couple of taxis and that they should arrive in ten minutes or so, but I was in no frame of mind to go to bed now and neither was Ugly John or the irrepressible Young Dave who had offered his tormentor Lemon the opportunity to spoof him for the bill.

The game of Spoof went on for longer than anticipated; eventually Young Dave prevailed and with the big hand on the large grandfather clock in the corner of the bar pointing at six and the little hand pointing at three Lemon sportingly paid the bill and elected to take the first taxi, in the back of which Geordie Jase had been asleep for the last ten minutes, back to the hotel.

'You go with them my darling,' whispered a hoarse Young Dave to Mrs Young Dave. 'I'll wait for the next cab with UJ and Marco... it should be here in a couple of minutes.'

Mrs Young Dave arched an eyebrow in that distrustful wifely way but said nothing and gave her husband a peck on the cheek before leaving the bar and getting into the back of the taxi.

Ugly John and I looked through the window as the taxi's tyres screeched impatiently. A cloud of smoke palled into the dank night air as the cabby took his foot off the clutch and the car lurched forward causing Geordie Jase to fly across the back seat like a rag doll.

Back in the bar Freddie Mercury tapped his fingers on the Red Erik beer tap and raised three fingers... we all nodded appreciatively and returned to our discussion about what we might do next.

* * *

'Shall we see if the Druids Rock is still open ? It might be you never know,' said Ugly John. He was still up for a few more beers and so was I.

'Yeah, I'm in,' I replied. 'What about you Young Dave?'

Young Dave nodded as we got out of the taxi which had just pulled up at our hotel.

'It's only round the corner... it won't do any harm to have a look will it?' he said, paying the driver and rummaging in his jacket for his cigarettes.

'Where do you think your going? The door to the hotel is to your left.' The unmistakable voice of Mrs Young Dave boomed down from the heavens threatening to wake up the entire neighbourhood. A small dog barked fearfully at the din and scurried for cover behind a row of dustbins whilst Ugly John and I grimaced at each other shrugging our shoulders sheepishly and shoving our hands in our pockets like a couple of errant school boys.

'Yes you Young Dave... don't you think you can stagger in here at daybreak and have your evil way with me... you can sleep on the streets.'

Young Dave was looking up at the fifth floor balcony where Mrs Young Dave's figure could be seen clearly silhouetted by the glow of the streetlamps.

'Shhh... you'll wake the whole street up... I'm hick... just hick... gonna hick have one more with the lads my love.'

There was no reply, just the slamming of the doors that led out to the balcony.

'Quick hick lads,' muttered Young Dave, trying to stifle his hiccups, 'let's run for it, she might be on her way down.'

*   *   *

By the time we got there the Druids Rock was closing, all the chairs were already on the tables and the floor had been mopped but the chief barman recognised us from earlier and beckoned us in.

'Alroight boys... well now y'know I can't serve youse here now... but if yer still want to have a craic loike... well oil tell ya about this other place.' The barman motioned us to come closer and as he did so he picked up a beer mat and carefully peeled off the back.

'Go to this place, it's so discreet even the locals have trouble foindin it... it's ten minutes walk away, away over der across de piazza and den second street on the left... about half way down... yous will know it when you foind it ha ha... and when you get der ring the door bell and yous tell 'em that the Druid sent ya... there's a few of your boys up there already loike.'

BLACK FALCON
Via San Martino ai Monti

We thanked the Druid profusely and made our way across the deserted piazza and, after a couple of wrong turns, found ourselves stood outside a large black door which had one of those Victorian style lamps above it.

The large brass plaque that adorned the door carried a detailed engraving of a falcons head and bore the inscription...

BLACK FALCON
ASSOCIAZIONE CULTURALE
DART CLUB

'Well this is the place innit... Dart Club eh... mmm, could be interesting,' I said, ringing the door bell.

'You don't reckon the Druid's tucked us up do you?' asked Ugly John, tugging at the loose flesh on his neck. 'I mean I've heard about these places... like you go in and they spike your drinks and then you wake up three days later with sixty four inches of stitches on your body and find out that some moody doctor has removed one of your kidneys and sold it on the black market.'

'Personally I don't care... what this place is as long as they let us in, I'm f f f fucking f f f freezing,' chattered Young Dave, hiccups replaced by the shivers.

The door, which was on a security chain, opened a fraction and I could just make out the face of a woman. She asked in Italian who we were and I told her that there were three of us and that we were friends of the Druid... as soon as I mentioned his name she unhooked the security chain and opened the door.

Cigarette smoke hung in plumes along the length of the narrow bar which skirted along one side of the room we had just entered. Hanging on the partition at the far end of the room was a dartboard; but nobody was playing darts, instead people were huddled around small tables talking loudly to make themselves heard above the sound of the Osmond Brothers heavy metal anthem 'Crazy Horses' which was booming from an impressive pair of wall-mounted Bose speakers.

Nobody had paid the slightest attention to our arrival apart from a couple of Chelsea shirted lads who gave us the thumbs up as we made our way to the bar. The landlady explained that we had to fill out a membership application form before we could buy a drink since this was a private members' club.

We hurriedly filled out the paperwork and I laughed as I saw that Young Dave had written his name down as Charles Windsor and his address as Balmoral Castle.

'Better to be safe than sorry eh Young Dave?' I said, nudging him and pointing at the piece of paper he was handing over to the landlady.

'Who are you then?' asked Young Dave, rubbing his hands and

blowing on them to get the circulation going again.

'You'll see,' I replied, nodding and winking at Ugly John as we both handed our forms over to the landlady who made her way through the room and disappeared down the stairs which were at the far end of the bar.

* * *

'Alora signori... Signor Charles eh Weendsor.' The landlady had returned with our membership cards and was calling out our 'names'. Young Dave put his hand up and gratefully accepted the card, inspecting it closely before handing it to the barman who handed him a very welcome pint of lager.

'Signor Donnee eh Hosmond eh Leetle Jeemee Hosmond which ees?' The landlady held out the two remaining membership cards and threw a harsh look over at the two Chelsea lads who were now laughing loudly enough to be heard over the music.

'I'm Little Jimmy Osmond.' Ugly John raised his right hand and smiled at the landlady.

'E mi chiamo Donny... grazie.' I offered politely.

The landlady gave us both a withering, I've seen it all before and I know your taking the piss, look before handing over our membership cards.

We stayed in the Black Falcon until 6.45am by which time we had managed to drink ourselves back sober. I knew it was time to go when I heard Young Dave state for the umpteenth time, 'Y'see that's what happens when the team clicks and becomes the sum of its individual parts.'

By the time we got to bed it was almost 7.30am, just time for a couple of hours sleep since Ugly John and I as we were booked on a midday flight back to London. Young Dave had the rest of the day in Rome to win back the affection of Mrs Young Dave. He'd already budgeted for the expense that would be incurred wining and dining her and maybe buying her an expensive item of jewellery as a peace offering.

Lemon and Geordie Jase, who'd missed out on the Black Falcon experience, would be returning home via the same route they'd arrived and I had no doubt that given half a chance Young Dave would be talking up our final adventure of the evening when he met up with them later in the morning.

* * *

The departure lounge at the airport was rammed with bleary eyed, hungover Chelsea supporters. All of them looked like they had several tales to tell to their friends about their escapades in the Eternal City.

I sat down with a copy of the famous pink Italian daily sports paper, Gazzetto dello Sport. I'd bought it as a souvenir for my mother and was flicking through it trying to summon up the concentration required to read it, but my mind kept drifting.

One thing was puzzling me about this whole Rome thing... that saying, you know it? 'When in Rome... do as the Roman's do!' Why Rome? Why not New York? Paris? or London eh?

What was it exactly that the Romans did? Eat too much? Shag too much? Put down peasant revolts and throw Christians to the lions? Snort cocaine in the toilets of the Black Falcon? 'Ah, fuck it,' I thought to myself, 'I'll find out next time.'

BESIKTAS JK
UEFA Champions League
Group G
Arena AufSchalke, Gelsenkirchen, Germany
Tuesday 9th December 2003

When Chelsea were drawn in Group G alongside AC Sparta Prague, SS Lazio and Besiktas JK, the general consensus was that by the time our final fixture was due to be played in Istanbul against the team known locally as the Black Eagles, we would already be assured of a safe passage into the next round.

Since Chelsea's famous and trouble free 5-0 victory over Besiktas's bitter rivals Galatasaray in the Turkish second city during our last Champions League campaign in 1999 an enmity had developed between English and Turkish supporters.

Initiated by the brutal slaying of two Leeds United fans, stabbed to death in April 2000 on the eve of their teams UEFA cup semi-final defeat by Galatasaray, relations had worsened following a series of incidents at Sunderland's Stadium of Light where England had played Turkey in a qualifier for Euro 2004.

More than fifty people were arrested and one fan was seriously injured when police on horses, backed up by officers with dogs, baton charged England supporters who were besieging the end housing 5000 Turkish fans.

By the time the return fixture was played in front of a capacity crowd of 42,000 at the Sukru Sarcoglu stadium, home to Besiktas, the FA had already banned English supporters from travelling to the match.

With the Turkish authorities imposing spot checks at all major ports of entry in order to ensure that the ban was properly enforced, there was no visible English fan presence at the game which consequentially passed off without incident, well off the pitch anyway.

As far as I was concerned if Chelsea, who had yet to announce ticket details for the Besiktas match, decided to follow this course of action then it would need a certain amount of ingenuity on my part and a great deal of good fortune to ensure that I got to see the game.

I remembered the T shirt I used to have which had the legendary slogan 'you can't ban a Chelsea fan' emblazoned across the front; those were the days, the ironic thing was that the travelling support when we were 'banned' from every ground in the country was greater than it was now in the post Taylor report all seated stadium era.

Initiative, that's what was required; I'd sat there evaluating the possible options open to me in the event that the FA recommended to Chelsea that they too decline to take up their allocation of tickets for the game.

Pretending to be a deaf mute Turk who'd lost his passport was one option, then there was the 'official press photographer' dodge which I'd used to good effect several times in the early eighties; realistically though, my best chance lay with 'Uncle' Robert and the promise he'd made to me when we were out in Zilina.

*   *   *

Not that long ago I would have tutted venomously at the very thought of leveraging any opportunity to experience corporate hospitality at a football match; my view was that most of the prawn sandwich brigade weren't real supporters, they were undeserving parasites, feeding off the underbelly of the club, dragging it deeper into the financial mire it had continued to squelch around in despite the best endeavours of Ken Bates.

Since Chelsea's very public rinsing of its financial affairs in the weeks leading up to the Abramovich takeover, my increased understanding of the ways in which corporate sponsorship played a part in keeping the football machine well oiled had shifted my stance on the matter from one of cynical suspicion to tolerant, albeit still slightly begrudging, acceptance.

That opinion was to change to one of extreme gratitude for its existence when, with still no decision having been taken on whether or not Chelsea fans would be allowed to attend the game, I received an email notifying me that I, along with a friend, had been invited by one of the club's sponsors to travel with the official Chelsea party.

I'm sure if the game had been against Real Madrid or Juventus then this opportunity would not have presented itself... but it wasn't, and it had... and I for one wasn't going to pass up on it out of some misguided belief that this wasn't the way genuine supporters followed their team.

'Uncle' Robert... top man!

*   *   *

The sombre news that greeted me as I switched on my TV at lunchtime on Thursday November 20th threw a cloak of gravitas over the churlish excitement I'd felt at the prospect of being so close to the heart and soul of the club I love.

Suicide car bombers had been responsible for two devastating attacks on the British consulate and offices of the London based banking conglomerate HSBC that had left 30 people dead and over 450 injured.

Turkey, with its mainly Muslim population, secular system, and pro-Western orientation, was a soft target for extremist violence. Claims for the atrocities had already been made by Osama bin Laden's al Qaeda network and a small Turkish terror cell called the Islamic Great Eastern Raiders Front.

This was the second wave of terrorist attacks inside a week and followed the bombings of two Jewish synagogues that had also resulted in a tragic loss of life and further served to destabilise international confidence that the Turkish government was able to control the situation.

Later in the day UEFA announced that two matches, Galatasaray vs Juventus and Maccabi Haifa vs Valencia, scheduled to take place in Turkey the following week, would be postponed whilst the overall security situation in the country was monitored.

Chelsea then issued a statement that it would not be taking up its ticket allocation for the match with Besiktas on December 9th. Paul Smith, Chelsea's interim Chief Executive, who had been working closely through UEFA with the Turkish authorities to ensure that it was safe for fans to travel to Istanbul, declared following the bombings that on the advice of the Foreign & Commonwealth Office, and given the generally unsettled situation in the country, it would be inappropriate for Chelsea supporters to travel to the match.

I knew that this would extend to corporate guests invited to travel with the official Chelsea party, and so it was no surprise when I received a telephone call mid-afternoon confirming that this was the case. I'm ashamed to say that at that very moment I felt gutted, cursing my misfortune without once pausing to consider the reasons behind the decision.

A newsreel I watched later in the day soon put things into perspective; a grainy shaky film graphically depicted a man stumbling across the rubble of the wrecked consulate building towards the person holding the video camera. Bewildered, shocked, face blackened and bloodied with vision and hearing clearly impaired by the blast, his voice trembled with fear as he spoke.

'I'm British,' he said, to no-one in particular before being led away by a paramedic to a waiting ambulance.

Suddenly football lost its relevance; the importance I'd assigned to attending the match seemed trivial and the legendary Bill Shankly quote that waxed lyrical about football being more important than life or death became an embarrassing irreverence.

*   *   *

On the following Tuesday the UEFA emergency panel met in Brussels and decided that all all three UEFA Cup and Champions League fixtures scheduled to be played in Turkey in the coming weeks should be moved.

The question was where? Besiktas had been given until midday on Friday 28th November to come up with an alternative venue, and in the interim period Ugly John, Young Dave and I pondered on the likely venue. Prague or Budapest seemed the most likely alternatives, and we readied ourselves to make travel plans as soon as the venue was announced.

Friday came and went, and by the weekend the rumour mill was working overtime. Besiktas had apparently lodged an appeal and were stalling for time. In the meantime, the chat room on the Chelsea website looked like it was going to melt down. Information from a variety of 'reliable' sources suggested that the fixture would be played in Germany.

The rumour was correct – on Tuesday December 2nd UEFA announced that the venue for the match was to be Gelsenkirchen in Germany. The stadium, home to Schalke 04, was the same one that would be used for the Champions League final.

The date for the fixture was unchanged meaning that we had less than a week to get flights, accommodation and tickets sorted... no problem!

Besiktas continued to protest to UEFA but their protests fell on deaf ears. Personally I couldn't see what the problem was; ok the fixture was no longer being played in Turkey, but with the Arena AufSchalke having a capacity of 62,000, reduced to 54,000 for European matches, and Germany being home to some 7 million football crazy Turks, they would have a larger support cheering them on there than if the game was being played on their home soil.

*   *   *

'Gimme a couple of hours, and I'll see what I can come up with,' crowed Ugly John down the phone to me. This was just the sort of challenge he loved, and with Young Dave and Geordie Jase again confirmed for the trip he busied himself with his schedules and a calculator.

Geordie Jase eh, that made me laugh. He had to be so close to turning now. After witnessing perhaps our greatest ever triumph on foreign soil, the 4–0 demolition of Lazio, he'd suffered the ignominy of having to sit on his hands in the Mathew Harding Upper whilst watching his treasured Newcastle United get taken to the cleaners... 5–0.

We had beaten Manchester United 1–0 at home at the weekend; mind you that was an understatement... we hadn't just beaten them, we'd choked the life out of them and then knocked them over. The previous week we'd also accounted for Southampton by the same scoreline in what historically would have been a banana skin of an away fixture... things looked good.

'Top of the league... we're having a laugh,' was the chant, as Chelsea had taken the field against Sparta Prague in a match we were overwhelming favourites to win. We were having a laugh all right; glorious unpredictability returned to Stamford Bridge that night in the form of dull 0–0 draw which was however still good enough to keep us at the top of Champions League Group G. Chelsea now needed just a point from our final match with Besiktas to ensure qualification for the knockout phase of the tournament.

* * *

'That's great son, a direct flight with Air Berlin eh... listen to this though mate... let me read you this email I've just received...' I could scarcely contain my excitement as I spoke to Ugly John on the phone.

'Further to my previous email, the above match is now taking place in Germany. We would like to extend an invitation for two persons to travel with the team... the flight departs Heathrow on the morning of Monday 8th Dec, staying two nights in Düsseldorf, returning on the morning of Weds 10th Dec... er... you still there Ugly my son?'

The email had been forwarded to me by 'Uncle' Robert's friend Charlie with the header... 'are you still interested Mark?' 'Still interested?... Still interested?' Does that big brown bear still shit in the woods? My God, it made me laugh; how could people be so blasé about something like this? Something which, in my cul-de-sac like world, was akin to waking up and finding Halle Berry in my bed and last nights winning lottery ticket under my pillow.

* * *

'Look over der boi the Starbucks kiosk... that's yer man Cudicini, the

Chelsea keeper dunno who the other fella is though, oi don't reccy him.'

I looked up from the magazine I was reading and smiled as I watched a group of three burly men in Irish rugby jerseys engage in an impromptu game of spot the footballer. They stood up and scanned the busy terminal, nudging each other as they espied more Chelsea players arriving for the chartered BA flight to Düsseldorf.

'Oh look yer man God... Duff... oim away to buy a football from de sports shop and get his autograph.'

Duff, accompanied by Bridge and Johnson, all three resplendent in cream coloured Chelsea tracksuits, seemed unfazed by the attention. He looked like an errant schoolboy, and the articles I'd read about him retiring early to bed and giving most of his salary to his mum for safe-keeping suddenly seemed very plausible indeed.

Contrast this then with the swagger and style of Terry and Lampard; the latter wearing a red leather strapped bling bling watch that probably cost him a weeks wages. Giggling female shop assistants craned their necks to get a better view as the lads sauntered past each store seemingly oblivious to the attention they were drawing to themselves.

The Irishman who went to get Duff's autograph returned with a triumphant expression on his ruddy face.

'Look oi've got all deese now on de football,' he proclaimed ecstatically. 'Oil have it on e-bay by the weekend ha ha.'

Holding out the football for closer inspection by his friends he pointed at each autograph in turn. 'Ranieri, yer man the Duff, Terry, Lampard, Bridge, Cudicini and Gr... Gron... Gronk... er the Danish bloke y'know the one that never looks up before he crosses the ball...'

I sniggered at the Irishman's perceptive description of Jesper Gronkjaer.

'Who's is that one then?' asked one of the other Irishmen, pointing at the ball.

The autograph hunter turned around and pointed to the man with Carlo Cudicini.

'Yer man there wit Carlo... the one who's just dropped that muffin on the floor... oi didn't catch his name.'

'It's Ambrosio ha ha,' I offered, unable to contain my amusement. 'He's our... er I mean Chelsea's reserve er keeper.'

The Irishman holding the ball turned to face me, bouncing the ball several times as he did so.

'Well moi friend... if the way he dropped that muffin is anything to go by, you'd better pray to sweet Jesus that yer man Carlo doesn't get injured ha ha.'

The Irishman was right, if Marco Ambrosio's iffy display in his one senior outing against Notts County in the League Cup was anything to go by then we would be in trouble if the Spider was ever ruled out through injury, given that the recent signing of Neil Sullivan wasn't an adequate solution to the problem either.

Sullivan had looked reasonably solid, and kept a clean sheet, on his debut in the 1-0 win away at Reading in last weeks 4th round League Cup tie... but it was Carlo who'd returned to keep goal against Leeds in a 1-1, top versus bottom thriller of a draw, at Elland Road three days ago.

*   *   *

Ugly John and I sat unashamedly in silence nudging each other as we watched management, players, officials, journalists and assorted hangers on make their way through to the departure gate in which we were now sat.

Amongst the players Crespo was a noticeable absentee. It was however good to see Stanic, who probably had the most imaginative chant in the history of chants dedicated to him, back in the fold. Whoever came up with the idea of using the old Deep Purple track Black Knight as the basis for a terrace anthem clearly had a little bit more in their roll up than plain old Golden Virginia.

The players looked very relaxed; Terry and Lampard were laughing and joking as they leafed through the tabloids whilst the Dutch boys, Hasselbaink and Melchiot flicked through the DVD's they had just bought.

The French contingent, Desailly, Gallas and Makalele along with Geremi were deep in what looked like a very serious conversation which contrasted markedly with the Duff, Bridge, Johnson triumvirate who looked like they were late for a games lesson.

Also on view, and diametrically opposed to each other in style, were a sheepish looking Joe Cole who had turned up with his dad George, a boisterous instantly likeable bear of a man, and the urban styled Celestine Babayaro, who this morning bore an uncanny resemblance to Craig David.

An immaculately attired Claudio held court with the journalists, amongst them the well respected Steve Curry, chief sports writer of the *Daily Mail*.

Ken Bates still looked every inch an influential cog in the Chelsea machine as he strolled around shaking hands with the players offering each of them words of encouragement and evidently sharing in their self evident collective enthusiasm for the testing task that lay ahead.

Chelsea goal scoring legend Kerry Dixon was present as well as Gavin 'if only' Peacock, both of them now carving out careers for themselves as media pundits in addition to being part of Chelsea's match day hospitality team.

'Ah, if only...,' sighed Ugly John, looking up from his mobile phone.

'Yes mate, if only... if only that shot had dipped under the bar... who knows what might have happened?' I replied, clasping my hands together.

'If only,' indeed; Ugly John was referring to Gavin 'if only' Peacock's dipping volley in the 1994 FA Cup Final. At the time the score was 0–0 and the game was fairly evenly poised; Chelsea had done the double over Manchester United in the league that season and there had been more than a hint of faint optimism that we might turn them over at Wembley as well.

But it wasn't to be; Gav's shot didn't find its way into the net, United rinsed us 4–0, and we got soaked to the skin in the torrential downpour that followed. I'd still enjoyed the day though, my first 'proper' Chelsea cup final at Wembley. Looking back on it now, even though we'd lost it felt more tangible than the hollow Wembley victories in the Full Members and ZDS cup finals against Manchester City and Middlesboro respectively.

'Poor old Gav, he must get bored being quizzed about that shot eh?' Ugly John said, shaking his head and tutting before returning to the text message he was composing.

*   *   *

Our welfare was checked on by a glamorous lady of indeterminate age who introduced herself as Clarice. She provided me with details on the hotel we would be staying at and an itinerary for the following evening. As she walked away I looked around the departure lounge and shook my head pinching myself just to be sure that this was really happening.

The one person missing from the whole ensemble was the man responsible for most of the expensively assembled array of talent before us... our benefactor Mr Abramovich. Whatever his reasons were for not travelling with the main party, I had no doubt at all that he would be at the match... that for me was a certainty.

I put a call in to Young Dave to appraise him of the situation. Oh he was envious. The jealousy he harboured was probably greener than that horrible jade coloured second strip that Chelsea used to wear in the mid eighties. Right now Young Dave was more jealous than a Rottenham Dropspur fan gazing achingly at the Premiership league table and wondering where it all went wrong.

To tell the truth, Young Dave was happy enough. He'd be out with us, along with Geordie Jase, in Düsseldorf tomorrow. As the flight was called, any lingering doubt I had about the street ethics of being a party to this high rolling way of watching the team evaporated...nobody in their right mind would knock back an opportunity like this on the grounds of terrace morals... would they?

'Fuck me son,' whispered Ugly John, as we walked down the aisle past the players to our seats which were at the rear of the plane, 'this is fucking brilliant... I owe you a pint.'

'Don't thank me son,' I replied courteously, 'Thank 'Uncle' Robert next time you see him... he's da man.'

*   *   *

Not that I'd ever been there before, but Düsseldorf was one of those place names I remembered from my childhood; Sundays as a kid for me comprised of getting up, going to church, playing football, and then going over to my mate Phil's house to watch the Big Match on LWT.

Phil wasn't really a friend as such... he was a quiet studious kid who shirked double games in favour of double history, and preferred going fishing to playing football. His parents however, were the only people on our estate who owned a colour television... once you'd watched football on a colour telly you could never imagine watching the game on a black and white set ever again.

I couldn't anyway. You see it was through watching the Big Match on Phil's parents colour telly that I first became aware of how smart Chelsea's players looked in their traditional royal blue kit. They had a swagger and a style about them that captured my imagination, and whilst the other kids in the school playground fancied themselves as Georgie Best or Charlie George... for me it was always Peter Osgood... even though I was always asked to play in goal.

My dear mother still has in her possession the note I'd handed her with my 1971 Christmas wish list scrawled on it in green biro. The request list numbered four items... Etch A Sketch, Spirograph, the Look & Learn annual and a Chelsea football shirt.

That was how my love affair with the Blues began. No familial peer group pressure, no football exorcism from the likes of Young Dave... when it came down to making a choice, mine was founded on the first verse of what remains, even to the most biased of all soccer fans, the original and the best football song of all time.

'*Blue is the colour... football is the game, we're altogether and winning is our aim... so cheer us on through the sun and rain, cos Chelsea, Chelsea is our name.*'

There was a trade off though, Phil would invite me round to watch Brian Moore and co provided that I stayed on and watched with him the documentary series World At War which followed immediately after.

The thing was, I didn't mind. Like most kids growing up in the seventies I was fascinated by the Second World War, however at the time I had no concept of the terrible price it had exacted on humanity.

In class I would merrily deface my school exercise books with swastikas, eagles, SS logos and other Nazi imagery; in the playground I was an enthusiastic participant in games of 'Army' and 'British Bulldog'.

Only in adult life did the legacy of this war become apparent to me as I found myself travelling to cities that were scarred in some way by the conflict. The odd thing was that on arrival my mind would be drawn back to the documentary series I'd watched as a kid, to its haunting theme music and to the information I'd absorbed into my subconscious as I sat transfixed by the grainy footage listening to the monotone narrator describing the horrors of the conflict in finite detail.

*   *   *

Düsseldorf, an industrial and administrative metropolis on the left bank of the River Rhine endured a catastrophic, seven week long bombardment during the spring of 1945 that just about razed the city to the ground. Round the clock air attacks transformed residential areas into piles of rubble claiming as many as 150,000 civilian lives.

Almost fifty years later I could see no evidence of this destruction as I took in the scenery through the windows of the coach we were on which was speeding us from the airport to our hotel.

The post-war British occupation of the Rhineland saw the city reconstructed from scratch and in 1946 it was designated the capital of the newly created county of Nordrhein-Westfalia.

Düsseldorf became a mecca for international companies keen to associate themselves with 'new' Germany and tap into the investment grants made available to reinvigorate the economy of the region.

I turned and looked at Ugly John who was shaking his head at me, he knew I was having a World At War moment and left me to it.

I wondered for a split second what I would have been thinking about had I never witnessed that TV series as a kid? Beer, girls and football in no particular order probably.

Further down the coach I could see King Kerry sat on his own gazing out of the window. He was rubbing his chin and seemed to be deep in thought. What about, was anyone's guess... but it probably wasn't anything to do with the World At War.

* * *

The hotel receptionist had given us directions to the 'Alstadt', which translated unsurprisingly into 'old town'. She'd gushingly described it as being the 'heart of Düsseldorf' and home to the 'longest bar in the world', news which I had already relayed back to Young Dave and Geordie Jase as they prepared to join us in Germany the next day.

'You turn left out of ze hotel and follow ze path along ze river bank,' she'd said, in a husky heavily accented voice which quickened my pulse and had me mentally removing the androgynous black and white uniform she was wearing on her skinny frame.

'At ze main bridge... you will see it... go left, zer you vill find ze old town,' she continued, giving me one of those witheringly suspicious 'I know what you're thinking looks' that women often do.

'She'd get it, that receptionist... lovely mate, keep you nice and warm on a cold day like today eh,' I said to Ugly John, scuffing at the gravel which crunched under my shoes as we walked along the towpath.

The late afternoon sunshine shimmered across the still surface of the River Rhine, its rays reflected into my eyes causing me to squint with their intensity. From the comfort of my hotel room it had looked deceptively warm outside, there were no visible signs of the icy wind that was pressing my clothes against my body trying to find a way in and making me wish we'd taken a taxi.

'Every bird with a saucy accent and an eating disorder would get it according to you,' replied Ugly John, grimacing and pulling the collar of his pea coat up against the ravages of the stiffening breeze.

Ugly John had a point, as I'd got older my taste in women had become more defined; I'd say refined to my mates, but they would always shoot me down in flames and recommend that I went down to Specsavers to get my eyesight checked out.

The Goldfingers girls in Prague were the barometer for beauty and set a standard which was hard to match for the average, run of the mill, drink on a stick type of girl that I went for. Having said that, most of my friends, with the exception perhaps of Ossie, preferred women of more voluptuous proportions arguing that they got better value for their money. It was all down to personal preference at the end of the day, and as the end of that day drew ever nearer for me the more finicky I seemed to have become.

I've been a born again singleton for a considerable period of time now, cast out from polite society, settling instead for the tranquillity and harmony that comes with living on your own and enjoying the freedom that goes with a lifestyle unaffected by the exacting demands of family life.

Very rarely would I view the domestic situations some of my friends found themselves in with envy. Despite my mothers protestations that their lives were normal, and that if I didn't buck my ideas up I'd end up like my favourite Uncle Salvatore, I continued with my bachelor lifestyle convincing myself that one day I'd bump into the love of my life in the old part of some town I happened to find myself in.

Anyway as far as I was concerned Uncle Salvatore, my boyhood hero, had it sorted. He'd lived a full life, travelled the highways and byways of life in search of, and finding the craic and now, in his mid seventies, he was looked after by his widowed sister and didn't want for too much at all.

I'd tried the marriage thing once, years ago, but it hadn't worked out; it hadn't worked out because the myopia and amnesia that began to affect me not long after I'd walked down the aisle soon transformed itself into a pharmacologically fuelled dereliction of marital duties of rock star proportions.

Maybe I'd had my midlife crisis a decade early. My life now though, unlike Chelsea Football Club, was stable and predictable albeit prone to regular bouts of self doubt and soul searching. Any self pity I felt occasionally as I rustled up dinner for one would soon vanish into the ether when I spent time at the home of my mate Ugly John.

Ugly John is a man who, in my simple eyes, travels the deepest gorge in the valley called despair. The fuck up fairy always seems to be waving her not so magic wand at him; Small kids, big mortgage, feisty wife, demanding boss... I don't know how he copes, but like countless others he does and he does it well, in fact I reckon he's the best dad in the world. Maybe my mother was right in her assessment of normality, maybe I did need to fall in line with the rest of society... yeah, one day maybe!

*   *   *

Tiffany was lovely, she had a sweetly natural smile and a visibly healthy complexion which grew rosier with every drink I bought her. Her tumbling blonde tresses fell across her face as she shook her head in time with the Thin Lizzy soundtrack blaring from the speakers in the Irish Pub that Ugly John and I had been sat in for the last few hours getting steadily drunk.

When Tiffany spoke, it was a heavy American accent or so I thought. The way she handled her customers reminded me of the electrically charged Violet Sandford character in the film Coyote Ugly although she stopped short of dancing on the bar and spraying us with water.

It turned out that Tiffany was half German and half Canadian, an interesting combination if ever there was one. She was living in Düsseldorf and studying at the local art school, which apparently had a reputation as being the best in the country.

She told me that she was single and that her last boyfriend had been fifty years old which I figured gave me some hope, although I wasn't exactly sure what I was hoping for. In the end I told her that we would return tomorrow after the match and if we progressed through to the final we would return in May and I would ask for her hand in marriage.

Tiffany was understandably unimpressed although she did promise to come to the bar the next evening which was in fact her day off. I remembered Ugly John telling me not to read too much into this as he bundled me into a taxi at the end of the evening, but by that point I was so drunk I was past caring.

*   *   *

I woke up to the strains of Kalinka, Chelsea's new Russian anthem, trilling from my mobile phone. It was Young Dave informing me that he and Geordie Jase had landed at the local airport and were en-route to town in a taxi.

It was nearly midday and I cursed as the pointed end of the ice pick that was my hangover headache, buried itself between my eyes again. Payback time, hangovers were as obligatory a part of the Chelsea in Europe experience as chatting up barmaids, waitresses, and hotel chambermaids... although slightly less pleasurable.

I assumed that none of players, who were staying in a separate hotel on the outskirts of town, would be in this state although several of them had occasionally found themselves in the tabloids as a result of the odd drink related indiscretion or two.

As I gulped down a couple of Nurofen I remembered reading an interview with Franco Zola where he'd attributed the longevity of his playing career to a healthy diet, sobriety and a disciplined fitness regime. I then remembered reading in Peter Osgood's autobiography the famous story about the night before an away match at Blackpool when several of the players had defied a curfew imposed on them by Tommy Docherty and gone out on the town.

Home grown players in the modern game respect what the foreign imports have brought to this country in terms of attitude and approach, but I'd wager a shiny sixpence that it's the hand me down dressing room stories about the extra curricular exploits of the old legends that they talk about whenever they get the opportunity.

I went into the bathroom and admired my dishevelled state in the mirror pulling my tongue out as I did so, if I'd been lucky enough to play professional football would I have been like Zola or like Osgood... neither probably, I'd have been more of a Merson or a Gazza with a bit of Bestie thrown in for good measure... that would really have given my mum something to moan about!

As I showered, I speculated on whether or not if I'd been a famous professional footballer I would have been able to pull Tiffany last night, probably not... but on the other hand she was an impoverished student and I'd be on at least fifty grand a week.

I remembered what Patricia, the Goldfingers girl in Prague, had whispered seductively in my ear as she'd lured me away for a private dance... 'every girl has her price.'

*   *   *

'Yeah, take the Lazio and Newcastle matches... that's what happens when Claudio gets the team selection right first time.' Young Dave who had been in full flow, paused to polish off the third pint of Guinness he'd had during the afternoons drinking session. He, along with Geordie Jase, felt obliged to play catch up having spent the last hour or so listening to Ugly John and I trot out our experiences from the previous day.

'So beating Newcastle 5-0 is the yardstick by which you measure your success then eh ha?' replied Geordie Jase, the rhetorical question asked with a snigger rather than any self pity.

'It doesn't matter son,' said Young Dave, whose stubble clad face bore the sort of smug look that you normally saw on the faces of Man U or Arsenal fans come the end of May each year. 'Last time I looked we were top of the league, cruising in an enviable holding pattern and still on course to win four major trophies,' he continued, making the most of the opportunity to milk the situation.

'Hold on... hold on, I don't want to be negative... but we only drew with Leeds on Saturday and its only the beginning of December... it's a bit early to be talking of trophies,' said Ugly John, who'd been waiting patiently to offer his opinion, an opinion which enveloped the discussion like a gloomy blanket of fog.

Ugly John was a realist, to him the cup of life was always half empty when it came to football matters. His pre-match forecasts always had a whiff of unease about them, the trouble was more often than not they were correct. It was Ugly John who should have turned his hand to gambling not me, with my flamboyantly optimistic and ultimately costly, betting strategies.

I looked at Geordie Jase, resplendent in his brand new Stone Island leather jacket. Here he was again, away in Europe with Chelsea. Looking at him, I really did begin to wonder how long he would be able to keep up the pretence that his allegiance still lay on Tyneside?

Geordie Jase was one of those guys who never seemed to let things get to him. Even when he had endured the 5-0 humiliation of his team from the 'comfort' of the Mathew Harding Stand he'd retained his sense of humour throughout, in fact I don't think I'd ever seen the bloke fazed by anything.

We were drinking in a bar called O'Reilly's, the Irish Bar that Ugly John and I had patronised the previous evening was closed and we had struggled to ascertain exactly where the 'longest bar in the world' which the hotel receptionist had referred me to yesterday was.

In any case since it was a cold Tuesday afternoon in December and none of us had the slightest inclination to go on a bar crawl. O'Reilly's suited our purpose and the music of course was right up Young Dave's Neolithic rock street. I couldn't help but laugh as I watched him crank up his air guitar to imaginary full volume and rasp out a passable impression of the tortured vocal delivery of the legendary long deceased AC/DC singer Bon Scott.

Young Dave cracked me up, one minute he'd be in full Young Dave 'I wanna tell you a story' mode and the next he'd park everything up at the side of the road and embark on five minutes worth of heavy metal mayhem before scratching his head looking at everyone with one of his famous 'now where was I expressions'. Fantastic!

With the exception of ourselves O'Reilly's was deserted; a few Chelsea veterans, including Scarface Sneddon, Fat Barry and Steve the puff, had been in the bar when we'd turned up at lunchtime but they had melted away when several men who looked suspiciously like undercover NCIS officers had arrived and sat down at a table close to the front door.

Depending on whom you spoke to the National Criminal Intelligence Service's strategic and specialist intelligence branch were still carrying out covert surveillance exercises when Chelsea played away from home.

A waste of money if you asked me; with so few supporters travelling these days, and those who did being away purely for the craic, it was difficult to see how the expense to the tax payer could be justified.

Take Steve the puff and Scarface Sneddon for example; they only ever watched Chelsea in Europe, both had been banned for life from Stamford Bridge as a result of their involvement in the riot which followed a dramatic 5-4 penalty shoot out defeat by Millwall in a 4th round FA cup replay in 1995.

Both men were well into their fifties now, grandfathers probably, clinging to hard earned reputations, proud of their heritage and happy to swap their favourite stories with anyone who had an ear for what they had to say and the price of a pint in their pocket.

It was always great to see them, all of them, and it was always funny to participate in the grim silence that ensued in a bar whenever the NCIS unit put in an appearance as they had done this afternoon.

I'd glanced over from time to time and watched as the NCIS officers sat there in silence with grouchy looks of self justification etched on their features, their shifty eyes scanning the bar for known 'faces'... knowing nods exchanged when they saw someone they recognised.

'How much is that lot costing us?' said Ugly John, shaking his head and frowning disapprovingly.

'Dunno mate, but it's a fucking disgrace innit,' Young Dave replied, nodding his head and tutting. 'Rapists, muggers, terrorists, all of em on the loose back in Blighty and they wanna waste money sending that little lot out here to keep tabs on a few decent blokes who are just out here for a beer, a game of football and the chance of pulling a couple of birds.'

'You sure about that?' asked Geordie Jase nonchalantly, 'I mean, well... Steve the puff he can't get away with saying he's out here to pull birds now can he?'

Young Dave stood up shrugged his shoulders and playfully slapped Geordie Jase across the face.

'Nah, nah, nah you thick Geordie pillock... ha ha... you don't think he's called Steve the puff because he likes to take a stroll down the Bourneville Boulevard do ya?'

Geordie Jase's exuberance was replaced by the lugubrious demeanour of a man who knew he'd made an embarrassing mistake but didn't quite know what it was.

'Well why is he called Steve the puff then?' he asked, stepping off his stool and squaring up to Young Dave in mock confrontation.

'Because he used to knock out ganja, you know? Weed, spliff... PUFF!' declared Young Dave jubilantly.

We all laughed uproariously which drew the attention of the NCIS officers, so we elected to move into the far corner of the bar away from their prying eyes. Not that we had anything to hide; none of us were career hooligans, out here plotting some major insurgence into the massed ranks of the 55,000 rabid Turks that would congregate in the AufSchalke Arena in a few hours time.

As far as we knew nobody was out here for that. Firstly it would be tantamount to suicide, and secondly there was a genuine belief that so far on our travels nothing had been pre-meditated, rehearsed or provoked by any Chelsea supporters. If there was to be any kind of trouble it would be at the instigation of over zealous policing of the type witnessed in Rome or local 'have a go' firms wanting to enhance their reputations.

*   *   *

The 45km coach journey from Düsseldorf to Gelsenkirchen was a fairly subdued affair; as we left the A40 autobahn, the traffic had virtually ground to a halt and Ugly John and I looked on with growing concern as the time ticked by and we seemed to be making little progress.

Young Dave and Geordie Jase had taken the train and were already on a transit bus en-route to the stadium. We, on the other hand, were being cut up by cars and transit vans festooned with Turkish flags and the scarves not only of Besiktas, but Galatasaray and Fenerbahce as well.

Youths clearly impervious to the cold were hanging out of car windows and sunroofs holding flares and sounding off air-horns. If this was a portent of what we could expect once inside the stadium, if we ever got there, then the team could expect a very hostile reception indeed.

'Fuck me it's Turkey United vs Chelsea... look at it,' muttered Ugly John, pointing at the pillion passenger on the back of a motorbike who was flying the flag of yet another Turkish club, Trabzonspor.

'You'd never get that back home would you eh?' I replied, laughing at the prospect. 'Imagine say if Rangers had to play their games in Liverpool, or Manchester where there are loads of Scots, you'd never see displaced Celtic fans going along to cheer on their bitterest rivals... it's mental.'

'Blimey look at that... it looks like Bluewater shopping centre.' Ugly John suddenly transferred his attention to the view from the window on the opposite side of the coach. Fortunately we were now making clear progress along a bus lane which was being monitored and kept freely flowing by a cordon of police motorcyclists whose blue flashing lights contrasted nicely with the smoky red haze of the flares being brandished by the Turks.

'That can't be it can it... surely?' I leant across the centre aisle and rubbed my eyes in the same way a small child would do when seeing something that defied belief.

'That's it mate, the AufSchalke Arena... if it isn't then we aint gonna see a football match tonight, because there's nothing else around here.' Ugly John shook his head and tweaked the folds of flesh on his neck before settling back in his seat and turning his attention back to the goings on outside.

The stadium looked more like an alien spaceship to me than a shopping centre. Symmetrical glass panels diffusing an eerie yellow light were held in position by polished steel girders which were in turn set into sculpted concrete blocks. The sci-fi facade was completed by a blue neon strip light which circled the roof of the structure creating a halo effect made all the more spectacular by the white light haze from the floodlights cascading down, roman candle style, from its hitherto unseen epicentre.

*   *   *

Our futuristic perception of the stadium as seen from the confines of the coach was well founded. The AufSchalke Arena, constructed from scratch in less than three years and opened in August 2001, was a masterpiece of modern engineering.

It featured a movable southern stand under which the grass pitch, housed in a reinforced concrete trough, could be slid from the inside outwards and back as required. This facility, combined with a fully retractable sliding roof had made the arena one of the most versatile multi-purpose venues in Europe.

Nothing could have quite prepared us for what we were about to witness as we entered the stadium and made our way through to the entrance gate for our sector. Imagine a rock concert being held in the middle of a war zone and you might just get the picture. Our senses were quite literally bombarded with an array of sounds, lights and colours.

It was difficult to know where to look first. To our left a steeply banked stand played host to the supporters of Besiktas. Swathed in a sea of black and white banners, flags and scarves, they were illuminated by red flares that burned brighter than a thousand suns.

Blaring from the tannoy, what I assumed must be Turkish pop music was being voiced over 'Stars in their eyes' style by a Gareth Gates look-alike who was prancing and preening around the perimeter of the pitch.

The opposing penalty areas were littered with ticker tape and toilet rolls which continued to rain down from the stands despite the attention

of both stewards and police who seemed to be finding it increasingly difficult to maintain order.

The other three sections of the stadium were a temporary home for
those Turkish fans who supported other clubs. Not to be outdone by the
fans of the Black Eagles they were whipping up a frenzy of nationalistic
fervour with the continuous chant of 'Turkey... Turkey.'

'Jeeesus fucking Christ Ugly John... look at our lot up there... that looks
like hell on earth, poor bastards.' I pointed at the opposite corner of the
stadium where a small triangular section of the wrap around stand was
playing host to no more than 400 of our top boys. In amongst them somewhere, Young Dave and Geordie Jase.

'Shit mate look at it... its like Zulu dawn,' said Ugly John, looking as
mesmerised as a small child would on its first visit to the circus.

I put a call into Young Dave to check on his welfare. 'Oi Oi son are you
all right?... It looks like a bad night in Basra up there... can you hear me
mate?'

'Yeah... just about, it's fucking bedlam in here,' came the reply, 'they
are throwing cartons of milk and bread rolls at us... as well as coins...
Geordie Jase already has enough to buy a few beers later.'

'Where abouts are ya? I can't see your yellow hat.' I had been scanning
the Chelsea section of terrace for Young Dave and Geordie Jase for the last
couple of minutes but I couldn't make them out. Another of Young Dave's
superstitions involved the wearing of a fluorescent yellow Valentino Rossi
baseball cap.

I couldn't remember the significance of the hat, what I could
remember though was Ugly John and I thinking that Valentino Rossi was
a designer label. I'd dug Young Dave out for championing some naff label
that no-one had ever heard of until he told us both that Valentino Rossi
was the undisputed king in the world of grand prix motorcycling!

'There he is... look,' said Ugly John, pointing to the left side of the
Chelsea section. 'Just there on the same level with that tasteful banner on
the Turkish side of the fence... the one that says FUCK THE QUEEN.'

'Yeah... Young Dave... you still there... yeah we can see ya... you be
careful in there... speak to ya in a bit mate.'

I ended the call and we both waved at Young Dave and Geordie Jase
and then stopped waving when we realised that we had drawn the
unwanted attentions of several hundred Turk's in the lower section of the
stand in which we were sat.

There was an element of Russian roulette fatalism about our situation;
In an ironic and glaring contrast to the corralled environment Young
Dave, Geordie Jase and the rest of Claudio's blue and white army found

themselves in, we were in an area of the ground that offered zero security.

I looked around to see what level of support we could expect if things kicked off. It didn't look good. Sat alongside us were several elderly members of Chelsea's executive travel club whose anxious facial expressions gave way to a neck twitching chronic bout of unease as they assessed the possible outcome of the drama unfolding in front of their eyes. The odds improved slightly when the robust looking George Cole and a couple of members of the aircrew that had flown us out here arrived... but not by much.

Just as things looked like they might get out of hand the teams took to the pitch and the Turk's in front of us redirected their attentions to the Chelsea players who were greeted by a hail of missiles, coins, bile and vitriol.

The atmosphere was poisonous and malevolent and as I watched the lads go through their final warm up routines I wondered how the younger, less experienced members of the team might react to this level of intimidation.

I should have known better than worry, the Tinkerman's starting line up was a blend of youth and experience with Marcel 'the rock' Desailly, who'd seen all this before, wearing the captains armband.

Carlo was in goal. In front of him were Johnson, Terry, Bill Gallas, Desailly, Lampard, Makalele, Babayaro, Geremi and Gronkjaer. Hasselbaink was preferred to Mutu who, most probably because he was one booking away from a suspension, had been relegated to a lively looking bench alongside, Joe Cole, Duff, Stanic, Bridge, Melchiot and the reserve keeper Marco Ambrosio.

The game kicked off and the toxic verbal abuse being launched by the sewage spill of lowlife in the stands around us seemed to have an adverse effect on the Black Eagle's strikers who were being physically bullied off the ball in the early exchanges by a very focussed looking Desailly and Johnson.

'Dare I say it son,' said Ugly John, clapping his gloved hands together to applaud a great cross from Jesper Gronkjaer, 'but we look good. Claudio's got it right, look at the grief Geremi and Baba are giving them on the far side.'

'I know... ooh shit that was close.' I hung my head in frustration as the Dane's cross beat the keeper and whizzed tantalisingly past Jimmy's outstretched boot.

For a few moments the Turkish fans were silenced. The overall picture however remained a shabby one with the players and staff sat on the Chelsea bench having to shelter under umbrellas which afforded them

Ugly John in front of the rabid Turkish hordes ...
Gelsenkirchen, December 2003

some protection from the wide variety of projectiles which continued to shower down from the stand behind them.

The distant chant of 'Chelsea' could be heard above the general hubbub, but only momentarily as the stadium announcer, Turkish I assumed, got the crowd going again with a series of tannoyed comments aired when Chelsea were on the ball.

Gronkjaer went close, and Lamps closer still with a flashing left foot shot that whistled just over the bar. The heavy burden of expectation was clearly getting to the Turks who mustered little, their only constant threat was Ibrahim who'd looked dangerous in the first encounter at Stamford Bridge.

'That'll do very nicely indeed,' said Ugly John, applauding the half time whistle. 'If we play like that in the second half I can't see 'em scoring and I think we might just nick a win.'

Ugly John's analysis was spot on. All we had to do was continue to play the way we were playing. If we stifled the Turkish midfield and thwarted their attacks we would be home and dry, winning Group G into the bargain.

We spent half time watching the German riot police marching into several sections of Turkish fans in the stand behind the goal to our left. They were trying to stop the constant stream of toilet rolls that were being thrown onto the pitch. They had their work cut out though because every time they quelled the problem in one area it would start up in another.

'Tell you what son,' I remarked to Ugly John, smiling as I did so, 'I wouldn't wanna go for a tom tit in that stand... there'd be nothing to use to wipe yer brown spongey eye with would there.'

'Yeah... be horrible that... mind you I think they're all Muslims so it won't bother 'em so much,' replied Ugly John, shaking his right hand in the air.

'Muslims... what's that got to do with it?'

'They don't use bogroll, they use their hands... now there's nothing good about that.'

How happy would the toilet roll salesman who supplied the AufSchalke Arena if he was watching the match on TV? Very happy... very happy indeed, a nice big repeat order would be coming his way at the end of the week.

*   *   *

Ugly John loved a conspiracy theory as much as Ossie did and his latest one I had to agree had some merit.

As the players took the field for the second half the referee promptly took them off again as the far corner of the pitch was covered in enough toilet paper to wipe the collective arses of the entire population of Gelsenkirchen.

During the five minutes it took to clear the mess up Ugly John explained that Besiktas would now have an advantage over Sparta and Lazio who were playing out their final match in Prague where the half time score was 0–0.

If things stayed as they were in Prague and the same here in Gelsenkirchen then Chelsea would win the group and Besiktas would qualify for the knockout phase as runners up. If however there was a result in Prague, and the score remained level here then Besiktas would be eliminated.

The delay in restarting the match meant that Besiktas would know the outcome of the other match well before the final whistle went here. If the other game finished in a draw then it didn't matter if the Black Eagle's lost they would still qualify. Ugly John's theory looked very sound indeed.

When the second half started Chelsea soon regained their tempo,

Gronkjaer continued to torment the Turkish backline whilst our defence remained resolute and impenetrable. Amongst the Turkish supporters it was only the Besiktas contingent who continued to try and intimidate our players.

Flares thrown onto the field of play became the latest tactic employed in an attempt to distract Cudicini and break his concentration. But Spider remained un-fazed by the attention, clearing away the debris in the same efficient manner that he cleared his lines when he was called on to do so.

The remainder of the Turks fell silent, a begrudging mark of respect for a team that was playing their countrymen off the park.

With the hardworking Gronkjaer being constantly thwarted by the Turks it was no surprise when, with a shade under twenty minutes left, Ranieri decided to change things and substituted him in favour of Damien Duff.

'Look Mutu's warming up now,' observed Ugly John. 'He'll come on for Jimmy for the last ten... oh... go on Jimmy... go on son Yesssss.'

The substitution didn't take place; Duff put a great ball through to Jimmy who rifled the ball into the net with his right boot.

The Chelsea players celebrated, the Chelsea supporters in the pen away to our right celebrated and Ugly John and I celebrated, leaping out of our seats and punching the air with scant regard for our own personal safety.

The Turks around us looked on with a mixture of bewilderment and disdain which fortunately for us failed to metamorphose into anything else. Elsewhere though, the goal was a cue for a meteor like shower of coins to come raining down on the Chelsea bench forcing everyone sat there to take refuge under umbrellas once more.

With time ticking down Bridge replaced Babayaro and within minutes he latched onto a square ball from the unflagging Hasselbaink and drilled the ball hard and low into the net for his first Chelsea goal.

Ugly John and I who had remained on our feet since the first goal stood on our seats to applaud the second which was a timely cue for the Turkish fans to head for the exit points.

We joined in the 'Carefree' chant which was now clearly audible from across the stadium and carried on singing right through until the final whistle blew. When it did so the stadium, which had been home to 55,350 mostly hostile Turks, was virtually empty.

The welcome news filtered through that Sparta Prague had scored a 93rd minute winner against Lazio thereby eliminating both the Italian side and the Turks in the process.

There was a finite sense of justice about the way that things had worked out and we looked on with great pride as the Chelsea players walked over to our resilient contingent of 398 fans and thanked them for their support.

Match Result

Besiktas Jimnastik Kulubu 0 : Chelsea FC 2

<u>Group G Final Table</u>

	P	W	D	L	F	A	Pts
Chelsea FC	6	4	1	1	9	3	13
Athletic Club Sparta Prague	6	2	2	2	5	5	8
Besiktas Jimnastic Kulubu	6	2	1	3	5	7	7
Societa Sportiva Lazio	6	1	2	3	6	10	5

*   *   *

'Baba one... Baba two... Baba three Babayaro...'

The chant, sung to the tune of the hideous holiday hit Macarena, had been started by Young Dave and everyone in the Irish Bar including the ever lovely ever horny Tiffany joined in!

'Baba four... Baba five... Baba six Babayaro...'

Brad the barman lined up a row of shots along the bar.

'Baba seven... Baba eight... Baba nine... Babayaro... Ohhhhh Babayaro!'

Young Dave, Geordie Jase, Ugly John, Tiffany, myself and six other Chelsea lads who were also in the bar each picked up a shot and downed the contents, slamming the empty glasses down on the counter and grimacing before joining in a reprise of the Baba chant.

Fortunately the 'Slippery Nipples' that we were imbibing as quickly as Brad could line them up were less destructive than the Absinthe that we'd experimented with in Prague, nevertheless they soon had a less than sobering effect on our constitutions and any lingering hope that I'd harboured about persuading Tiffany to become the new love of my life evaporated when I went to kiss her tenderly and belched instead, almost throwing up in her mouth.

*   *   *

'How did you leave it with Tiffany last night son?' enquired Ugly John, an inquisitive smirk forming on his face.

'To tell you the truth son,' I replied, inhaling deeply before continuing,

Back at base camp, the Irish Bar in Dusseldorf, celebrating the victory
over Besiktas

'I really don't know. I think I said we'd be back in May for the final and I
vaguely remember asking her if she'd go out with me when I was sober.
What I do know is that I haven't got her number or her email address so
I'm gonna put that one down to experience... er basically I think she blew
me out.'

Ugly John removed his camera from the holdall he was carrying and
held it out in front of me.

'She's in here mate... so you'll soon be able to work out if her blowing
you out was a blessing in disguise or not eh.'

'Yeah... anyway there's not exactly much I could do about it now... so
it's probably just as well, shame though... whaddya reckon?'

Ugly John shrugged his shoulders and laughed. 'Ha... ha well son, to
tell you the honest truth... I thought she was a bit loud, she'd drive you
bonkers after a while... mind you it depends what you're after innit...
white wedding or emptying yer pods and doing a runner.'

*   *   *

If the truth be told I hadn't really thought too much about Tiffany this morning a 'Slippery Nipple' hangover had taken care of that and a full English breakfast had in turn given me indigestion.

We'd arrived at the airport in good time for the flight only to find out that because of fog at Heathrow there was a knock on delay to departures and our original take off time had yet to be re-scheduled.

Düsseldorf airport had little going for it in terms of things to do, in fact its only saving grace was its newness. It owed this newness to the fact that the worst fire in Germany's post war history, a disaster that left 17 people dead, had destroyed most of the main terminal building. The remnants were bulldozed and a minimalist modern structure had been built in its place.

The dynamics of the Chelsea party in the departure lounge were pretty much the same as they were at Heathrow; the cliquey gangs were all laughing and joking with each other, pausing only to take time out and make calls on their mobile phones.

The only player not participating in the high spirited jocularity was Jesper Gronkjaer. He was receiving treatment for what looked like an injured knee, the pained expression on his face giving ample clues to what he thought about it all.

'Poor Forrest, look at him,' whispered Ugly John, as he leant across the table we were sitting at. 'He got a right kicking last night... played well though eh.'

I nodded in agreement. Ugly John was right, Jesper had displayed a gutsy level of determination to match his wayward mercurial skills which last night had given Chelsea the edge over Besiktas. It was a shame that this edge had only been exploited in the final phase of the game when he had been substituted.

After an hour or so we finally boarded the plane but any new found optimism this may have given us that we would soon be on our way was dashed when we were informed that air traffic control at Heathrow were still not permitting planes to land there because of the fog.

Ugly John elected to get some much needed beauty sleep and I found myself drawn into an interesting conversation with Steve Curry who was sat across the aisle from me.

For a big man, Steve had a quiet engaging and eloquent speaking manner. This coupled with a crisp Mancunian accent seemed to give him a level of credence and sincerity that you wouldn't normally associate with any Fleet Street hack, let alone one that made a living from scooping football stories the like of which Nobby Enfield could only ever dream of.

He told me about Claudio and how much the players respected him.

He told me that behind the charming courteous public face there lay a glacial resolve which could chill opponents to the marrow.

I told him that the Tinkerman had long since won the fans over and that his tactics, once maligned, misunderstood and jeered from the stands were now applauded and viewed as being well planned works of strategic genius... well most of them!

I asked him about Sven, and the so called 'done deal' that Nobby Enfield had alluded to in Prague. He told me that nothing had been signed. I believed him because I knew that he was a personal friend of Ken Bates and as such would have a clear insight into what was and wasn't going on in the Chelsea boardroom.

Steve informed me that he had written an illuminating article on Ranieri which was to be published in the Daily Mail the next day and I sent a text message to Ossie and Young Dave to let them know because they love that sort of stuff.

* * *

The plane was sat on the tarmac for two hours before eventually being given permission to depart. As a result of the delay the players, who had been scheduled to train that afternoon in preparation for Saturdays home game with perennial strugglers Bolton Wanderers, were informed they would be allowed to take the rest of the day off since the flight would not arrive back in London until at least 3pm.

I reclined back in my seat and relaxed, drifting in and out of sleep as I did so. It had been an exceptional and unforgettable trip and I felt privileged to have had the opportunity to glimpse the real Chelsea Football Club.

To those who sought to light a bonfire under Claudio Ranieri and his glittering team of superstars with their stories of discontent and rumours of managerial changes I raised the middle finger of my right hand... fuck 'em.

What I had witnessed was a well organised, disciplined and motivated team which exuded a true sense of kinship both on and off the field of play. It would be almost three months before we embarked on the next leg of our European adventure and I hoped that in the intervening period the club would continue to 'build', as Claudio referred to it, on the success it was now deservedly beginning to enjoy.

VfB STUTTGART
UEFA Champions League
First Knockout Round
Gottlieb Daimler Stadion, Stuttgart, Germany
Wednesday 25th February 2004

A week is a long time in football, eleven weeks is akin to a lifetime. The draw for the first round of the Champions League knockout phase had been made on the Friday following our defeat of Besiktas in Gelsenkirchen.

As group winners Chelsea were guaranteed a home fixture in the second leg; the dynamics of the draw meant that we could face one of seven teams that had finished the first phase as runners up in their respective groups.

Amongst these teams were Bayern Munich and FC Porto but it was VfB Stuttgart, a team that had made a very strong start to their domestic season and also beaten Manchester United 2–1 at home in this competition back in October, that Chelsea were paired with.

Ugly John had wasted no time in getting things organised, within a couple of days of the draw having been made he'd put together a trip costing £170 which incorporated a return flight to Munich with BA from Heathrow and one nights accommodation at Stuttgart's intriguingly named TOP Kongresshotel Europe.

On arrival at Munich we would then take an ICE train to Stuttgart which would cover the 225km distance in around two hours. The flight out was early the flight back was late; it was a good deal all round and it was little surprise to find out that ten of Gate 17's finest had signed up for the trip.

The three usual suspects; namely Young Dave, Ugly John and myself would be accompanied by Ossie, Lemon, Roger Socks, Big Chris, Sir Larry, Baby Gap Brian and Geordie Jase who, on account of his continued enthusiasm for watching the Blues in Europe, was on the verge of being rechristened Chelsea Jase.

Despite the fact that we had all the right paperwork we had wildly underestimated demand for match tickets which had gone on sale on the morning of the home game with Birmingham City. I had casually strolled up to the box office just before midday and been informed that Chelsea's allocation had sold out by mid morning and that people had queued through the night to be sure of getting a ticket.

It made me laugh; in recent years, online booking complemented by an efficient postal application system and the fact that we didn't 'travel' in the same numbers as we used to had all but banished from my memory the hours spent queuing for tickets for various 'big' games in the past.

The official line from Chelsea was that the only way to guarantee a ticket for away European fixtures was to book an official trip with the club. Ironically the last time I went on an official trip with the club was when Chelsea had played Stuttgart in the 1998 Cup Winners Cup Final in Stockholm.

The return leg of that journey was a complete farce for those supporters, myself and Ugly John included, who were scheduled to fly home after the match. On arriving at the airport we were told that our planes were not were they were meant to be. In the chaos that ensued people ended up boarding the first flights that became available to their destination airport.

Fortunately for the authorities, everyone was on a high following the victory; this coupled with the fact that the airport bars were shut and everyone was knackered ensured that order was maintained and that protests were restricted to pen and paper.

By the time some of these engrossing epistles found themselves onto the pages of Chelsea's official monthly magazine 'Onside', with each of them being granted a few sanctimonious lines of verbiage by way of a reply from the 'editor', it was the middle of the summer and I had long since decided that I would never pay the clubs inflated prices for the privilege of being treated like a little piggy on its way to market ever again.

Ugly John Travel was the way forward now, the small matter of arriving in Germany without a ticket just made things that little bit more exciting.

For Ossie however things weren't quite that cut and dried. He had immediately become suspicious about the precise manner the tickets had been sold and proceeded to conduct his own personal stewards enquiry in a vain attempt to uncover the truth.

Stories abounded that Chelsea had sold parcels of tickets to a number of 'agencies'. It was a fact that tickets were liberally available on the internet at prices ranging from £140 to £200 and it was also alleged that the box office had flagrantly disregarded the rule regarding the number of tickets able to be purchased by a single person, namely five with supporting documentation ie:- name, address, season ticket and passport number supported by flight and accommodation details. Ossie had heard from a reliable source that one individual had managed to acquire ninety tickets through the open box office sale.

Wherever the truth lay, the bottom line was we didn't have any tickets. Our main hope now lay with Young Dave who'd made an internet connection with a German ticket tout who went by the menacing name of Wolfman.

* * *

Being ticketless for the match was the least of our problems, we were all more concerned with the alarmingly erratic form being displayed by the team. One act of 'glorious unpredictability' such as the home defeat by Bolton Wanderers immediately following the fantastic team effort against Besiktas could have been forgiven... the League Cup exit away from home at the hands of a resurgent Aston Villa side could have been excused, but there had been other disasters; a major one away at Charlton Athletic and a painful one at home to Liverpool.

It wasn't all gloom though, Chelsea by and large continued to excel away from Stamford Bridge and victories against Fulham, Leicester City, Blackburn Rovers and Portsmouth had enabled us to keep pace with Arsenal and Manchester United. Although we were now in third place in the Premiership, there was considerable daylight between the top three and the remainder of the pack.

In the FA Cup, Watford after a replay and Scarborough had been accounted for and the playing squad had been bolstered by the £10 million arrival during January's transfer window of the much coveted Scott Parker from Charlton Athletic. The other notable signing was that of the young, highly rated, Czech international goalkeeper Peter Cech, who would complete his £7 million move from the French club Rennes at the end of the season.

Parker it was, who had been largely responsible for Chelsea's ignominious 4–2 defeat at the hands of his old club on Boxing Day. A clause in his new Chelsea contract rendered him ineligible to play in the return match at Stamford Bridge several weeks later, a game which his new team-mates had laboured their way to a 1–0 victory.

A welcome win, but the main talking point on the day had been the omission of Ken Bates wonderfully acerbic column from the matchday programme. Everyone agreed that it would only be a matter of time before Kenyon edged his old adversary out of the club altogether.

On one hand, with the notable exception of the stultifying objections voiced by lifelong Chelsea supporter and Labour MP Tony Banks, the close season arrival of Roman Abramovich and his billions had been met by a unanimous display of solidarity amongst the fans; on the other hand, Peter Kenyon's hiring as CEO at the expense of the immensely popular Trevor Birch was clearly going to take a little more getting use to, especially now that he had completed his period of gardening leave and would now become eminently more visible as he took over the day to day running of our club.

Glorious unpredictability... yeah right... there was something inglorious and alarmingly predictable about the draw for the fifth round of the FA Cup. For the fourth year in a row we would have to play Arsenal in the competition, and with the match scheduled to take place at Highbury the week before we played them in the league at Stamford Bridge there was much optimistic idle chatter about this being the year that Chelsea finally overcame their Gooner whodo.

Oh the injustice of it all; déjà vu... groundhog day... the cries of 'you'll never beat the Arsenal' ringing in my ears... sniggering taunts from my mate Sex Case... the banal statistics... the excuses.

The only injustice I'd witnessed was Gronkjaer's headed goal in the cup tie being ruled offside. Both games saw Chelsea fail to defend a 1-0 lead; Arsenal always looked vibrant in attack, Chelsea always looked vulnerable in defence. In both matches as soon as Arsenal equalised I knew in my heart of hearts that we would end up losing.

At 1-1, we were in Ugly John's world... the glass wasn't half full, it was half empty; the pre-match concerns, dulled by a few beers and an early Chelsea goal, returned to collectively dampen our enthusiasm and soberly prepare us for the defeat that would surely follow.

Ranieri had spent more in seven months than Wenger had in seven years but it was still the same old Chelsea out there, kicking and rushing against an Arsenal team who, over the course of 90 minutes, were superior in every department.

How much of it though really was down to psychology? 'Together with all our hearts', was the endearing sign off used by Claudio Ranieri in his programme notes and I for one believed him. Despite continued media speculation linking Sven Goran Eriksson with the Chelsea managers job, Ranieri continued to enjoy the public support of the players but the pressure was growing game by game.

The manner of Chelsea's back to back defeats against Arsenal had once again opened up the debate about the tactics employed by the Tinkerman and whether or not he had the ability to gel his expensively assembled stars into a team capable of realising the dizzyingly lofty ambitions of Roman Abramovich.

A confidence boosting victory in Stuttgart was of paramount importance; if the doom-laden, nebulous ruminations of the press were to be believed, elimination at this stage of the competition would hasten Claudio Ranieri's, rumoured to be inevitable, departure.

* * *

'You're not gonna leave that are you?' Without waiting for a reply Big Chris reached across the table and helped himself to the breakfast croissant on Lemon's plate.

Big Chris, with his fresh face, foppish fringe and home-counties accent was a dead-ringer for the chubby, cake-loving, 'cripes' uttering work-shy Greyfriars schoolboy Billy Bunter.

In the modern world inhabited by Big Chris the school tuck shop had been replaced by McDonalds whilst crisps, peanuts and lager were a comparable calorific substitute for cream buns, jam tarts and lashings of ginger beer.

'Oi Fatty Fatkins,' snapped Lemon, pulling the plate away from Big Chris's outstretched hand, 'I haven't finished with that yet.'

Big Chris blushed ashamedly and frowned as he watched Lemon pick up the croissant and take a large bite from it.

'Oh go on then... here you are, go on you have it.' Lemon shook his head as he handed the half eaten croissant back to his old Athletico Dunkerton team mate.

'Can't have you going hungry eh Big Chris... I mean God help us... what would happen if you went ten minutes without any food?'

Big Chris said nothing as he gratefully devoured the remainder of the croissant before turning his attention to a brown sauce smothered rasher of bacon which was looking forlorn and neglected in the middle of the otherwise empty plate which Baby Gap Brian had just placed back on the table.

'Go on Big Chris you have it mate... I'm full, and besides I wanna leave some room for this stuff today know what I mean'

Baby Gap Brian nodded at Big Chris and then took a swig from the bottle of Becks Young Dave had just handed him. 6.30am was a little on the early side to start drinking in anyone's book and Baby Gap Brian knew that today was going to be all about pacing yourself or facing the prospect of being comatose well before kick off time which was still over fourteen hours away.

'I dunno where you put it all mate,' quipped Ossie, looking up from the tabloid size version of the Times he was reading.

'Who me?' said Big Chris, licking his fingers.

'No not you fat boy,' replied Ossie, tutting in a manner which raised a chuckle from the rest of us who were sat around a couple of tables that we'd pushed together in the concourse area outside Est Est Est in London Heathrow's Terminal One.

'It's fairly obvious where you put it all innit... No mate, I'm talking about my mate the mighty atom here... Baby Gap Brian.'

Ossie had a point, for a man of such diminutive stature Baby Gap Brian had a capacity for alcohol to rival the legendary Sir Larry himself.

'Yeah... ha ha the mighty atom,' said Ugly John, opening out the back page of Baby Gap Brian's passport which, along with everyone else's, he was holding together with all the relevant travel documentation. 'Look Baby Gap is so small he's got a full length picture of himself as his passport photo.'

Everyone laughed at the joke, and Baby Gap Brian laughed loudest of all. In that imaginary world of dogs he was a Jack Russell, barking enthusiastically and wagging his tail whilst scampering around and snapping at everyone's heels in a friendly bid to gain attention.

Baby Gap Brian had a serious side though; a lovely wife, a beautiful daughter and what Sir Larry would often refer to as a 'proper job'. The good thing was he always left his sober hat at home in the wardrobe when he came to the football and our world was a more entertaining place because of it.

Baby Gap Brian shuffled to his feet and picked up Geordie Jase's brand new Stone Island jacket, a hooded cream number that sported two large patch pockets and internal windproof cuffs. The jacket, which was lying on top of an equally new Louis Vuitton cabin bag adjacent to the table, had caught his eye as soon as we'd all met up at the ticket desk.

'Oi leave off the jacket man... it's brand new.' Geordie Jase pretended to look concerned as he watched Baby Gap Brian don the jacket which was at least six sizes too big for him and made him look like one of Fagin's urchins in the film Oliver Twist.

'Junior Stone Island...'

We all turned to look at Roger Socks, a man whose mellow baritone voice had a the kind of school masterly timbre to it that was able to silence any chatter. Even when he said nothing he had an eloquent quality about him that made us all want to listen to the occasional pearls of wisdom that would pass from his lips.

Roger Socks narrowed his sleepy eyes and scratched his lantern jaw before elaborating further. 'It's a shame they don't have a junior Stone Island range of clothes for ya Brian,' he drawled, knowing that his audience was hanging on his every word, 'then you could get out of those Baby Gap denims you're always wearing and look more like the real deal.'

'The real deal... and I suppose you is da real deal aincha Socksy?' retorted Baby Gap Brian, removing the jacket, handing it over to Geordie Jase and twitching his neck in the manner of Del Boy Trotter. 'Look at you... man at Matalan... styled by Stevie Wonder... go on... here's 50p son, go and buy yourself a new wardrobe.'

Roger Socks had no answer to Baby Gap Brian's verbal assault but he half knew that it was just a joke. Right now everyone was laughing at him but then we were all aware that the wheel of misfortune was spun frequently on away trips and sooner or later anyone of us would become the next in line for a good digging out.

It's like being in the school playground again, and everyone thrived on it; for a short period of time the shackles of responsibility were unlocked and a youthful, carefree approach to life returned. Whether you are young or old, to retain youthfulness is an acquired skill in much the same way that conducting oneself with maturity is. It's not about looking older or younger, it's about choosing how to behave and in what spirit... and the spirit we had all chosen this morning was one of exuberant immaturity. Fantastic!

As the laughter died down Ugly John informed us all that we had about fifteen minutes to spare before we needed to make our way down to the departure gate.

'Seriously son?' said Sir Larry, beckoning the waitress over and ordering another Bloody Mary.

Ugly John nodded, furrowing his brow and pointing at me and then at his watch. In his eyes Sir Larry was my responsibility; a professional when it came to the consumption of alcohol, his drinks of choice were lager and vodka. Rather than bingeing he was a maintenance drinker who kept himself topped up throughout the day and it was my job to ensure that he didn't peak too early or go AWOL thereby throwing Ugly John's carefully laid travel plans into jeopardy.

Sir Larry took his nickname from the great actor Sir Laurence Olivier; not because he was a star of stage and screen himself, but because in his less sober moments, of which there were many, he would become expansive and prone to making melodramatic sweeping gestures with his hands.

By way of an example, one afternoon in the One Bar several years ago, news reached us that Frank Lampard was about to sign for the club. Sir Larry had reached out his arms and tossed back his head in a grandiose theatrical manner ensuring he had our undivided attention before uttering the immortal line, 'give me a ball and one month... and I... yes I... Sir Larry of Sexual, will become a better footballer than Frank Lampard.'

Sexual was play on words and related to the London borough in which Sir Larry lived... Sexual Ealing.

A few months later he'd made the same bold claim about David Beckham, although this time the requested timescale had been three months. Fortunately nobody had given Sir Larry a football to practise 'keepy uppy' with, which in some respects I'd viewed as a shame since the resultant stage show would have been as entertaining as the fantastic Peter Kay 'av it' TV commercial for John Smith's bitter.

Sir Larry and I went back half a lifetime, he was like a brother to me and I'd shared his grief when his mother had passed away recently after a long illness. This trip was his first opportunity to get away from Sexual and the sorrowful task of having to put her affairs in order and as such I was prepared to cut him as much slack as he needed to ensure that he enjoyed the craic.

When finally it arrived, Sir Larry polished off his final Bloody Mary with customary aplomb... now he was ready for Germany but would Germany be ready for Sir Larry

*   *   *

Not content with being the finest actor of his generation, Sir Larry was also fluent in five modern languages and several obscure Indian dialects. His command of German was such that he'd been able to negotiate a group discount for the ICE (Inter City Express) train we had boarded in Munich which was now on its way to Stuttgart speeding along the twin ribbons of steel that cut a swathe through the Bavarian countryside.

From the warmth and comfort of the buffet car we had taken over, I found my eyes drawn to the changing countryside landscape scenes that were perfectly framed by the carriages large rectangular windows.

Once out of the Munich conurbation we passed through several villages each characterised by churches with onion shaped spires. Corner after corner, hill after hill, idyllic pine and snow scenery flashed by occasionally interspersed with narrow green patches that tapered out into larger meadows.

Sat next to me was Geordie Jase, chattering away in his trademark stumbling staccato, laughing and joking frequently as he exchanged anecdotes with Ugly John, blissfully unaware of the fate that is about to befall him.

Big Chris, ever the public schoolboy, with his rosy cheeks and floppy hair, looked like he'd just finished a smashing game of hop scotch. He was locked in a three way argument about the new offside rule with his regular partners in crime Lemon and Roger Socks who had clearly conspired to ensure it was one debate he wasn't going to win. The more Big Chris argued, the rosier his cheeks became.

Sir Larry was stood at the bar on his own smoking reflectively. The vacant expression on his face was soon replaced by a cheesecake grin as he saw Young Dave dressed head to foot in the liturgical vestments of the Latin Rite, enter the carriage flanked by Ossie and Baby Gap Brian.

Young Dave, Chelsea megastore carrier bag in hand, made his way over to our table and stood directly in front of Geordie Jase whose characteristic lopsided smile had now been replaced by a frown which amply conveyed the formless sense of apprehension he was beginning to feel.

With Ugly John and myself sat either side of him and the rest of the lads fanned out behind Young Dave, Geordie Jase quickly realised that his escape options were pretty limited.

'W... W... Whats g g goin on like?' he stuttered nervously, looking up at the impressive blue and white mitre Young Dave was wearing on his head. 'Yer aint gonna throw me off the train cos I'm a Geordie like are ya?' he continued, sitting back in his seat and folding his arms, 'cos if yer are I'm gonna knock a couple of ya oot before ya manage it... I used tae be a boxer eh... and I'm that hard.'

Young Dave, the football exorcist, reached into the megastore bag and produced a neatly folded Chelsea home shirt which he placed on the table in front of Geordie Jase; reaching into the bag once again he produced a dog eared old exercise book which he opened up and began to read from in a bogusly bucolic manner.

'Most glorious Prince Roman of the heavenly armies, Saint Claudio the archangel, defend us against the red scum of the world and the snares of the north-eastern devils.' Young Dave motioned Baby Gap Brian to hold up the Chelsea shirt in front of a bemused looking Geordie Jase before continuing with the exorcism.

'Behold the shirt of Chelsea, flee bands of enemies. The lions of the tribe of Millwall the offspring of Ken Bates hath conquered... as wax melts before the fire so the wicked did perish at the feet of Zola.' Young Dave picked up a bottle of beer and took a swig from it before handing it to Geordie Jase.

'Do you renounce Sir Bobby Robson?' asked Young Dave.

'Why aye man,' replied Geordie Jase, gulping down a mouthful of the amber nectar.

'And all his works?'

'Why aye man.'

'And Alan Shearer?'

'Why aye man.'

'Do you renounce the fog on the Tyne and agree that Peter Beardsley is an ugly twat.'

'Aye.' Geordie Jase took another swig from the beer bottle and handed it back to Young Dave.

There was a hushed silence in the carriage and I noticed that the ticket inspector and a couple of similarly attired colleagues were stood at the far door looking on with some bewilderment as Young Dave concluded the exorcism.

'Do you believe in Chelsea Football Club?'

'Why aye.'

'Repeat after me... if she don't come...'

'If she don't come.'

'I'll tickle her bum.'

'why aye'll tickle her bum.'

'with a lump of celery Geordie Jase?'

' why aye with a lump of celery Young Dave.'

Geordie Jase's final response was met with a chorus of 'celery, celery' from our small worshipful congregation.

Young Dave held out his hands in a priestly manner and gave the final blessing.

'We rejoice with thankful hearts that you have renounced the Magpies and received the teachings of Chelsea... you are absolved of your sins, go in peace to love and fly the blue flag.

* * *

'Who is Mr Lemon?' asked Frau Ochs, the hotel front of house manager, an air of desperation creeping into her voice.

'I'm Mr Lemon.' Lemon stepped forward and placed his hands on the reception counter drumming his fingers in time with the old Nena hit '99 Red Balloons' the video for which was currently being screened by MTV on the hotel lobby TV.

'No... I am Mr Lemon,' said Big Chris scooping up a handful of complimentary fruit bonbons from a large crystal bowl on the counter and cramming them into his mouth.

'No... no... you are Mr Big Chrees... he is Mr Lemon.' Frau Ochs, unfazed by Big Chris's attempts to re-enact the Kirk Douglas / Tony Curtis piece de resistance from the film Spartacus, narrowed her eyes and adjusted the top of her cream coloured blouse so that it accentuated the form factor of her pert breasts. Then, with a determined look in her lagoon blue eyes, she extended the index finger of her right hand in a businesslike fashion and pointed at Ugly John.

'You... Mr Mare, you are responsible for zees boys and zer bookings?... I vill not have zees English foolery of the tom in my hotel yes.'

For a split second my mind wandered and I imagined Frau Ochs, clad in the uniform of the Waffen SS, fulfilling my darkest desires. But the split second soon passed by as Sir Larry emerged from the bar lager handed and burst into song.

'*Ninety-nine, Decision Street, ninety-nine ministers meet, to worry, worry, super-scurry, call the troops out in a hurry...*'

Ugly John shook his head and made his way to the desk.

'*This is what we've waited for,*' trilled Sir Larry, oblivious to what was going on, '*this is it boys, this is war... the president is on the line as ninety-nine red balloons... go by... la la la la la la...*'

Frau Ochs arched her left eyebrow and glared at Sir Larry.

'Singing is not permitted in ze hotel sir.'

'How do you know my name?'

'I don't know your name.'

'But you just called me Sir... that is my name... Sir... I am Sir Larry.'

At this point, with a confused Frau Ochs about to lose control of the situation, Ugly John stepped in and displayed the kind of maturity that I'm some way off attaining myself.

'Ok ok... listen lads, lets give the woman a break... the sooner we can get this sorted out the sooner we can get into town... remember we haven't got a match ticket between us yet at the moment... we've still gotta find this Wolfman bloke of Young Dave's.'

I looked at Ugly John and then at Frau Ochs; I wasn't thinking about giving her a break, more about giving her 'one'. She would definitely get it.

* * *

I remembered Ossie remarking at the Arsenal match that as a city Stuttgart had little to offer the accidental tourist. Having done his research on the internet he even went as far as likening it to the north east

England's very own city of culture... Middlesboro. I thought he was being a bit harsh at the time but not anymore.

Zilina, Prague and Rome had been easy on the eye. Even a cultural philistine like me couldn't have failed to have been impressed by their picturesque historical splendour, refulgence made all the more agreeable by the warmth of the sun.

Düsseldorf had had its moments, in particular the walk along the scenic left bank of the River Rhine when sadly all I kept thinking about was Barnes Wallis and his legendary bouncing bomb. Thoughts that had been accompanied by the memory of seeing several thousand Chelsea fans, arms outstretched and swaying, pretending they were Lancaster bombers as they hummed the theme from the Dambusters movie.

Strangely enough those memories were of the time when we had beaten VfB Stuttgart in the Cup Winners Cup Final at the Rasunda Stadium in Stockholm back in 1998.

'There's nothing good about this,' muttered Ossie, voicing his discontent and breaking the silence as we traipsed along Stuttgart's main shopping street following the directions we had been given to Bar Amadeus. The wind lashed the falling snow into our faces with a spiteful vengeance and the thickening glaze of sleet gathering on the pavement cruelly exposed the limitations of the un- seasonal footwear that most of us were wearing.

'How much further is it Marco?' bleated a sober Sir Larry, inadvertently shaking the snow from his Elvis-like shock of black hair as he slipped and slithered his way along the icy cobbles.

'Just up here on the left,' I replied, waving the map I was holding and trying to sound confident.

'You said that fifteen minutes ago... this weather is dread man,' complained Big Chris, sighing as he looked at the spicy sausages that were hanging in the window of the butchers shop we were walking past.

'Why do we have to go all this bloody way anyway,' he continued, peering lovingly into the shop window.

'Oi Mr Blobby stop moanin will ya... we have to find this bar cos it's where we are gonna meet the Wolfman,' squawked Baby Gap Brian, emerging from behind Big Chris whom along with Ossie he'd been using as a wind break as we trudged through the snowstorm. 'Bloody Hell that was a bad idea,' he chattered, shivering as he jumped back in line.

Big Chris stopped in his tracks and stepped into the doorway of the butchers shop.

'Look will you all please stop calling me fat,' he implored, the wind permeating his puffer jacket, inflating it and making him look positively obese. 'I know that fat isn't beautiful but for most people it is sooner or later inevitable... as you will all one day find out.'

'Blimey look... it's the Michelin Man,' chortled Young Dave, as he brushed the snow away from his collar. 'Very philosophical...,' he continued, before being interrupted by a familiar voice.

'It's down there lads... look I can see it, Bar Amadeus.'

Fortunately for Big Chris everyone turned their attention back to the street and the whitening figure of Sir Larry who was stood fifty metres away, looking increasingly like Frosty the Snowman, and pointing at some obscure point in the distance.

There's nothing that appeals to your average Chelsea fan more in atrocious weather conditions like this than the traditional confines of an unpretentious, cosy, drinker and fortunately for us Bar Amadeus more than matched our requirements which had been getting less and less exacting with every snowy minute that passed.

From the outside, with its garish pink and blue neon lit signage, Bar Amadeus could quite easily have been an ultra modern bordello. However, once we had pushed open the impressive solid oak door and made our way inside any thoughts we may have had about buxom, corseted ladies offering to take us upstairs for a generous consideration were dispelled by the olde world English pub environment we found ourselves in.

Bar Amadeus, with its grey stone floors, oak beams and large open fireplaces in which huge logs crackled and burned with a fierce intensity, was not only redolent of the past but also possessed charm, atmosphere and character.

It was the type of place where religion, race and social class held no sway at all. The people of Stuttgart came here to have a good drink and judging by the thigh slapping, glass chinking behaviour of the VfB supporters gathered in one corner, they were under no obligation to conduct themselves in a sober manner... it was just like being at home, except the beer tasted better.

'Who is this Wolfman geezer then Young Dave?' asked Lemon, wiping away the frothy moustache that had formed on his top lip as he'd sipped away at the Weiss beer in the large Stein glass he was holding with both hands.

Young Dave sparked up a Marlboro light and chugged away on it a couple of times before answering.

'His names Axel Wolf and he's Stuttgart's answer to Stan Flashman, he's got the ten tickets we need and if we're lucky he'll be here at 6pm... I sorted it all out on the internet.'

Everyone looked at their watches, it was 5.45pm... just three hours to kick off.

'Looks like we'll only need nine if I know someone,' I said, pointing over at the main bar where Sir Larry was already embroiled in a deep conversation with an alarmingly pretty girl, whose raven hair and porcelain features made her look even younger than she probably was.'

'Vo F B... Vo F B...'

We all turned our attention to the far side of the pub where a group of thirty or so Stuttgart fans attired in replica shirts were chanting and pointing at a haggard looking character whose grey beard I thought likened him to the Stench From The Trench, the pitiful beggar we'd come across in a Prague doorway.

'Vo F B... Vo F B... Vo F B.' The chant continued until 'grey beard' acknowledged the fans with a thumbs up which was met with a large round of applause.

'I bet that's the Wolfman,' whispered Lemon to Big Chris, who was thoroughly enjoying a large plate of Schnitzel and paying little attention to what was going on elsewhere in the pub.

'Grey beard' looked around the bar clocking our group several times before eventually swaggering over with two accomplices. One of his accomplices had a beard identical to his and the other was clean shaven.

'Fuck me, it's ZZ Top!' I said to Young Dave, as the men approached us.

'Who is ze Young Dave?' said 'grey beard', eyeing each one of us avariciously. 'I am ze man zat zey call Volfman and I av zumzink zat you vant,' he continued, in an accent that had me thinking about the Colditz TV series again.

'I am Young Dave,' said Young Dave, getting to his feet and raising his right hand whilst winking at Wolfman who had made his way around the long narrow table at which we were sat.

'Looks like a scene from The Great Escape,' chuckled Baby Gap Brian, as we all looked on waiting to see what would happen next.

Sir Larry, who'd been watching proceedings from the bar, sauntered over and gave Young Dave a hearty slap on the back before exchanging pleasantries in German with Wolfman who seemed mightily impressed with his command of the language.

'She looks a bit young mate,' I said, pointing at the bar.

'Old enough son,' replied Sir Larry, clicking the fingers of his left hand.

'You know what they say Sir Larry dontcha?'

'What's that?'

'Ask Young Dave.'

'What do they say Young Dave?'

Young Dave tutted and shook his head in a fatherly manner. 'If there's grass on the wicket... let's play cricket.'

We all chinked our glasses by way of approval as Wolfman and his accomplices looked on disdainfully.

'Vee do ze football business now ya? I av no time to talk about ze cricket.'

Young Dave, Wolfman and Sir Larry made their way over to an alcove which was near the main entrance to the bar to conclude negotiations and sort out the paperwork. Five minutes later they returned. The tickets, which each had a face value of 50 Euros, had been purchased from Wolfman for 60 Euros which was as Lemon put it... 'a right result!'

As ever, Sir Larry elected to remain in the pub and watch the match on TV with his intended paramour for the evening, the waiflike Helga. The rest of us had three lots of two tickets and one lot of three to divide up... game on.

Our 60 Euros investment would afford us the pleasure of watching the match from assorted sections of the ground which housed the Stuttgart supporters, something which Wolfman had assured us would be completely safe.

'Vo F B... Vo F B... Vo F B.'

Wolfman's return to the other side of Bar Amadeus was greeted once again by the Stuttgart fans raucously chanting the V F B prefix letters to their teams name which Sir Larry had knowledgeably informed me stood for Verein fur Bewegungsspiele or something like that!

The German's pronounced V as Vo and the whole lot translated as 'association for movement' and if this enthusiastic Vo F B crew were anything to go by, we'd be in for a very lively evening indeed.

*   *   *

We'd followed Wolfman and his cohorts out of Bar Amadeus leaving Sir Larry alone with the alluring Helga but vowing to return at the end of the match. Maybe Sir Larry had the right idea, it was positively glacial outside. Fortunately though it was just a short walk to the metro station and I managed to make the journey without complaining too much.

Like most things in Germany, Stuttgart's metro service is timely, efficient... and best of all free. This last factor was of course not strictly true, in fact it wasn't true at all. Stuttgart's metro service operated on what was called a trust system; trust was placed on the commuter to purchase a valid ticket for the journey they wished to undertake thereby reducing operating costs by negating the need for inspectors and ancillary machinery.

It was a great idea and I'm sure it worked reasonably well with certain cross sections of Stuttgart's populous, a cross section that clearly didn't include Wolfman and the rest of the VfB boys who had beckoned us onto the tram which was about to depart from Charlottenplatz station.

'Fuck me U-15... that's a bit scarey,' huffed Young Dave, as we bundled each other into one of the carriages.

'Why's that then Young Dave?' asked Baby Gap Brian, his voice piping up from somewhere around the navel level of a large, middle aged woman who seemed to be deliberately pressing herself up against an increasingly concerned looking Big Chris.

'The U-15 was the first German submarine to be sunk in World War One...,' replied Young Dave, his voice tailing off slightly as he realised he had an audience slightly larger than he anticipated.

I shook my head and began to laugh, only Young Dave would have known a piece of trivia like that.

'Vo F B... Vo F B... Vo F B.' The now familiar chant commenced again as the tram pulled into the next station and more red and white clad fans crammed themselves into our carriage.

It was beginning to feel uncomfortably hot and for a moment I thought about the crew of the doomed U-15, marooned at the bottom of the North Sea suffering an agonising death, bodies writhing as their lungs cried out for air.

'Yeah, it was rammed by the British cruiser HMS Birmingham,' said Young Dave, tilting his head backwards and taking a deep breath before resuming our history lesson. 'Cut clean in half by all accounts... and the funny thing is right... that the skipper of the Birmingham... was called Duff.'

'Your full of shit Young Dave... stop trying to scare everyone.' Baby Gap Brian emerged by the central doors in the carriage, his face flushed with the exertion of preventing himself from being trampled on.

'I'm telling you mate it's the gods honest... seriously, and you know Duff's gonna make his comeback tonight.'

Fortunately after ten extra long minutes, and two more stops, the tram arrived at its final destination and the carriage doors opened disgorging us gratefully onto the platform.

As we regrouped I looked at the number displayed on the side of the tram,

U-16 it said clearly in a traditional gothic typeface that could be mistaken for nothing else.

'Oi Young Dave... it's a 16 not a 15 you muppet,' I said, pointing back at the tram as we walked along the platform.

'Yeah I know... but the story of the U-16 is less interesting,' he replied, grinning at me as he offered me a Marlboro and sparked one up himself.

*   *   *

The impressively named Gottlieb-Daimler Stadion, home of VfB Stuttgart turned out to be a bit of a disappointment. Originally built in 1933 for the German gymnastics festival it had been modernised several times subsequently; in 1986 for the European Athletics Championships, in 1993 for the World Athletics Championships and now further work was being undertaken to improve facilities in time for the 2006 World Cup Finals.

Whilst the stadium had the same wonderful sense of symmetry as the Stadio Olimpico, it was much smaller than the home of Lazio and as I looked around I couldn't help feeling that the place hadn't really been designed with football in mind.

Call me old fashioned but a running track around a football pitch just doesn't look right. Not only that, but as a spectator you are just that little bit further away from the action.

The old Stamford Bridge was a prime case in point, in days gone by the original track around the pitch had been used for a variety of sporting events. From my old vantage point high up on the Shed by the tea bar, the players looked Subbuteo size and whilst there was plenty of hostility generated on the terraces the opposing team rarely felt intimidated by the home support in the way they would at places like Upton Park or Loftus Road.

If the Gottlieb-Daimler Stadion didn't feel like a proper football ground, it did nothing to dampen the ardent fervour of the supporters who came here to cheer on VfB Stuttgart.

Ugly John and I took our seats half way up the wrap around section of the main stand, in line with one set of goalposts and directly opposite the section housing the 2300 Chelsea supporters who'd officially made the trip.

'Vo F B... Vo F B.'

Ugly John pointed at a man who was balanced on a low wall directly behind the goals nearest us. In his hand he held a megaphone and with it he was noisily orchestrating the chanting around the stadium, it was Wolfman.

The chanting alternated between both ends of the ground creating a fantastic hi-fi effect which was made visually impressive by the red and white scarves which were being twirled above thousands of heads.

The teams were out on the pitch going through their final warm up routines. Thankfully Cudicini, who despite not being fully recovered from the leg injury that had kept him out of Saturday's home defeat by Arsenal was to play behind a counterattacking defensive partnership of Terry, Bridge, Bill Gallas and the boy wonder Johnson.

Makalele, Geremi and Lampard made up the midfield with Gronkjaer to be used as the wide player. Up front; Gudjohnsen, who'd scored and then been sent off against Arsenal, was preferred to Hasselbaink and Hernan Crespo had responsibility for leading the line.

Along with Hasselbaink on our multi-million pound subs bench were Duff, Joe Cole, Parker, Desailly, Melchiot and the calamitous reserve custodian Sullivan.

'Fuck me Marco, check this lot out,' exclaimed Ugly John, pointing at the massed ranks of the VfB supporters, red scarves outstretched above their heads, who were now treating us to a perfect English rendition of the traditional Liverpool anthem You'll Never Walk Alone.

'Even the Scouser's would be proud of that,' I replied, genuinely impressed, 'in fact look at it, we could be at Anfield.'

It was impossible to make ourselves heard above the noise so we just sat down and absorbed the atmosphere. In the far corner I could see, but not hear, the Chelsea fans, arms aloft, clearly responding to the home supports vocal efforts.

There wasn't a hint of trouble in the air. The German's we were sat with knew by now we were Chelsea fans and they shook our hands with genuine warmth. The old boy sat next to me told me that when Stuttgart had beaten Man U earlier this season in the group stages of the competition the United fans had jeered and whistled when they'd sung You'll Never Walk Alone so I spent a couple of minutes explaining that there was plenty of 'previous' between United and Liverpool and that the United fans probably thought that the VfB supporters were singing it to deliberately wind them up.

'Tonight my friend vee make a good match ya.' The old boy nodded at me and twirled the ends of his handlebar moustache. I'm not sure if he'd fully understood what I'd said but who cared.

'Yes mate... lets hope so,' I said, scanning the stands to see if I could see Young Dave and his Valentino Rossi hat.

From the first minute it was all Stuttgart both on the pitch and off it. On the pitch the first ten minutes saw Cudicini produce a truly world class save, unbelievably getting his finger tips to a terrific shot from the lively looking Stuttgart midfielder Meissner.

Chelsea Gate 17 ... Stuttgart ... February 2004

Left to right ... Ugly John, Marco, Lemon, Baby Gap Brian, Ossie,
Geordie Jase, Sir Larry, Big Chris and Roger Socks ... the girl in the ad
would definitely have got it!

Worryingly, despite the Spider being back to his agile self he still wasn't fit enough to take goal kicks and I'm wondered what might happen if he had to run out of the goalmouth to make a sweepers clearance at any point in the match.

Off the pitch Wolfman continued to lead the chants, which were non stop and occasionally in English.

'You're shit and you know you are... you're shit and you know you are.'

There was no trace of a foreign accent as the chant reverberated around the ground. Forty odd thousand Germans voicing their partisan opinion on a Chelsea side that now had Wayne Bridge to thank for not falling one goal behind as he cleared a Kuranyi effort off the goal line.

'This doesn't look too good mate does it... they're all over us.' Ugly John's lucid observation was impeccably ill timed as we both got to our feet to follow a Chelsea counter attack away to the right.

Bill Gallas sprayed a neat ball to Glen Johnson, clearly reinvigorated following his 'rest' period, who then played a lovely one-two with Geremi before flashing a low cross towards the advancing Crespo.

The ball was then spectacularly sliced into the Stuttgart net, not by Crespo but by one of the home teams players panicked by the space the Argentinean had created for himself in the box.

'GOAL... ha ha... oops fuck me... shit!' Momentarily forgetting where I was, I punched the air and jumped on top of an equally euphoric Ugly John. If we'd have been in a similar position at an opposing ground in England our celebrations would have been met with a flurry of fists. Here instead, as we hastily reviewed our potentially perilous situation, we realised that the VfB supporters were far more concerned with the ramifications of the own goal their team had just conceded rather than the actions of a couple of foolhardy Chelsea fans.

Wolfman, megaphone in hand ensured that the home support continued to vocally rally behind their team. Corner after corner, free kick after free kick rained in on Chelsea's goal and we were perfectly placed to see Cudicini and the rest of the defence deal efficiently with each threat as it was posed.

'They aint gonna score... you know it.' Ugly John jabbed me in the ribs as we watched Spider cleanly catch another Stuttgart corner ball that floated into the five yard box.

I had to agree, the more the game went on, the more I got the feeling that Chelsea were not going to concede a goal. To counter that I also felt that we looked highly unlikely to score a goal by orthodox methods since by the time the referee blew the whistle to end what had been a breathless first half Chelsea's counter attacks, with the exception of a Gudjohnsen effort which sailed hopelessly over the bar, had yet to result in a shot on goal.

'Tell you what m m mate,' said Ugly John, stammering slightly as he shivered in the plummeting temperature. 'Claudio's got the tactics and the strategy for European football aint he... how mean is our defence eh? We still aint conceded a goal away from home in Europe.'

'Yeah... it goes further than that son,' I replied, blowing into my cupped hands and rubbing them together. 'We've kept clean sheets in more than half of all the games we've played this season,' I continued, sounding more like Young Dave than myself, 'it's the Italian way innit, ugly football... nicking 1-0 wins away from home making the defence the foundation of the team... Vialli started it buying Cudicini, Desailly and Melchiot and Claudio's continued it with the addition of Bill Gallas, Bridge and Johnson.

'Yeah, that's right,' agreed Ugly John, 'and don't forget as well that it was Claudio who gave John Terry his chance in the first team and look how well he's come on... gotta be the first name on the team sheet innit... and who is it that always jumps to the defence of the manager when the media question his tactics and strategy?... John Terry.'

As the players took to the field for the start of the second half Ugly John and I came to the conclusion that Abramovich would soon have to decide whether or not he wanted Chelsea to evolve into a trophy winning side playing the frugal, some might say boring, style of football advocated by the AC Milan coach Ancelotti or a more swashbuckling outfit that won over the critics with a Brazilianesque debonair attitude and approach to the game.

Roman could buy all the best players in the world if he wanted, but ultimately it would be down to the coach to fashion the style of play. If Ranieri was ultra cautious, how different would the tactics of say Eriksson be?

'*Chelsea... Chelsea... Chelsea.*'

At last we could here the chants of our own supporters, but not for long as Wolfman the conductor was soon on his perch again with his back to the game, orchestrating the German riposte.

* * *

The second half started much as the first with Stuttgart pressing forward, looking to exploit any weakness in a Chelsea defence being superbly marshalled by a demonic tackling John Terry.

Ugly John and I were on our feet again as Crespo struck the ball into the Stuttgart net only to see his effort ruled offside, this time our antics attracted the attention of a steward who politely asked us to sit down.

Stuttgart made a couple of ineffective substitutions and by the time Claudio had sent on Duff for Gronkjaer and Hasselbaink for Gudjohnsen they were being restricted to shooting from distance.

Joe Cole replaced Crespo in the penultimate minute but Stuttgart were by now a spent force. Cudicini was called on to make one last stunning save and the final whistle when it came was accompanied by a chorus of boos from the home fans whose unstinting support deserved better than it got.

Match Result
Verein fur Bewegungsspiele Stuttgart 0 : Chelsea FC 1

*   *   *

Ugly John and I stayed behind to applaud the Chelsea players from the pitch. Another clean sheet, 450 minutes of football played away from home and not one goal conceded. It was a consummately professional performance from a team of players determined to give the increasingly beleaguered Claudio Ranieri just the fillip he needed following the demoralising league and cup defeats against Arsenal.

*   *   *

'Yeah... and you know what's gonna happen next don't ya?' said Young Dave, as he reached for another Marlboro, 'we're gonna get Arsenal in the quarterfinals... I'd bet money on it.'

I must admit I hadn't thought about that as a possibility, I'd thought that Man U would draw Arsenal and that maybe we'd get a nice trip to Spain or Italy... somewhere warm for a welcome change.

The news came through that FC Porto had beaten United, who'd also had Roy Keane sent off, 2–1. United were going through a shaky patch at the moment and although they would be favourites to go through following the return leg in two weeks time that outcome was by no means a foregone conclusion.

'That would be a fucking nightmare,' said Big Chris, his eyes widening as he saw the waitress approaching our table with a large bowl of chips. 'Getting tickets for the away leg... how difficult is that gonna be eh? The touts will make a killing...'

Big Chris paused, realising that if he was talking he would not be able to make a decisive strike on the chips which had now been placed on the table.

'I reckon the Chelsea allocation... will be less than 3000 for that game,' said Young Dave pointing at the collection of three quarter empty beer glasses on the table and then holding up nine fingers to the waitress who nodded and smiled at us as she walked away.

We had all made it back to Bar Amadeus as agreed. Well everyone who'd gone to the match had made it back to Bar Amadeus, Sir Larry, who we'd left in the company of his new German girlfriend Helga, was nowhere to be seen. I'd tried him on his mobile a couple of times but that had just gone through to voicemail, so I sent him a text message telling him we were back in the drinker.

The massive bar was virtually empty; the Stuttgart fans, Wolfman included, had clearly decided that with nothing to celebrate they might as well go home to bed, it was after all 11.50pm on a school night. Wolfman had told us of a couple of places we could visit that would be quite lively into the small hours, but the early start, cold weather and adrenalin buzz of being at the match was beginning to take its toll.

'It's bollocks innit,' I said, elbowing Ossie in the ribs and pointing at the black stocking clad legs of the waitress who was leaning over the bar.

'What is?' said Big Chris, wiping tomato sauce away from his lips and licking his fingers.

'We took over 6000 to Highbury in the FA Cup the other week they should allow the same number of away fans for all matches, ah fuck it... I'll be interested to see what rules Eddie Barnett dreams up for fairly allocating tickets if we do draw em in the Champions League.'

The more we talked about it, the more the conspiracy theorists amongst our number suggested that UEFA would 'fix' the draw so that it would be impossible for two English teams to play each other in the final. What a shame, I had this fanciful dream that we were going to return to Gelsenkirchen in May where Chelsea would thrash Man United 4-0 in the final and I would enjoy a steamy night of unbridled passion with Tiffany the barmaid who'd made such a big impression on me in Düsseldorf.

The dewy, almost rhapsodic, freshness that I associated with Tiffany when I thought about her, which to be quite honest wasn't that often, was a stark contrast to the sight which greeted us as the main entrance doors to Bar Amadeus swung open Wild West saloon bar style.

The waitress had just politely informed us that no more beer would be served and as she did so a man who was deaf to the words 'last' and 'orders' staggered into the bar. It was Sir Larry.

The next edition of the Oxford English Dictionary might think about including the adjective 'wankered'. A modern expression used to describe someone who is beyond the stage of drunkenness normally referred to as being pissed.

Sir Larry took a few more unsteady steps forward before stopping in his tracks and punching his right fist skywards.

'Good result all round,' he said, lowering his hand and thrusting it into his coat pocket, knees buckling slightly as his body tried to remain upright.

'1–0 to the Chels and 1–0 to Sir Larry.' Sir Larry pulled out a pair of miniscule white panties from his pocket and held them to his nostrils before tossing them theatrically at Lemon who placed them over his head.

We all got to our feet and applauded and as we did so Sir Larry passed out and collapsed unceremoniously to the floor.

'Blimey!' exclaimed Ugly John, 'that Helga looked like such a sweet girl, you'd never imagine her minge could smell that bad.'

*   *   *

'Have you read this?' I said, pointing at the article in the *Evening Standard* I'd just finished reading.

'Yeah,' replied Ugly John, nodding and smiling.

'Good to see that Lampard thought pretty much the same way as we did... what was it exactly he said? Oh yeah "We could be drawn against Arsenal? Oh fuck it". Fantastic! What a top man.'

We were strapped into our seats aboard BA 955 which had been scheduled to depart Munich airport some while ago. The problem was it had begun to snow quite heavily and our plane had to join the queue to be hosed down with de-icer to ensure that it could take off safely.

I sat back and as I relaxed I felt my mind drifting. Today had been fairly uneventful. We'd slept in, had a late breakfast and got the midday train back from Stuttgart to Munich. During the course of the journey there had been no horseplay, no ribald banter and no drinking.

In Munich, Ugly John purchased his first item of Stone Island casual wear. A retina burning bright orange shirt that would ensure if he ever got lost Mrs Ugly John, his kids, his mates and the emergency services, if they were required, would have absolutely no trouble in finding him.

Sir Larry and I had fallen in love with an exotic looking beauty called Tamara who'd waited on our table in a very pleasant little café come bar we'd wiled away a couple of hours in before catching another 'free' train to the airport.

Security at the airport had been reassuringly strict. We'd undergone a rigorous screening procedure which unfortunately for Roger Socks also involved everyone removing their shoes.

Baby Gap Brian's specially trained eyes had been quick to spot a major infringement of the Gate 17 dress code; Roger was wearing a pair of Daz white Hi Tec socks... guilty as charged your honour.

Baby Gap Brian had been in his element, mercilessly lampooning Roger Socks for his fashion faux pas, finally suggesting that he might consider a secondary career as children's entertainer or failing that a circus clown.

My train of thought was derailed by the aircraft tannoy which hissed into life with the voice of the captain informing us that we had been given clearance for takeoff.

As we taxied down the runway and began to gather speed, I became acutely aware of only being able to hear the roar of the planes engines. The treacherous conditions had muted even the most seasoned travellers, even the cabin crew seemed nervous.

I looked out of the window, at the large flakes of snow flurrying in our slipstream and then at Ugly John sat next to me, eyes shut, hands gripping the armrests of his seat so tightly that his knuckles had visibly whitened.

I too closed my eyes. Mentally I made the sign of the cross and bit into the middle knuckle of my right index finger. 'Here we fucking go,' I muttered under my breath, clenching my fists and taking a deep breath as the plane began to take off.

Of course as soon as the planes wheels had left the ground and that momentary stomach churning weightless sensation that accompanies take off had abated the chatter of voices could be heard again. I looked out of the window once more at the twinkling lights on the ground that very quickly became obscured by the snow clouds we were rapidly climbing through and began to laugh uncontrollably.

'What you laughing at mate?' asked Ugly John, opening his eyes and cracking the knuckles of his left hand. 'There was nothing funny about that.'

'Ha, I just remembered what Lemon said last night ha ha when we were having a drink after the match,' I replied, still chortling.

'What was that then son?' Ugly John cracked the knuckles of his right hand and looked at me expectantly.

'He said, "If you have a mid-air wank on a plane... does it count you in as being a member of the mile high club?" now that's fucking funny innit.'

GIANFRANCO ZOLA
Cagliari FC vs Como FC
Serie B Italia
Stadio Sant' Elia, Sardinia, Italy
Saturday 3rd April 2004

'Put a brandy in that will you love,' said Sir Larry, pointing at the beer glass on the table in front of him and pushing his fingers comb-like through his greying mane of black hair.

'Is that a Miriam son?' he continued, adjusting his spectacles so he could focus his eyes more intently on the sylphlike figure of the olive skinned waitress who was endeavouring to take our order as we sat outside the Antico Caffe in Cagliari's Piazza Costituzione.

'Well it looks like a Miriam mate,' I replied, rubbing at the stubble on my chin, 'but I reckon that underneath that tight black skirt, partially concealed by the flimsiest of G strings, you'll find a regular black box as opposed to the meat and two veg that Miriam was hiding from her suitors.'

'Right... right, but she'd definitely get it yeah,' replied Sir Larry, sparking up a Marlboro and smiling as he watched the waitress pour the brandy he'd just ordered into his beer glass.

'Grazie love... this ought to do it... cheers lads... happy birthday Ugly John.' Sir Larry raised his beer glass, as we did ours, and drained the contents.

* * *

The occasion was Ugly John's 40th birthday. Before Christmas we'd made a plan to celebrate it in style by making a pilgrimage to Sardinia... a trip that hopefully would include watching Gianfranco Zola playing for his hometown club Cagliari against Como in the Italian Serie B, the equivalent of England's 1st Division... and here we were!

I looked around the table; it was a good turn out, even if the slightly botched travel arrangements had meant that a couple of lads had dropped out at the last minute. Originally we'd all been booked on a return flight from Luton to Cagliari but then the carrier, Volareweb, decided at the last minute to cancel the return flight back to London leaving us slightly snookered.

Ugly John eventually manage to sort things out so that we still flew from Luton out to Cagliari with Volareweb but inconveniently the return leg of the journey would involve driving to the north of the island and taking a Ryanair flight from Alghero back to my favourite airport in the whole wide world, Stansted.

We hadn't planned on hiring a couple of cars, but in the end it turned out to be a blessing in disguise as our hotel was a fair distance from town and the weather could at best be described as variable.

Right now though, the sun was so intense I could feel my bald pate starting to protest at the lack of protection I'd afforded it. Fuck it, I thought to myself, we're only here for a couple of days... if I burn, I burn.

Ossie didn't look too concerned about the potentially harmful effects of the midday Sardinian sun either, stretching himself out along the length of his chair and rolling up his jeans to his knees. All he needed now was a knotted hankie on his head and he'd complete the perfect image of the English tourist abroad.

Young Dave's leathery skin had long since lost its elasticity and was probably impervious to the suns injurious ultra violet rays. He could bask lizard-like for hours, sitting in silence as he was now, studying Ugly John's Lonely Planet guide to Sardinia, speaking only to confirm what he wanted to drink next.

Sir Larry was Sir Larry. Extremes of temperature didn't faze him, quite simply he was a human phenomenon whose alcohol soaked body was resistant to a wide number of ailments ranging from the common cold to Malaria. Recently he hadn't been so lucky with the Poison Ivy but he'd figured an extra brandy with his beer would soon clear that up enabling him to wax his dolphin with any Miriam that took his fancy.

Ugly John was sat there next to Sir Larry with his eyes closed and a broad grin on his upturned face. Ossie had cruelly suggested that it was Ugly's 50th birthday not his 40th, but from where I was sitting he seemed to be wearing reasonably well. At least he still had a full head of hair, which was still the same dirty blonde colour as it had been when I first met him twenty odd years ago.

Ugly John's locks had been the topic of a lengthy discussion in the bar at Luton airport the previous evening. It had a synthetic nylon-like quality to it which reminded me of the Action Man dolls of my childhood. 'Suedehead!' Ossie had proclaimed, garnering support for a new nickname for Ugly John. But Ugly John, 'Brutto Gianni' as I'd introduced him to a couple of Miriam's we'd chatted to over breakfast this morning, was Ugly John in the same way that Sir Larry was Sir Larry although I had to admit that the nickname Suedehead was a pretty good one.

Augmenting our impressive line-up of middle aged, itinerant thrill seekers were a couple of battle scarred veterans whose friendship I'd nurtured during the early halcyon days of the rave scene.

Neither Sergeant Barnes or El Jocko had a great deal of affinity with Chelsea FC, but they did share with us a genuine love of the game and of course the birthday boy, Ugly John.

Sergeant Barnes was razor thin and absurdly youthful in both his appearance and outlook on life. The youthful looks he attributed to a spartan lifestyle that was dominated by a love of cycling and the fitness regime that went with it.

Barnes was my conscience, pulling me back time and again from the precipice when my recreational drug abuse threatened to become something more habitual. Always sharply dressed, he had the gait to accompany the militaristic moniker by which he was known.

This had been the first time that Ossie and Young Dave had met Sergeant Barnes and they had both automatically thought that he was known as Sergeant Barnes because his surname was Barnes and he'd achieved the rank of sergeant during the course of an army career.

They were right about the surname, but little else. Young Dave's whimsical notion that Barnes was a war hero who's face had been scarred during active service in the Falkland's or the Gulf was way off track.

Sergeant Barnes was the Tom Berenger character in the film Platoon. At the time Barnes and Berenger bore an uncanny resemblance to each other, well according to my ex wife anyway... the same ex wife that thought my 'Uncle' Robert looked like Mel Gibson. It was all easy... the surname of the character in the film and our mate were the same and so plain old Jonathan Barnes became known as Sergeant Barnes.

With the passage of time Barnes's personality had become aligned to the character he was named after. Our Sergeant became prone to belligerent outbursts, provoked more often than not by the sight of a lardy girl wearing ill fitting clothes that had been purchased from Top Shop rather than the shabby behaviour of the fellow members of his 'platoon'.

A recent mishap hadn't helped his temperament; the scars Sergeant Barnes bore on his face were not old shrapnel wounds but the legacy of a life threatening road accident that had also seen him break his back in two places and dislocate his left shoulder. The main thing was he was alive, most definitely kicking, and here with us today to celebrate Ugly John's landmark birthday.

If the scythe of the Grim Reaper had missed Sergeant Barnes by the narrowest of margins then it had missed El Jocko by a cat's whisker. El Jocko should have been rechristened Lazarus, for his was the greatest comeback of all. Less than a year ago, whilst on a climbing holiday in South Africa, he'd fallen fifty metres down a sheer cliff face.

It had taken twelve hours for the rescue team to reach him and a further twelve hours to get him down off the mountain. His injuries were so grave that it was thought for some time he might never walk again. It was a full month after the fall before the neurological unit at the Cape Town hospital El Jocko found himself in, pronounced him well enough to be flown to a hospital in Paris the city he'd called home for the past decade.

The dreadful accident had taken its toll on El Jocko. His right leg and lower back were held together by a Meccanoesque assemblage of metal pins, screws and plates and he now walked with a pronounced limp and a slight stoop. His once powerful frame had been decimated by muscle wastage resulting from the lengthy period of inactivity which El Jocko, a hugely talented all-round sportsman, had found maddening to endure... but he was back, and it was great to have the pleasure of his company again.

*   *   *

If my memory served me well enough I'd only ever been to three football matches with El Jocko and it had rained heavily on each occasion. The first time I'd taken him down to the Bridge, we'd got soaked to the skin watching a one sided 5–0 demolition of Sheffield Wednesday.

The second time El Jocko had invited a few of us to his home town city of Edinburgh where we had watched the team he'd followed as a callow Scottish youth, Heart of Midlothian, take on the mighty Bayern Munich who'd fielded a side which included a very young future defensive stalwart of the successful Chelsea cup side of the late nineties, Erland Johnsen.

I don't remember much about that game, a UEFA Cup tie, but I do recall it pissing down with rain and El Jocko taking us to a drinker called the Athletic Arms where he introduced us to the delights of a potent Scottish brew called Eighty Shillings and the local delicacy of Mars Bars deep fried in batter.

The final time I'd attended a match with El Jocko oddly enough was here in Italy, Genoa to be precise... Italia 90. Since El Jocko had been sporting enough to come and watch England play on more than one occasion, it was only fair that we reciprocated. Unfortunately for El Jocko the game we went to see was Scotland's embarrassing defeat at the hands of the football super power that is... Costa Rica, and it had tipped it down then.

* * *

Piazza Costituzione is located at the top of a gentle hill that slopes down to the sea. I sat there nursing my beer and watching the rays of blazing sunshine streaking through the branches of the poplar trees lining the uneven flagstone road which led down to the sprawling port of Cagliari.

As the afternoon shadows cast by the trees lengthened, I couldn't help but notice the dark, brooding clouds out to sea which seemed to be creeping slowly inland bringing with them a murky malevolence which El Jocko wryly commented on.

'Looks like we might have a bit of rain to the west later,' he drawled slowly, sounding like a TV weatherman, his lilting Scottish accent adding a bizarre level of credence to the forecast.

El Jocko looked at Sir Larry and then at the waitress who was hovering nearby before leaning over and whispering in my ear, 'Will yae order me a stiff brandy Marco, get her tae pour it in ma beer like Sir Larry has it and then for the love of Jesus Christ tell me who the feck this Miriam is yae all keep talking aboot.'

* * *

Despite the ominous looking clouds which blackened the horizon, the sky above our heads remained holiday brochure blue. As we walked down the hill to the port area it became obvious to me that the wealth which was so clearly flaunted on mainland Italy, and which had been clearly visible in the elegant and stylish city of Rome, seemed to be missing from Cagliari.

Sardinia may be rich in history and culture but Cagliari as a city is an agglomeration of bland apartment blocks, modern office buildings, medieval walls, baroque churches and a centre that is characterised by a maze of narrow cobbled streets and a castle.

An article I'd read recently about Sardinia described it as being the 'land of magic full of designer views.' Everywhere I looked though all I could see was graffiti. It wasn't even in the artistic style of the hip hop urban 'tag' graffiti that we are so used to seeing back in London, this was just plain old vulgar, political sloganeering. Nothing was sacred, every wall, statue and monument that we passed was sprayed up; the only tagging in evidence here was the ubiquitous and strange stencilled image of a lady's red halter neck brassiere.

We walked past a group of North African men were stood outside the upmarket department store La Rinascente on Via Roma selling the usual range of fake designer goods.

'Y'know Sardinia is nearer to Africa than Italy,' said Young Dave, giving us the benefit of some more of the knowledge he'd absorbed from Ugly John's Lonely Planet guide.

'Look at the Miriam's in there,' said Ossie, pointing excitedly at a group of young women with dark tresses and film starlet looks who were gathered at a cash desk just inside the main entrance to the store. 'Would they get it Marco?' he asked, looking at me knowingly.

'Not half son,' I replied, wolf whistling my approval to accompany the enthusiastic round of applause the women were receiving from Sir Larry and Sergeant Barnes in particular.

* * *

'Yeah so anyway son,' I said to El Jocko, pausing briefly to light one of Sir Larry's Marlboro's, 'basically it's to do with this reality TV programme they've been showing these past few weeks on Sky One. The programme was called There's Something About Miriam and it was all about these blokes trying to win the affection of this gorgeous looking Mexican model... who happens to bear a striking resemblance to all the birds we've seen so far out here... including those chicks in the shop back there.'

El Jocko looked slightly perplexed as he poured himself a generous glass of red wine from the carafe that Ugly John had just handed him.

'Oh I see, fair enough,' he said, as he picked up the wine glass and put it to his lips... 'well what was it then, this something about Miriam?'

'Well like all these reality TV shows, eventually there are just two geezers left and Miriam has to pick the one that has impressed her most... so she picks this bloke Tom who she's had a few snog's with... and he's well happy cos he gets ten grand and a week with Miriam on a luxury yacht cruising around the Med... thing is Miriam then reveals that she is in fact a transsexual who still has a full set of tackle... poor Tom's crushed and all the other blokes piss themselves laughing.'

'I still dinnae get it though,' said El Jocko, rubbing his index finger around the top of his wine glass. 'So if this Miriam's really a geezer then why are you lot all raving on about her and likening all these lovely Sardinian birds to her... I mean er... it?'

'I dunno son... from the chest up... you would mate... what can I say eh lads?' I looked around the table for support and received approving nods from everyone apart from Sir Larry.

'It aint bleedin normal that... er scusi signore ancora Brandy inna that please.' Sir Larry punctuated his lambaste with a request to the waiter to put a brandy in the carafe he was holding close to his chest. 'I reckon you're all sausage jockeys... never mind G17 you lot should call yourselves the Chelsea poofters.'

* * *

We were having an early tea in a run down trattoria at the far end of Via Roma. At the far end of Via Roma was the Cagliari club shop where we'd been reliably informed we could purchase tickets for their match with Como which was taking place later in the day. The reason that we were in the trattoria and not the club shop was simple... the club shop was closed.

In Italy, a country renown for putting off until domani what should be wrapped up today, pretty much everything shut down between 1.30 and 4.30pm.

'Jeeeesus Christ!' exclaimed Sir Larry, throwing both his mobile phones onto the table. 'Listen to this for a win double.'

'Go on then,' said Ossie, trying to grab one of the phones.

'United have done Arsenal 1-0 in the cup and the Chels are 1-0 up at the Lane.' Sir Larry puffed out his chest proudly and poured the brandy the waiter had handed him into the carafe he was holding swirling the contents around to make absolutely certain they blended well.

There was a certain amount of kudos attached to being the first to disseminate welcome news such as that which Sir Larry had access to through his new 3G mobile phone.

'That's fucked 'em for the treble then, cocky Gooner shits,' I said, clapping my hands and clenching my right fist and waving it at the others.

'Now all we've got to do is something we haven't done for the last eighteen times of asking,' retorted Young Dave. 'Beat the fuckers ourselves on Tuesday night and we'll be off like as not to Madrid in the semi-final of the Champions League... and what a laugh that will be... no treble for them, no double even... lovely... all easy... all gravy ha ha.'

* * *

That's the way things were working themselves out. Following our tenacious victory in Germany we had beaten Manchester City 1-0 in the league and then drawn the return leg with Stuttgart 0-0 at the Bridge.

Claudio had been given a hard time by the press for his tactics but none of us gave a flying fuck because Chelsea were through to the Champions League quarterfinals. Surprisingly Manchester United had been knocked out by FC Porto, but Real Madrid were in the draw as were AC Milan... and Arsenal.

It was inevitable that Chelsea would be paired with Arsenal when the draw was made, gloriously predictable in fact. I'm sure you could have heard the rumble of collective groans and cries of 'fix!' across the whole of West London when what was inevitable became a reality.

The draw for the semi-finals of the competition had been made at the same time; the winners of our tie with Arsenal would meet the winners of the tie between Real Madrid and Monaco. Elsewhere, AC Milan faced Deportivo La Coruna and FC Porto had been paired with Lyon.

The pressure drop on Claudio Ranieri was immediate. In the face of growing media speculation that he was to be sacked at the end of the season he remained concretely resolute.

Back to back league victories against Bolton Wanderers and Fulham had done little to change things. Kenyon was in for Sven who was stalling on signing a new England contract and despite Chelsea being a comfortable second in the Premiership it looked like Claudio Ranieri would soon be on the outside looking in, just like Ken Bates who'd finally resigned from the clubs board and stormed off in a huff aiming many a tabloid broadside at the new Chelsea board.

Worse still Carlo Cudicini had injured his hand in training and whilst Marco Ambrosio had turned in a surprisingly capable performance in keeping a clean sheet at Bolton, he'd looked slightly less composed in the local derby with Fulham.

The Spider was not going to be back between the posts for the visit of Arsenal in the first leg of the Champions League quarterfinal, in fact he was going to be out for a good few weeks... the portents for the match hadn't been good.

'Ranieri's blue and white army... Ranieri's blue and white army...'

The atmosphere at the Bridge that night had been electric, the support for the team and the manager unparalleled.

'Your support is fucking shit,' we'd chanted at the Arsenal fans strung out silently along the lower tier of the East Stand.

When Eidur gave us the lead, I'd thought that the roof of the Shed was going to lift off. I wasn't too happy about being in the Shed, we'd originally been told that, as with the Stuttgart match, the section that we normally occupied in the Mathew Harding Upper Stand would be closed in accordance with the wishes of UEFA.

What a load of old toffee apple, I'd reflected. What exactly was Peter Kenyon playing at? I wondered if Roman was pleased with the way his new CEO was performing... what exactly had he achieved since he'd joined us from Manchester United?

Probably quite a bit, but from where I was sitting all he'd managed to do was alienate and annoy every single Chelsea supporter in the ground. In a two page interview that had appeared in the Chelsea magazine Onside, there hadn't been one single mention of the burning question that was on every fans lips. Would Claudio Ranieri still be the manager of Chelsea FC next season?

Kenyon had been responsible for the signing of Peter Cech, and more recently the highly rated Dutch winger Arjen Robben... so what? The Robben signing, what was that all about? Trying to put one over on his old club United? What about Damien Duff? Wasn't he good enough? What was going to happen to him?

'We don't want Eriksson... We don't want Eriksson.'

The chant was as defiant as it ever had been; the England manager watching from the stands wasn't deaf... he'd just put pen to paper on a contract extension. If Roman had hired Kenyon with the proviso that he deliver Eriksson then what now?

The absolute bottom line was the simple fact that we didn't need Eriksson... and I'd wondered if Mr Abramovich had finally realised that. He'd won us over with his money... but now the talk about him was less approving, and as I'd contemplated what his next strategic move to enhance the fortunes of my team would be... the Arsenal only went and fucking equalised. 1-1 it finished and as I'd watched the players troop off the pitch I'd thought to myself that it wasn't over. The difference was that the players weren't just playing for themselves or the club, they were playing for their manager... our manager, the man Ranieri. "Together with all our hearts"... Come on!

Chelsea went through the month of March unbeaten, rounding things off with an emphatic 5-2 drubbing of Wolves at Stamford Bridge. Kenyon must have all but choked on his prawn sandwiches when he'd heard the news that Claudio Ranieri had been voted 'manager of the month'.

We'd had our letters from Eddie Barnett informing us that we'd seen enough away games in Europe to merit a ticket for the return leg at Highbury... and we'd be there, and I could hardly wait.

This pleasantly distracting trip to Cagliari to watch Gianfranco was a welcome sideshow. I looked at the people sat around the table with me; at the lads who were going to be at the Arsenal game and I felt confident. Something gloriously unpredictable was going to happen on Tuesday night... Chelsea were going to beat Arsenal in their own backyard.

'You ok son?' said Ugly John, poking me in the ribs. 'You were a bit quiet in the restaurant earlier... is everything all right?'

'No I'm fine mate... I was just thinking about Tuesday night... you know I really think we might do it... I've just got that feeling.'

'You gonna put a bet on then?'

'Fuck off, don't be silly... that'd be the kiss of death, and besides I don't gamble anymore.'

'You will.'

Maybe I would, but I was on tenterhooks enough without risking a monkey on Claudio and the boys. If I got back into the gambling it would be some other time... next season maybe.

*   *   *

The Stadio Sant' Elia had played host to England in the 1990 World Cup Final's but I didn't remember it looking like this. El Jocko's weather forecast had been unerringly accurate; the shadowy clouds that we'd seen gathering over the port earlier in the afternoon had made their way inland, bringing with them the type of incessant rain you would normally associate with a tropical monsoon.

Each of us had wisely invested the princely sum of 3 Euros to procure plastic Macintoshes which we had donned to protect us from the elements... we may have looked like nerdy trainspotters, but at least we were dry.

The bowl shaped stadium, originally built to house 40,000 spectators, had been modified on its three open sides using a combination of secure scaffolding and pressed steel to create temporary stands which brought the fans closer to the action. This had probably halved the capacity to 20,000... tonight the visit of Como had attracted a crowd approaching 10,000 at best.

'Como, Como... vafanculo... Como, Como... vafanculo.'

The continuing deluge did nothing to dampen the passion of the Cagliari supporters whose most vociferous elements were gathered at each end of the ground. The local Ultra's to the right, their end bedecked in red and blue banners and flags, led the unremitting chanting inviting Como to go and fuck themselves.

When the players took to the pitch, it was to a fanfare from the brass band located amongst the fans in the end to our left. Their cacophonous trumpeting along with the flares which shrouded both ends in billowing blankets of red smoke served to create an atmosphere which reminded me of the time Chelsea had played AC Milan in the San Siro.

Through the gloom I could make out the pint-sized figure of Gianfranco Zola who was stood by the halfway line wearing the number 10 red and blue halved shirt of Cagliari.

As the game started and I watched him make his first mazy run at the Como defence it was clear that he hadn't lost the magic. The hair was shorter and maybe he lacked just that extra yard of pace, but this was still our Franco; the little man who'd brought so much pleasure to tens of thousands of Chelsea supporters.

'*Gianfranco Zola... la la la... Gianfranco Zola... la la la.*' Young Dave got us all at it, and our singing attracted the attention of a group of bedraggled Cagliari supporters who came over, shook our hands and offered us swigs of the cheap red wine they were drinking from litre sized plastic bottles.

These hardy Sardinians, wearing customised black bin liners to keep themselves dry, were an interesting looking bunch. Their leader, a tall Arabic looking man with coal black eyes and a long grey beard bore an uncanny resemblance to the worlds most wanted terrorist, Bin Laden... which led to Sergeant Barnes christening him Osama Bin Liner.

*   *   *

Cagliari are Sardinia's principle club. Founded in 1920, they have spent most of their life entrenched in Serie B or the lower reaches of Serie A. Their moment of glory came in 1970 when they lifted their one and only Scudetto.

As champions of Italy, Cagliari numbered amongst their ranks the legendary Luigi Riva, and the team formed the core of the Italian side that reached the final of the World Cup in Mexico that summer.

Franco spent the formative years of his career with two of Sardinia's lesser teams, Nuorese and Torres before moving to the mainland to join a Napoli side managed by a certain Claudio Ranieri who coincidentally had previously been responsible for the stewardship of the team we'd come to watch today, Cagliari.

Initially the understudy to the legendary Maradona, Zola's career had flourished in Naples once the Argentinean left for Spain. In all he made 105 appearances for Napoli scoring 32 goals, a period during which he also won the first of 35 international caps.

Success with Napoli earned him a transfer to big spending Parma for whom he made 103 appearances and scored 49 goals. When he moved to Chelsea for £4.5 million in November 1996 he was already 30 years of age and few people, myself included, thought that he would go on to become the greatest player in Chelsea's 99 year history.

Zola, wearing the number 25 shirt, played the first of his 312 games for Chelsea, a 1–1 draw away to Blackburn Rovers, alongside Gianluca Vialli and Mark Hughes. In the six years that followed he gathered enough plaudits and winners medals to satisfy the ambitions of most players and was voted 'footballer of the year' by his fellow professionals in 1997.

Of the 80 goals he scored in the blue of Chelsea, three sprang readily to my mind which exemplified the compelling genius of Gianfranco Zola.

January 1997
Chelsea were trailing 2–0 at half-time to a cocky Liverpool side in a fourth round FA Cup tie; Zola inspired a famous recovery, scoring the equaliser with a wicked left foot shot from the edge of the penalty area. Chelsea went on to win the match 4–2 and several months later Denis Wise lifted the FA Cup at Wembley.

May 1998
Zola entered the fray as a seventieth minute substitute in the Cup Winners Cup final against VfB Stuttgart in the Rasunda Stadium, Stockholm. With the game evenly poised at 0–0 and heading for extra time, Zola latched onto a Wisey pass and dribbled the ball towards Stuttgart's goal before unleashing a venomous shot into the roof of the German outfits net. The match ended in a 1–0 victory to Chelsea.

January 2002
Chelsea were 2–0 up and cruising to a 4–0 FA Cup third round replay victory over Norwich City when Graeme Le Saux hit a corner straight to Zola at the near-post. With a shimmy of his feet Gianfranco deftly back-heeled the ball into the net on the volley for a stunning goal which looked doubly amazing when we'd watched the replay on the scoreboard.

*   *   *

Now in his 38th year and rapidly approaching the career landmark of 700 first team appearances I wondered if Franco was going to add to the 200 odd goals he'd scored by obliging us with one of his gems here in the Sant' Elia tonight.

Ossie, Marco and Ugly John flying the flag ... Cagliari ... April 2004

Sadly it wasn't in the script. What we were treated to for our 12.5 Euros admission money was a pulsating encounter between two desperate teams. The home side pushing for promotion and the away side striving to avoid relegation.

Whilst Cagliari pressed for an opening in the difficult conditions with the lively, highly rated Esposito going close twice and the majestic looking Honduran international Suazo hitting the post, it was Como who took the lead against the run of play.

Despite having had a man sent off in the 17th minute Como always looked dangerous on the rare occasions they were able to breakdown the Cagliari midfield. On the half hour mark Como scored and the home support were momentarily silenced, all that could be heard was the sound of the rain beating down onto the reinforced steel gantry that we were stood on.

Geographically, Como is located to the north of Milan, 425 kilometres from Cagliari. The forty odd supporters that had travelled all this way to watch their team understandably went ballistic in response to the goal. Already soaked to the skin, they removed their shirts and began to dance in the rain invoking the wrath of the Cagliari ultras who responded by pelting them with eggs and tomatoes.

On the pitch, Cagliari continued to press forward; the atrocious playing conditions and the fact that their opponents were playing with only ten men began to work in their favour and, following a neat little one two with Zola, Esposito drilled the ball home from the edge of the box.

The home support cheered wildly and celebrated in some style by launching firework rockets into the air and igniting flares. The smoke from the flares billowed down onto the pitch mixing with the mist that was already present because of the rain to form an opaque fog which hung in the air for several minutes forcing the referee to postpone the restart until it had cleared.

At half time we took refuge from the elements under the stand and cracked open a welcome beer as we listened to Young Dave's summary of proceedings thus far. The general consensus was that Cagliari were well on top even though this wasn't reflected in the score-line.

Whatever Como's manager said to his players during the lemon break inspired them sufficiently to re-take the lead five minutes after the restart. Cagliari, buoyed by the fervent support of their own fans, continued to play with passionate verve and it wasn't too long before the crowd favourite, Esposito, equalised once again with a close range volley which saw the ball skid along the wet surface, hit the post and just evade the outstretched fingertips of the Como goalie on its way into the back of the net.

That goal seemed to break the spirit of the Como team who began to look jaded; niggling fouls crept into their pattern of play with Zola and Esposito becoming the main targets on which to vent their frustration.

Como, with ten men camped in their own half behind the ball were now playing for the draw and as the minutes ticked by it became clear it was going to take something special to break the deadlock.

With less than ten minutes to play Zola chipped a ball square across the centre circle to the second half substitute Langella who advanced into the Como half, beat two defenders and from a distance of at least 35 metres rifled the ball into the top left hand corner of the net. Goal!

Langella, removed his shirt and sprinted to the home supporters gathered behind the goal who responded with a pyrotechnic display of Bonfire night proportions. It was pure football theatre; everyone, ourselves included, rejoiced.

'Serie C... Serie C... Serie C,' chanted the Cagliari supporters, taunting the now forlorn looking Como fans.

The ultras unfurled a huge flag, which one of their numbers ran with from corner to corner behind the goal.

'Fuck me,' said Sir Larry, pointing at the flag, 'that looks like it could have been a Chelsea Headhunters flag dunnit... look at it.'

Sir Larry was right; the flag, a St George cross on a white background, was characterised by four black heads in each quadrant. Each head, tilted slightly back, was facing to the right and wore a headband.

'That's the flag of Sardinia,' said Young Dave, with the confident air of a man who knew what he was talking about.

'Fuck me... page the bleedin Oracle,' interjected Ossie, slapping Young Dave on the back.

Young Dave, unfazed by Ossie's actions continued with his explanation. 'The heads are those of four Moors and are said to represent defeated Arab kings... although there is a school of thought that suggests that they may have represented slaves...'

'Bleedin ell Young Dave,' said Ugly John, shaking his head and showering water everywhere, 'how the fuck do you know that?'

'All in here mate,' replied Young Dave, pulling out Ugly John's copy of the Lonely Planet guide to Sardinia which he had shoved down the back of his jeans in order to keep it dry.

The discourse ended when our attentions were drawn once again to the action on the pitch. A free for all, handbags at ten paces, fist fight had broken out between both sets of players. It took the match officials a few minutes to sort everything out and restore order, a process that involved another red card being shown to a Como player.

At the final whistle the Cagliari players went to each end of the ground to applaud their own supporters and as they left the pitch I noticed something strange had happened... the rain had stopped.

Match Result
Cagliari Calcio 3 : Como FC 2

*   *   *

We left the stadium and went to get a beer and a hamburger from one of the many kiosks outside. I removed my plastic Mac and threw it into a bin, it had served me well enough. Although my jeans were soaking wet from the knee down and the cuffs of my shirt were damp I was still reasonably dry although my hands had gone all crinkly in the manner they used to when I spent too much time in the bath as a kid.

The car park behind us was alive with the sound of revving engines and bibbing horns which cut across the excited chatter of the supporters still streaming through the exit gates we were now facing.

The youngsters among them delighted in jumping into the huge puddles that had formed on the surface of the stadiums perimeter road they had to cross to reach the car park, but nobody cared. Everyone was far too wet already, a few splashes here and there wouldn't make much difference.

Half an hour passed by as we mulled over the match and Franco's performance. The car park behind us was almost empty now and the floodlights in the stadium had been switched off leaving us standing in the gloomy yellow half light of the street lamps.

I looked at my watch, it was 11pm.

'Right lads,' I said, pointing at the large wrought iron gates that spanned the entrance to the players car park at the rear of the stadium, 'that should have given the little fella enough time to get changed, come on lets see if 'Uncle' Robert's worked his magic yet again.'

I'd told 'Uncle' Robert about our little trip and he'd promised to have a word with one or two people about the possibility of organising a meet with Zola after the game. It wasn't something that any of us normally got involved with but we'd bought Ugly John a Chelsea shirt with UJ 40 on the reverse for his birthday and thought it might be a nice touch if we could get Franco to sign it.

'Uncle' Robert had sent me a one line email which read, go to the players entrance at 11pm and when Franco comes out tell him Gary sent you. That's what I liked about 'Uncle' Robert, there was never any flannel in the way he communicated, he always got straight to the point.

The Gary that 'Uncle' Robert was referring to was Gary Staker. Gary did the majority of the translation work for Chelsea's Italian contingent and was known to be a good friend of Zola's, so it was quite possible that if he'd remembered to tell Franco we were coming then the little man might well grant us our wish.

There were twenty or so Cagliari fans gathered at the gates which were being marshalled by the local Carabinieri and a couple of stewards. The players came out in ones and twos, getting into their X5's and ML's, pausing at the gates to wind down their windows and sign autographs.

The Cagliari goalkeeper Pantanelli, a tall strikingly handsome man with a mane of long black swept back hair walked across to the gates drawing adoring sighs and gasps from several teenage girls who reached out their hands to touch him.

'He's over there look.' Ugly John pointed at the diminutive figure of Gianfranco Zola who had emerged from the players' entrance and was now walking towards us.

He made his way over to the right hand side of the gate and shook the first of many hands that were thrust his way between its bars. He spent some time talking to Ken and Nicola a father and daughter combo from Kent whom we'd met earlier in the day before eventually making his way across to us.

'Gianfranco, we are all Chelsea fans,' I said in English, wondering if the little fella ever got sick of the attention. 'Did Gary mention to you that there were a group of lads coming out to see you play?' I asked hopefully.

'Yes... of course, Gary did tell me... you have a friend who is having his 40th birthday today.'

'That's me Franco,' said Ugly John, propelling himself through the scrum of people now gathered at the gates.

Franco spoke to the stewards and then nodded at Ugly John. The gates opened slightly and we bundled Ugly John through the gap. The lads with cameras took several pictures of Franco and Ugly John shaking hands and then Franco signed the shirt we had given Ugly John for his birthday.

He also signed a Cagliari shirt that Sergeant Barnes had bought for his nephew and a menu that Young Dave had brought with him from his own restaurant. Number 25 on Young Dave's menu is Spaghetti Gianfranco Zola.

Gianfranco Zola is a Chelsea legend; I could wax lyrical, but the inimitable Claudio Ranieri, in his own personal touchline tribute to the little fella said everything I wanted to say, and so much more.

"Zola," said Ranieri, "is not only a great player, he is a man. First of all you must look at the man... and when you look at Zola you know what you have. You have somebody who you know will give you everything he has, and with him you know there is so much. I'm privileged to work with him, and I knew that when I first worked with him back in Italy many years ago."

ARSENAL FC
UEFA Champions League
Quarterfinal Second Leg
Arsenal Stadium, Highbury, London N5
Tuesday 6th April 2004

'Bertie Mee said to Bill Shankly... have you heard of the North Bank, Highbury... Shanks said no, I don't think so... but I've heard of the Chelsea aggro.'

They say the road to hell is paved with good intentions, but then that's the road. They, whoever they maybe, never said anything about the London Underground.

To the uninitiated, the atmosphere on the crowded platform would have appeared tough, energetic and endlessly provocative. Nervous, apprehensive tourists were stood next to equally nervous commuters; all of them looking up expectantly at the LCD display board, collectively counting down the time to the arrival of the next Piccadilly Line service bound for the twilight zone.

Their uneasiness was borne out of the fact that Leicester Square tube station was rammed with Chelsea supporters. Some, like us, had been drinking in the West End during the afternoon; others, travelling from South London and its suburbs were changing here from the Northern Line trains which served Waterloo mainline station and hotbeds of Chelsea support such as Balham, Tooting and Morden.

Those supporters travelling from Southwest London on the District Line would be changing at Earls Court to pick up the Piccadilly Line which snaked as far as Heathrow Airport to the west and Cockfosters to the north. Some of them would be on the next midnight blue line service we were all impatiently waiting for.

Sighs of relief emanating from the regular passengers would be clearly audible seven stops north of Leicester Square when the train pulled into Arsenal station, opened its doors and spewed forth onto the platform the massed ranks of vociferous Chelsea supporters who by now would be positively bristling with anticipation.

*   *   *

'*Forever and ever... we'll follow our team, cos we are the Chelsea and we are supreme...*'

I could see Seagull, Ronny Cutlass, Fuck Off Colin and a few of the Wandsworth boys gathered at the far end of the platform; the throaty vibration of their voices filtered through the air on a wave of macho attitude which amplified itself as it reverberated off the low ceiling inviting others to propagate the chant.

'*... we'll never be mastered... by no northern bastards... we'll keep the blue flag flying high...*'

A cooling rush of air gusted down the platform signalling the imminent arrival of the next train and I stood my ground as people began to jockey and jostle each other in attempt to secure a decent position from which they would endeavour to board one of its carriages.

'*Flying high up in the sky... we'll keep the blue flag flying high... from Stamford Bridge to Wembley... we'll keep the blue flag flying high.*'

'Please allow the passengers off the train first,' boomed the tannoy, 'move right along inside the carriage... thank you... mind the doors, this train is now ready to depart.'

The sliding doors opened and closed several times as bodies and bags were dragged through them; when they closed for the final time I found myself pressed up against a huge, Neanderthal browed middle aged man with right angled ears and a blocky body; I imagined that he would have a fat neck to rival that of Ugly John or Big Chris but I couldn't tell because tied around it was a red and white Arsenal scarf.

As the lights in the carriage flickered and the train finally juddered into motion I looked down the carriage to see if everyone I was with had made it on board.

All present and correct; in addition to myself, tonight's class register comprised of Young Dave, Ossie, Big Chris, Ugly John, and Vegas Dave.

Vegas Dave had called me on my mobile at lunchtime just as I was preparing my scalp for an encounter with my trusty Mach 3. He wanted to find out where we were going to be partaking of a few pre-match aperitifs since the rest of his regular crew, the Carshalton Casuals, had been unable to get tickets for the game and would be staying south of the border to watch it on TV.

'We'll be in the Spice of Life on Cambridge Circus,' I'd told him, thinking at the time that Vegas Dave turning up out of the blue as he was so often prone to do might just be a good omen. 'You know it yeah... it's the big drinker right next to the theatre where Les Mis used to be on, yeah... see you in there at teatime son,' I'd said, finishing the call and returning to my ritualistic match day ablutions.

* * *

I still found it refreshing to think that as middle-age loomed large in front of me, I still got a childish thrill out of playing truant. As a youngster I'd only ever played truant on special occasions, well apart that is from double French on Thursday afternoons and Religious Instruction on Friday mornings.

My Dad had sat me down on my eleventh birthday and said he wanted to have a few words with me about some of the things that really mattered in life; information that I would find useful as I embarked on the next stage of the perilous journey towards becoming an adult.

Dad liked to keep things simple; without offering any explanation he'd told me that all I needed to know right now was that God didn't exist, and life was too short to learn French. Dad also told me that if I did well in my other subjects at school, he'd buy me a Raleigh Chopper bicycle for my birthday.

So I'd played both ends off against the middle, getting gold stars for the three R's whilst becoming an adept truant whom by the age of twelve had denounced Christ and firmly believed that one day everyone would be able to communicate in English.

Needless to say, Dad was true to his word and I'd spent that summer proudly riding around our estate on my brand new electric blue Chopper which 'Uncle' Robert christened Harris.

Years after Dad had passed away, my kid brother had informed me that he suspected our mother had a new boyfriend... a certain Mr Connaught, who'd oddly enough taught French and Religious Instruction at my secondary school.

This illuminating piece of information got me thinking about some of the other philosophical jewels Dad had foisted on me as I passed through puberty. "Never trust a hippy," he'd said, a year before Johnny Rotten and the Sex Pistols exploded into my life preaching the same message in their vitriolic, sputum filled mantras.

"All politicians are queer," he'd opined, one evening whilst chain-smoking his way through another packet of Capstan Full Strength as we'd watched the snooker on the little black and white television 'Uncle' Robert had sold him for a fiver.

If I remembered rightly, according to Dad, David Bowie, Cliff Richard, the Pope and even 'Uncle' Robert were all as gay as twenty leprechauns doing a jig on a tombstone... all of which drew my mind back to what my brother had told me about our mother and Mr Connaught.

If Dad's credo was founded on his suspicions that Mum was putting it about with all these people... and even if only half of it were true, then no wonder my old girl still had a devious little twinkle in her eye.

I looked at my reflection in the mirror, wiping away the shaving foam from the back of my head and wondering who the hippy might have been that my Dad had referred to? Richard Branson maybe? Nah surely not.

In the end the Capstan Full Strength did for my Dad what they had done for my Grandad and cut short his life just a few months into his fiftieth year.

I sometimes wonder if Dad were still alive today what he would make of the Anglicisation of Western Europe and the fact that kids today know more about computers than they do about the teachings of the Bible.

With such a fine pedigree you are right to suppose that I'd feel as guilty about playing truant now, as I had when I was a kid. As an adult I restricted my truancy to mid-week match days when the Blues were playing at home or elsewhere in London; this meant I probably gave my boss the slip maybe five or six times a year... er well maybe ten or eleven. But then who doesn't?

My boss is an honest, decent working class bloke more inclined to conciliation than confrontation. He's not into football nor is he into golf, but when the days get warmer come the Spring I always knew where I could find him if I was inclined to do so. But I wasn't, if I didn't do a decent job for my boss then he'd dig me out about it regardless of my attendance record; the odd spot of truancy never harmed my productivity, in fact I'd say that when things went according to plan then the guvnor got more out of me than he was paying for.

*   *   *

I'd had to keep an eye on the time though as I shirked my way through the afternoon. If I caught the 15.26pm South West Trains service from Worcester Park to Waterloo and then took the Northern Line to Leicester Square I would be in the Spice of Life by 4.30pm... two and a half hours drinking time... all easy. Perfect!

Life on the road with Chelsea this season had yielded precious little on the female front. Maybe I'd missed an opportunity with Tiffany the barmaid in Düsseldorf... maybe if the god I didn't believe in bestowed great fortune on both myself and my team, then I'd get to meet her again in May.

Then there were the Goldfingers girls in Prague; they had been some-

Big Chris prepares for the arduous trek to Highbury under the watchful eye of his personal fitness trainer Lemon.

thing else, but then like most things in life... especially women, they came with a price tag.

Apart from that there had been a lot of chauvinistic talk about various women and how they'd 'get it' but unlike the Blues, who'd so far won every match away from home in the Champions League this season, my away form was, to put not to fine a point on it, shite!

Mind you, when it came to the home fixtures, I'd put the ball in the back of the metaphorical net every single time... which was more than could be said for Claudio's boys.

Any moral female philosopher that tells you men are devious, dirty, conniving wretches who will sell their souls to the devil in return for a few unrequited minutes of lustful pleasure has clearly never watched an episode of 'Sex and the city'.

I wanted to personally thank the makers of that wonderful piece of television for unwittingly reprogramming the minds of a whole legion of career girls who now believed that it was the height of cool to have in their life what the American's amusingly called a 'fuck buddy'.

Sex without commitment, is what I am talking about here. For an uncouth bachelor boy like me who can't get a girlfriend, and probably wouldn't have the time to spend with her if he did... it's the perfect low cost solution to ensuring that my reproductive system is serviced regularly and remains in full working order.

I'd known Annie for a good number of years. I'd first met her at a club in London when we'd both been so pilled off our faces we could hardly speak. All we'd done that night is gurn at each other across the crowded dance-floor for a couple of hours before embarking on one of those 'love you... no, love you more' conversations which fizzled into nothing as the beats wore on and the E vibe wore off.

She'd given me her number which I'd promptly lost and had all but slipped from my memory until a couple of months later when I'd clocked her at Gatwick airport checking in for the same night flight to Milan that I was booked on.

Oozing laid back sophistication and looking eclectically stylish in a belted coat and evening trousers, Annie, with her waiflike figure, short spiky black hair, peachy complexion and perfectly manicured fingernails looked every inch the perfect Marco 'drink on a stick... she would definitely get it' type of woman.

I, on the other hand looked every inch the stereotypical Chelsea boy; exuding as I did a cockiness fuelled by several pre-flight Stella's and the knowledge that I had a ticket for the following evenings Champions League match with AC Milan in the San Siro.

Unprompted, Annie had then proceeded to tell me that she was tired of the banality of family life, and the constant bickering that now dominated the strained relationship she had with her husband and their children.

She told me she didn't want the hassle or the risk of financial penury that she might incur in leaving home and eventually getting divorced. What she'd said she needed was a different kind of hedonistic escapism, something one step beyond anything she'd previously enjoyed as a clubber.

By the time we headed down to the departure gate I had my first 'appointment' with Annie pencilled into my mental diary where I logged football fixtures and the birth dates of my friends and my family.

*   *   *

What Annie expected from me in the physical sense, Annie got. She would marvel at my rock hard permanent erection, and I would be grateful for the fact that I had a plentiful source of remarkably cheap Viagra.

'Who are you playing tonight darling?' she'd said, as I'd bent her over my knee and thrashed the lilywhite globes of her tight little Janet Reger clad bottom.

'Arsenal love,' I'd replied, slapping her even harder and smiling as her butt took on the same rosy red hue as the shirts of our Champions League opponents.

'Is it an important game?' she'd asked, snorting another line of the old Gianluca from the surface of the mirror in her make-up compact.

'Just a bit,' I'd said, thinking about what I was going to do to her next and checking the time on my watch.

'I'd better do something about this now hadn't I,' she'd said, sliding off me after I'd been going at her for ten minutes or so and was having to resort to the tried and trusted method of naming various trophy winning Chelsea teams from days gone by to prevent myself from coming.

I loved Annie for her sassy wise cracking humour and I'd smiled as she knelt down in front of me, caressing my aching cock with one hand and passing me the bottle of poppers she'd just inhaled from with the other.

'Five minutes Annie, then I've gotta get going yeah,' I'd said, ruffling her hair and pushing her willing mouth over the crimson, artificially swollen, throbbing head of my penis.

I held the bottle up to my right nostril and took several deep breaths, almost passing out with the immediate rush that the Amyl Nitrate afforded me.

'Five, four, three, two, one... gentlemen we have lift off phew,' I'd panted, as she'd got to work... oh yeah Annie knew how to make a man feel good about himself, she could suck a golf ball through a hosepipe.

Annie's special talent was the blow job. She gave it all she had to give, and so did I... and when I came, which was always within the prescribed time limit, she swallowed every last single drop.

'Who's next after Arsenal?' she'd shouted from the bathroom over the whine of the hairdryer she'd bought especially to leave at my house. I'd long since ceased needed to own one for myself.

'Dunno love,' I'd replied, looking over my shoulder and eyeing the red weals that Annie's rakish fingernails had striped across my buttocks, 'maybe Real Madrid, but we've gotta win tonight otherwise its all over.'

'You'll win tonight,' she'd said, walking back into the bedroom and helping herself to another couple of lines of the Percy she'd paid for before sitting down at the dressing table and fixing her make-up.

'Yeah, you know what Annie... I think we just might do it,' I'd replied, opening my wardrobe door and contemplating what to wear for the big occasion.

Within minutes Annie was fully attired, fully made up, and ready to return to her suburban wife-style. She'd walked over to me, squeezed my lazy lob through the Calvin's I'd just pulled on and kissed me on the cheek taking care to rub away the lipstick traces she'd left there in the same way a mother would with her five year old child she'd just dropped off at school.

With a "come on you Blues" and a "see ya next time hon", Annie was gone. I'd pulled back the curtains and watched her walk out to the gleaming BMW X5 she drove grabbing my cock as I did so, it's regained rigidity caused me some consternation as I wondered if I'd overdosed on the blue fellas and might have to endure the journey into the twilight zone with a chubby for company.

In the end I'd had a couple of liveners, a snort from the little brown bottle and played back the best bits of the afternoons action which I'd recorded on the discreetly hidden camcorder that Sex Case loaned me from time to time.

Emptying my pods once again with a flourish whilst I'd watched Annie's fuck face grimacing at me from my TV had had the desired effect on my libido and enabled me to get myself sorted out in time to be able to take a leisurely stroll down to the station.

I'd had a little chat about my Annie session and the match with Sex Case who'd sportingly wished me luck... but not too much. He was good like that was Sex Case, unlike the mouthy armchair Arsenal supporters at work who delighted in reminding me as often as possible that, in their less than humble collective opinion, there was only one team in London.

If we pulled it off tonight I'd already drawn up an email address short list of every Gooner who'd ever shown me disrespect for supporting Chelsea and I was going to be in work first thing tomorrow morning, no matter how wankered I got after the match, informing them that London was a small place and there was now only one team in Europe.

*   *   *

The Spice of Life is one of those drinkers that holds special memories for me even if, like many of central London's public houses, its internal refurbishment has completely transformed it from a place of true character to one of any town any place anonymity.

Its location at Cambridge Circus, where Shaftesbury Avenue bisects the Charing Cross Road, on the fringes of Soho made it the perfect meeting place and launch pad for a many a large night out in early eighties clubland.

Sweaty, dirty sexy memories of the upstairs bar, with its art deco jukebox pumping out London Calling by the Clash. Where working girls, all spiky peroxide hair, fishnet stockings and leather miniskirts would trade insults with West London ragamuffins whose joints made the air thick with fuggy grey-blue aromatic smoke. Where punks, mods, soul-boys, rockers and new romantics would joust across the pool table fired up by amphetamine sulphate, Holsten Pils and rum and black depth charges.

It all seemed so normal to me back then, and as I'd walked up to the Spice and pushed open the heavy brass framed door I'd wondered briefly what might have become of all those people who brought so much colour into my life. Had they all just drifted into a grey suburban life of drab normality? I supposed that in a way I had, but where they like me now? Defective escapists, with one foot entrenched firmly in the gutter and the other squelching around in the muddy mire of social acceptability.

'Fuck it... who cares?' I'd muttered to myself, as I spotted Big Chris stood over by the bay window that looked out onto Greek Street, cramming a large forkful of mashed potato into his mouth.

I'd checked out who was in the bar as I'd made my way over to the bay window and I'd wondered if any of the suited types that patronised the Spice now were veterans of twenty years standing like myself. Nah, not likely... but then you never can tell, that's what makes life just that little more interesting. It's all about getting the balance right and being happy with things... well most of the time.

*   *   *

'Tell you what, we weren't half all right at the Lane on Saturday,' Vegas Dave had said, winking at a couple of women who were looking in our direction and nudging each other. I'd glanced at them out of the corner of my eye, espying them as Ossie had raising their eyebrows and nodding in the way females do when they confirm their suspicions about someone or something to one another.

'What d'ya think their game is then?' Ossie had said, as I'd taken a steadying drink from the Stella top Sir Larry had just bought for me. The session with Annie had becalmed my PMT, but the after effects of the Nikki Lauda, combined with too many prying eyes were making me feel more than a little paranoid.

'It's him I think,' Young Dave had said, shaking his head as he'd pointed at Big Chris whom having finished off a large portion of shepherds pie was now tackling an equally large portion of chips. 'That's the second plate of chips he's had since we got here an hour ago, those birds have probably just realised what we've all known for years.'

'What's that then?' Ugly John had asked, enjoying the fact that someone else was being dug out about their excess weight.

'That Big Chris is Britain's greediest man,' Young Dave had replied, ducking to ensure that he missed the playful right hook that Big Chris had aimed at his head. 'Now finish off telling us about Saturday Vegas Dave yeah.'

'Hold on... hold on,' interrupted Big Chris, 'we're in Europe now... respect where its due please.'

'Ok... ok Europe's greediest man, happy now?'

'Yeah... I'm happy... very happy.'

Vegas Dave had looked on with some amusement, before lighting up one of Sir Larry's Marlboro's and continuing with his account of our defeat of Spurs.

'They never came close... I tell ya, y'know Ronnie Biggs's was still on the run in Brazil, and Wayne Rooney's parties ended with a game of musical chairs rather than a tear up the last time they beat us in the league.'

That remark had made us all smile and we'd continued to listen to Vegas Dave as he'd told us how well Scotty Parker had played and how sharp Jimmy had looked despite his match winning goal only being a tap in.

The 1-0 victory had been our sixth consecutive away win and 28th clean sheet of the season a further boost for the confidence of stand in custodian Marco Ambrosio who surely couldn't be too far away from having a serious chant dedicated to him.

With only an hour to go to kick off we'd helped Big Chris finish his chips and left the Spice with our spirits uplifted, confident that Chelsea's players were in the best possible frame of mind and form to tackle Arsenal on their home patch in what I'd billed myself as the most important match... ever!

*   *   *

'Carefree, wherever you may be... we are the famous CFC...' we chanted, as the train pulled into Arsenal station and juddered to a halt causing us all to jolt first to the left, and then to the right.

'... *and we don't give a fuck, whoever you may be... cos we are the famous CFC.'*

The doors slid open and the first person out of our carriage was the Neanderthal Gooner; I smiled as I watched him weave and bob his bulky frame through the crowd heading for the exit, his red scarf hidden from view concealed under his jacket which he had just zipped up maybe to hide his identity, or maybe because there was a nip in the air.

The *'Carefree'* chant was raucously continued by Seagull, who was among a group of lads headed up by Spangle and Ronny Cutlass walking just in front of us as we made our way through the station.

'Ah aahh... ah aahh... ah aahh,' we screeched, mimicking the sound of the common or garden seabird, as we watched Seagull going through his routine.

'What's all that about?' asked Vegas Dave, as we exited the station and crossed over Gillespie Road. 'Sounds like the middle of the Shed circa 1985, that wasn't you lot then was it?'

'Ha... nah mate,' I chuckled, 'we used to be tea bar Shedites, not... middle or white wall... but we did used to do the Seagull screech as it goes.'

In those days the screeches had heralded the arrival of a flock of seagulls that always seemed to fly over Stamford Bridge during the second half of our Saturday afternoon fixtures. Thinking about it, I couldn't be sure if they still did... but then the ground was far more enclosed now than it ever used to be before those days it was redeveloped.

'Y'gonna tell me then?' asked Vegas Dave again, as we walked up Highbury Hill towards the Clock End entrance to Arsenal Stadium which was a stones throw from the underground station.

'Yeah... yeah, sorry mate,' I said, as I surveyed the scene and looked at the vacant stares on the faces of the Arsenal supporters in the queues that were already forming at the entrance turnstiles to the West Stand which we were walking slowly past.

'Basically, matey boy over there,' I continued, pointing at Seagull, 'is only known as Seagull by our little mob. The reason he's called Seagull is because when he stands up to chant he always thrusts his arms out so they look like wings. Ossie over here, actually christened him Jesus at first cos he looked like Christ on the cross... but then Big Chris noticed that when Seagull stretched his arms out he tilted the palms of his hands downwards rather than having them open, which our mate Lemon said wouldn't be possible if you were nailed to a cross like that poor cunt Jesus was.'

'Fucking brilliant,' said Vegas Dave, as he looked in his wallet for his ticket. 'Seagull ha ha, wait till I tell the Casuals they'll love that... when I hear you screeching at the next match I'll make sure we join in too.'

* * *

By the time Ugly John and I had taken up our position in the Clock End, there were less than fifteen minutes to go to kick off. Our seats were adjacent to the dividing rails that split the end in two and separated us from the Arsenal fans who were currently chanting their own versions of 'Over land and sea' and 'Fuck em all'. The funny thing was, they were using exactly the same words as we would for the original Chelsea versions.

'*Thirty thousand Muppets... thirty thousand Muppets,*' we chanted, until the home support was silenced.

I looked for Young Dave and his yellow hat and spotted him stood in the lower middle part of our section of the Clock End. Vegas Dave was down by the front and Big Chris and Ossie waved at me when I sent them a text message, they were sat together in the West Stand were it looked like about 500 Chelsea supporters had been allocated seating.

Our Chelsea contingent of just over 2800 in an overall crowd of 35,486 struck up the chant which had now come to symbolise the unity of the team and the supporters. A unification of overwhelming support for the manager Claudio Ranieri.

'*Ranieri's blue and white army... Ranieri's blue and white army.*'

Arsenal Stadium; Highbury, to give it the name by which it is most commonly known, is a tired looking place these days. In its hey day it would have hosted 50,000 plus for the big games; but now, in the age of the 'all seated' stadia, it was able to boast a capacity of only 38,000 which had been further reduced for Champions League fixtures.

For the club, with its giddy Abramovich like ambitions to rival Manchester United, the move to the new stadium complex in Ashburton Grove couldn't come soon enough. The question was, by the time they moved to their new ground, would the team of winners that Arsene Wenger had so successfully crafted over the last seven seasons still be together?

If so, by that time would our multi million pound team have finally gelled into a championship winning outfit that no longer viewed trips to play their opponents tonight with fear and trepidation?

'What you laughing at son?' I said, patting Ugly John on the back as I side- stepped a steaming pile of freshly dumped police horse shit.

'Ha... ha,' he replied, still laughing, 'I was just having a bet with myself that you and Young Dave don't buy Arsenal pennants for your little collection.'

I'd actually thought about the pennant thing earlier on in the day and decided that if Chelsea got to the final of the Champions League competition then I would buy an Arsenal pennant since it would mean that we'd have knocked them out tonight and it would be nice to have a visible reminder of such a momentous occasion.

'Oh West London... is wonderful... Oh West London is wonderful... it's full of tits, fanny and Chelsea... Oh West London is wonderful.'

Thoughts of pennants evaporated as our Chelsea collective got into its stride on the vocal front and once again drowned out the Arsenal chorus.

'We don't want Eriksson... we don't want Eriksson...'

Once again the message was loud, clear and audible to everyone in the stadium, including the man himself who was watching from the stands. My mother had told she could hear the chant when she'd watched the first leg on TV, and if she could hear it then everybody watching would have heard it. The English love an underdog and Claudio Ranieri fitted the bill perfectly.

The players were on the pitch going through their final preparations and as both team selections were announced, the guy stood next to me said we were fielding the same starting eleven as we had at Spurs on Saturday. Tinkerman just loved to keep the surprises coming.

The full line up was, Ambrosio in goal playing behind a four man defence of Melchiot, Bill Gallas, Terry and Bridge. Parker, Makalele and Lampard were at the heart of our midfield with Duff the wideman looking to put balls into the twin strike-force of Eidur and Jimmy. Options on the bench included Joe Cole, Crespo, Gronkjaer and Mutu.

Stirring renditions of 'Carefree' and 'One man went to mow', kept the atmosphere bubbling along nicely. The match got under way and was soon being played at the same frenetic pace that had left everyone breathless during the first leg a fortnight ago. Lamps went close to scoring, but with action happening at the opposite end of the ground it was difficult to see just how well the Arsenal keeper Lehman dealt with his shot.

'Chelsea... Chelsea... Chelsea.' The chanting was incessant and directed at the Gooner's on the other side of the dividing rails, but their response was relatively muted and greeted with howls of derision which even the Old Bill, who were stood in the narrow sector of 'no-mans land' separating both sets of supporters, found mildly amusing.

Despite Chelsea's bright start, and the compact Ranieri style of play that had initially contained Arsenal's endeavours and seen us take the game to our opponents, as the half progressed I became more and more concerned with the way Ashley Cole, cleverly overlapping from left back, was continually exposing Scott Parker.

It was worrying to watch, and when Henry shot over the bar and then just wide of the post I began to wonder if we would be able to cope with the constant pressure that was being exerted on our defence.

'Clear it... Ambrosio... catch it... fuck!... Oh no.' I buried my head in my hands as I watched Reyes drill the ball into the back of the net right in front of us. Arsenal's goal had come not, as had been looking increasingly likely, from a move involving Ashley Cole on the left, but from a right sided Lauren cross that Ambrosio had flapped at and missed allowing Thierry Henry to head the ball back across the box where it eventually fell at the feet of advancing Spaniard.

'1–0 to the Arsenal... 1–0 to the Arsenal,' chanted the home supporters, the goal having finally awoken them from their catatonic state.

'Your support is fucking shit,' was our swift riposte.

The goal, the first that Chelsea had conceded away from home in the competition this season, came deep in stoppage time and as the players trooped off the pitch at half time Ugly John and I wondered what the Tinkerman would do to try and salvage something from the game.

*   *   *

'Well that's gonna solve our problems innit!' exclaimed Ugly John, as Chelsea took to the field with Jesper Gronkjaer taking the place of Scott Parker.

'Well I agree with taking Parker off,' I replied half-heartedly, 'but Forrest... Jeeeesus Christ... why? Why not use Joe Cole?'

'We are the famous... the famous Chelsea... We are the famous the...'

'Go on Maka shoot son... ohhhh,' the 'Famous Chelsea' chant was curtailed as Makalele hammered a shot from the edge of the box at Lehman. I couldn't see how the keeper dealt with the ball because he had his back to us.

'Go on Lamps... Yes... ha ha ha... YESSSS!' The ball rebounded off Lehman's body and Lampard flashed it into the back of the net. It all happened in a split second and our travelling army cheered, clapped and punched the air with joy. 1–1... game on.

That goal seemed to knock the stuffing out of Arsenal and their supporters knew it. Gone was the cocksure confidence they'd displayed in the first half. Chelsea were now hassling and harrying and being first to the ball when it mattered.

The whole gamut of Chelsea chants were rinsed by our choir and our players self-belief and poise on the ball became more and more evident as normal time ebbed away.

Tinkerman had got his strategy right; Gronkjaer not only stifled the threat that Ashley Cole had posed on the left but also started to use his speed and guile to outwit Arsenal when Chelsea pressed forward.

Makalele went close again and so did Arsenal who had Ambrosio at full stretch twice, first he denied Reyes and then he athletically tipped over a long range effort from Toure.

Chelsea's fourth choice keeper, the man my Godson Josh had christened the Leopard, a man of whom many questions had been asked, was demonstrating he was capable of rising to the occasion unlike his high profile opposing number who looked jittery and nervous every-time he was put under pressure.

Bill Gallas was doing a brilliant job in keeping Henry on a leash, however it still came as a surprise when Wenger substituted the prolific French striker with Bergkamp. Not to be outdone, Claudio, who was once again enjoying our braying support, replaced Duff with Joe Cole and Hasselbaink with Crespo.

'Go on son... go on...' I took a sharp intake of breath as Joe Cole skinned Toure and knocked the ball through to Eidur... 'Yes... Fuck!'

Eidur's effort was blocked on the line by Ashley Cole. I watched the replay on the electronic scoreboard away to my right and thought to myself that the game would now turn in Arsenal's favour and that they would now chase up to the other end of the pitch and score a dramatic late winner.

At 1–1 extra time was looming when Wayne Bridge played a one two with Eidur Gudjohnsen and received the ball back on the edge of the box.

'Shoot... Shoot... Yessssssssssssssssss... Fucking brilliant YESSSSSSSS!'

Delirious pandemonium on the left side of the Clock End... deathly silence to the right. Ugly John and I hugged each other and everyone else in our vicinity as we celebrated the goal. 2–1 to Chelsea and now, with just minutes remaining, Arsenal now had to score twice.

'Where's your treble gone... where's your treble gone,' we chanted, but the Arsenal supporters had already begun to drift away and by the time the referee blew the final whistle to signal on and off pitch celebrations, the like of which I had last witnessed in May when we had defeated Liverpool to qualify for the competition, the stadium was half empty.

Match Result

Arsenal FC 1 : Chelsea FC 2

Chelsea win 3–2 on aggregate

* * *

'One team in Europe... there's only one team in Europe... one team in Europe... there's only one team in Europe,' we sang to the tune of the old Sandpipers hit, Gauntanamera.

Another huge cheer greeted the surprise news flashed up on the scoreboard that Monaco had overcome Real Madrid to become our semi-final opponents. The police elected to keep us locked in for a quarter of an hour or so after the match had ended... they could have kept us there all night for all I cared.

I watched the last of the Arsenal supporters trickle away and then began to work my way through the stream of text messages I had received following the final whistle. The messages conveyed the congratulations of fellow Chelsea fans and also the supporters of other teams who had delighted in seeing Arsenal's dramatic reversal of fortune.

SCHADENFREUDE

The message was from 'Uncle' Robert. I didn't understand what it meant, so I replied asking for clarification.

YOU WHAT?

'Uncle' Robert, human lexicon that he was, replied swiftly

THE VERY HUMAN PLEASURE TAKEN IN OTHER PEOPLES MISERY

His definition of the word Schadenfreude was succinct and summarised the elation I'd felt as I'd glanced across the security railings when Bridge had scored.

Seeing all those Clock End Gooner's hanging their heads and burying their dejected faces in the same hands that earlier had been signalling 1-0 when their team had taken the lead I'd defined as "fucking priceless", but Schadenfreude was a nice big sexy fuck off word that just looked like it meant something sinful. As we left the ground and made our way back to the tube station I made a mental note to use it as often as possible the following day, the only problem being that it would have to be used in written communication because I didn't have a fucking clue how to pronounce it.

'Sch Sch Scha... ahh fuck it, it felt fucking great! Now give us a light and lager Eric mate will ya,' I'd said, trying to explain how I felt when I'd got back to my local drinker for a celebratory lock in just before midnight.

'Happy days eh.' Eric had said as he poured my drink for me. 'On the house Marco mate... enjoy it son,' he'd continued, tossing me over a free bag of Mr Porky pork scratchings into the bargain.

*   *   *

I spent the next day at work basking in the reflective glory of Chelsea's magnificent achievement. As my hangover wore off I began the Schadenfreude task of digging out every Arsenal supporter I knew and forwarding them via email the 'end of season... Arsenal dinner dance' invitation which some wag had put together and sent out most likely seconds after the final whistle had been blown the previous evening.

The 'dinner dance' was being held early due to 'unforeseen' circumstances and invitees were notified that the clubs European tour had now been cancelled. On the menu was Jens Lehman's 'catch of the day' and the guest speakers were Claudio Ranieri, and Alex 'treble winner' Ferguson.

I watched highlights of the game on line and clenched my right fist at the Chelsea goals smiling at the differing reactions of both managers and also of Roman Abramovich.

Claudio Ranieri's usual veneer of composure had been momentarily replaced by a marvellous study of unbridled joy... or was it relief. He summarised the achievement in his own inimitable way, "Fantastic... we had more power, more stamina, more vitamins."

During the post match press conference Ranieri had said, "I have players with fantastic character. They never give up. I like that... It's difficult to kill me," he'd continued, happy in the knowledge that the success which he had so deservedly earned through his shrewd tactical acumen had very publicly blunted the axe of his would be executioner Peter Kenyon.

The players mirrored the medias praise for their manager. Match winner Wayne Bridge said, "I'm not too sure what to believe about the manager and I'm not sure what's going to happen. Maybe this result will persuade the board that he should stay. He's been great to me and I can't ask for much more. All the lads get on very well with him and there's a possibility he might stay on. Ranieri talks to us about the speculation, tells us to put it to the back of our minds and seems to get on with it."

Lampard spoke of the "incredible feeling in the dressing room" and described beating Arsenal as "the best night of my career."

That evening I watched AC Milan get hammered out of sight by Deportivo La Coruna, a result which saw Chelsea instilled as the new favourites for the competition.

"Can we win the Champions League?," said Claudio, "Why not? Anything is possible now."

Why not indeed, I thought to myself as I picked up my mobile which had bleeped to alert me to the fact that I'd received a new text message. It was from Ugly John.

FLIGHTS TO NICE BOOKED 6.10AM EASYJET FLIGHT
FROM GATWICK 20TH APRIL

I keyed in my reply.

BRING IT ON

AS MONACO FC
UEFA Champions League
Semi-final First Leg
Stade Louis II, Monaco
Tuesday 20th April 2004

'Seriously... is that what the cab driver said?' I asked, raising my eyebrows to indicate my genuine surprise.

'I'm telling you son, that's exactly what he said, didn't he Baby Gap,' replied Ossie, kicking a small pebble along the concrete esplanade on which we were walking.

Baby Gap Brian skipped after the pebble and back heeled it me.

'Yeah,' he drawled, squinting into the warming rays of the mid-morning sun and adjusting his sunglasses, 'he said, "You are Chelsea yes... then you must fuck Monaco, they are a bad team, bad people, bad money, fuck zem for ze rest of France yes", which seemed a bit on the harsh side knoworrimean.'

'Just a bit mate,' I replied, kicking the pebble into the crystal clear water of the adjacent marina. 'What is it about these teams eh? When we were in Rome it was the same with Lazio... mind you, I suppose back home if you'd spoken to a Porto supporter over here for their game with Man U the other week, you would probably have said the same sort of thing.'

'Funny thing is though Porto did fuck Man U ha ha,' said Ossie, looking back across the yacht basin to see if Ugly John and his mate Jogger were still on their own by the hire car.

*   *   *

It was 10.30am and we were kicking our heels in Beaulieu sur Mer, one of the many picturesque resort towns that are dotted along the entire length of the N98 coastal road which snaked along the entire length of the French Riviera.

It had been a particularly early start for me today; being awoken at 3.55am by the cacophony created by several alarm clocks, the alarm function on my mobile phone and the TV which I'd programmed to switch itself on at this time was not conducive to putting you in the best frame of mind.

"There's nothing good about that", Ossie would have bleated, if he'd been misfortunate enough to have to rise at this time of the morning... but he hadn't. Both he and Baby Gap had flown out to Nice from Luton the previous evening and kept me awake until 1.00am with a barrage of text messages each detailing in increasingly lurid detail the quality of the local female talent that was dancing the night away in a bar called Le Havane which they'd happened on as they'd returned from a late evening stroll along the Promenade des Anglais.

Setting a new personal best for the time it took me to get up and get ready, I'd then managed the drive to Gatwick in a license threatening thirty minutes which enabled me to rendezvous on time with Ugly John and his mysterious acquaintance Jogger at the easyJet check in desk.

The flight to Nice had departed without delay, arriving on schedule an hour and a half later at 9.30am local time. On arrival we'd picked up a hire car that Ugly John had secured a special deal for and Jogger got behind the wheel and drove the short distance from the airport into the city centre.

Ugly John, sporting a new particularly bristly suedehead haircut, was becoming increasingly adept at putting our travel packages together and wheeling and dealing on the final price. Not only had he booked our trip, but he'd also sorted out Ossie and Baby Gap and also the rest of the Chelsea Gate 17 boys who were flying out from Bristol and scheduled to arrive in Nice at around midday.

Jogger, a lean suntanned balding man who bore more than a passing resemblance to Michael Stipe the lead singer of REM, was an ex work colleague of Ugly John's and an occasional Chelsea supporter. When questions had been asked about his Gate 17 pedigree, Ugly John had told us that Jogger knew the south of France like the back of his hand and more importantly he'd also agreed to do all the driving.

Being navigationally challenged when it came to driving on the continent, I was more than happy that the mantle of vehicular responsibility now lay with Jogger who'd confidently found his way to the Kyriad Hotel in Nice where Ugly John had booked our accommodation.

As it turned out Ugly John had played his Joker in bringing along Jogger whom, after we'd checked in and met up with Ossie and Baby Gap, had made a call in fluent French to a ticket tout who had five tickets for sale for this evenings match.

Jogger had sourced the tickets on the French version of E-Bay and had arranged to meet the tout in Beaulieu sur Mer to complete the transaction. The tickets were not going cheap. Geordie Jase had paid a London based ticket agency £200 for a ticket with a face value of 30 Euros, which at the prevailing exchange rate converted to £21.28!

The five tickets Jogger had sourced were going to cost 150 Euros (£106.38) each. Young Dave had a contact that worked in Monaco who had told him he would be able to get us any further tickets we required for the same price.

Young Dave and I had acquired two tickets from Chelsea directly through the same 'Eddie Barnett letter system' that had seen us secure tickets for the Arsenal away match. The club still had the audacity to load the price, charging us £25 for a 30 Euro ticket and profiting once again from those fans that represented their most loyal support.

Chelsea's official ticket allocation for the match was a meagre 1400 which reflected the low capacity of Stade Louis II. With 2500 blues fans anticipated to make the journey it was obvious that black market tickets would be priced at a premium and that the touts would rake in a handsome profit.

*   *   *

'Oi Marco, over here son... oi lads come on.'

I looked back down the promenade now shaded by the low-hanging mulberry trees that were planted evenly along its perimeter with the marina and saw Ugly John beckoning me over to where he was stood with Jogger.

As we walked back I could see that a black VW Golf had parked up alongside our car and two youngish looking lads were talking to Jogger whilst Ugly John looked on with a worried expression on his face.

'Show me your ticket Marco,' said Ugly John, clicking the fingers of his right hand impatiently.

I got my ticket out of my wallet and gave it to Ugly John who held it up to the light and closely inspected the security hologram.

'Yeah... spot on,' he said, handing me back my ticket and nodding at Jogger and the two touts who couldn't have been aged more than seventeen or eighteen.

Ugly John and Jogger concluded the transaction whilst we looked on. The two touts counted out the money to each other and then the four of them shook hands.

'Enterprising little bastards,' said Jogger, as we watched the touts get into their car and speed out of the marina car park. 'They told me that they were still at school and had to get back for a maths lesson,' he continued, shaking his head as he shuffled the five match tickets in his hands.

'Nice work Jogger,' I said, giving him the thumbs up, 'at the end of the day, who gives a fuck... everyone's happy, you lot now get to see the match and they've probably just made more cash in ten minutes than their maths teacher makes in a fortnight... all easy.'

*   *   *

Jogger suggested that we drive back a couple of kilometres towards Nice and have a few beers at a terrace café he knew in a place called Villefranche sur Mer.

As he drove slowly back along the cliff top road and then negotiated the hairpin bends that eased our descent into the town, I looked down across the red tile roofs of what was sign posted *vieille ville* (old town), and my eyes lingered on the yellow washed walls of the tall narrow bell-tower that formed part of a medieval looking church.

The view was picture postcard perfect. I followed my line of sight down the steep slope, along the narrow cobblestone streets that cut through quiet looking squares and across the long sandy strip of beach that flanked the Mediterranean Sea.

'Fuck me, that's a view innit,' I said, inarticulately voicing my opinion as I marvelled at the way the suns rays shimmered and sparkled on the tranquil surface of the sea which was the type of blue that you always imagined the sea would be when you were a small inner city child.

Chorus lines of gangly palm trees fringed the beach and completed the panorama which began to narrow in my perspective as Jogger drove the car the last few hundred metres down into the town.

*   *   *

'They got that right didn't they the old Frog's,' said Baby Gap Brian, as we made our way through a vaulted passageway that led us into the chocolate box square which was home to the terrace café Jogger had spoken of.

'What?' asked Ugly John, rubbing his stomach as he spotted three elderly couples sat outside the café sipping what was most probably ice cold beer from thin stemmed crystal glasses.

'Calling it er er that er er the Cote d' Azur... the blue coast,' replied

Baby Gap Brian hesitantly, distracted as we all were by the nut brown tanned, raven haired beauty who exhibited catwalk style deportment as she sashayed passed us.

'It's called the blue coast not cos of the colour of the sea but cos they make a lot of blue movies here, with birds like that in em,' I said nonchalantly, smiling as I watched the female halves of the couples arch their eyebrows disapprovingly as their partners drooled at the girl as she walked on by.

With the sun high in a cloudless, pastel blue sky and the gentlest of sea breezes fanning our faces we sat, continental style, outside the café savouring the chilled out atmosphere that Villefranche sur Mer afforded us.

'Tina Turner lives here,' said Ossie, as he drew our attention to a couple of exquisite looking women who were stood at the top end of the square talking to one another.

'Funny aint it,' I said, as I perused the menu contemplating what to eat, 'we're here to watch Chelsea and we haven't even spoken about the match yet.'

I shook my head as a youngish woman rode by on one of those vintage looking 'sit up and beg' bicycles. Her long blonde hair flowed behind her as she pedalled effortlessly past us and as she did so I wanted to call out 'excuse me' so that she would look my way allowing me to put a face to the youthful vitality she exuded.

'Well since you've mentioned it,' said Ugly John, pursing his lips and blowing a kiss after the girl on the bicycle, 'whaddya reckon?'

'I think we're gonna lose 3–1,' I replied, lighting up a Marlboro and inhaling deeply before expanding on my prediction. 'And I'll tell you why I think that, it's a confidence thing... like a Chelsea thing, like you never know what's gonna happen. We won at Arsenal and Claudio Ranieri and the lads were drenched in a waterfall of positive publicity... then what happens?'

'We aint won since,' answered Jogger, moving his chair in such a way that he now had the best vantage point to view the comings and goings in the square. 'A couple of dour 0–0's and a beating away at Villa... and all of a sudden the same old questions are being asked of Claudio, his team selections and strategy.'

Jogger was right, one minute the papers were full of praise for Ranieri, the next they were full of stories about Peter Kenyon flagrantly courting other managers, the latest rumoured to be the Aston Villa boss David O'Leary and FC Porto's highly regarded young coach Jose Mourhino.

'I reckon Marco's got a point,' said Ossie, signalling the waiter to bring five more beers to our table. 'Bill Gallas being out worries me, and we miss out not having Duff as an option... dunno about conceding three goals... mind you, they can score this lot and that Morientes is proper tasty up front.'

'Exactly,' I said, licking my lips with hungry anticipation as our waiter placed the plate of freshly fried squid I'd ordered on the table in front of me. 'Don't get me wrong, I'm no prophet of doom but I've just got a bad feeling about this one cos I'm not feeling anything, no pmt nothing... fuck me this squids lovely, drizzled in a lime and chilli sauce ooooh,' I continued, speaking with my mouth full as I began to eat my lunch.

'Well lads,' said Ugly John, looking up from his mobile phone, 'it looks like we might as well stay here for a bit cos the Monaco plod have ordered all the bars to stop serving alcohol between 3 and 9pm... just had a text message from a mate of mine who lives there saying that they are coming down hard on anyone behaving rowdily and wearing colours.'

'Well that suits me son,' I said, voicing everyone's opinion for them. 'Young Dave and that lot don't land in Nice for another hour or so... let's wait for them to call and then we can arrange to meet up in Monaco at around 4pm.'

No one objected in the slightest, so we remained a while longer sitting in the sunshine enjoying our lunch whilst swapping anecdotes and theories which were occasionally interspersed with comments about the ladies of Villefranche and what we'd to do to them.

'Kipling!' said Ossie, stirring us from the daydreaming we had succumbed to following lunch and several sunshine beers.

'Where!' said Baby Gap Brian, jolting forward in his chair as if he'd just been poked with an electric cattle prod.

'Uh... huh, they won't have them cakes here,' I said, yawning and hoping that the adrenalin buzz of being away with Chelsea would kick in soon to rid me of my soporific mood.

Jogger looked on, his poker face inscrutable. I waited for him to pass comment but he didn't. Ugly John removed his sunglasses and rubbed his eyes before cracking the joints of his knuckles one by one. He knew that Ossie was about to volunteer some profound piece of trivia related to Chelsea that would leave us scratching our heads in a bewildered manner.

'Not Mr Kipling of exceedingly good cakes fame,' said Ossie, pausing to stretch his arms Seagull style, an act which prompted a series of squawks from Baby Gap, Ugly and myself that had everyone sat nearby drawing their sunglasses down the bridges of their noses and peering at us suspiciously. 'No... no, I mean Rudyard Kipling... the geezer that wrote Jungle Book.'

'What about him then?' I said, wondering what tenuous link there might be between a famous poet and Chelsea. It had to be a link with Chelsea as that was to be Ossie's specialist subject should he ever be asked to appear on Mastermind.

'His poetry inspires Claudio,' replied Ossie, sitting forward in his chair knowing that he now had our full and undivided attention.

'Fuck off,' said Baby Gap Brian, smirking, 'what like his team selections are inspired by Balloo the fucking bear and that irritating little kid Mowgli... I should bleedin coco... mmm mind you though.'

'I'm being serious,' said Ossie, standing up and making a theatrical gesture with his left hand that Sir Larry would have been proud of. 'If you can meet with triumph and disaster and treat these two impostors just the same and all that and everything er er then something and er... you will be a man my son. It's from Kipling's poem 'If'. Claudio said, he'd read it as a kid and he continued to read it now when he needed to reassure himself about what he was doing and why.'

'Good story,' I said, looking at the time on my watch. 'And your prediction Ossie for tonight is?'

'1–1,' said Ossie, gaining the agreement of everyone except Ugly John who flicked V signs with both hands to indicate his prediction of the match result was 2–2.

At that point my phone rang; it was Young Dave calling to inform me that he and the rest of the crew were on the ground in Nice and mobilising themselves for the final push to Monaco... by helicopter. A 20km journey that would take less than ten minutes and cost each of them 50 Euros.

*   *   *

The Principality of Monaco is a sovereign and independent state that shares borders on its landward side with several communes of the French Department of the Alpes-Maritimes. Seawards, Monaco faces the Mediterranean.

The Principality, renown for being the playground of the rich and famous, is no bigger than Hyde Park and yet has more police per square metre than any other country in the world. Normally their function is to protect the riches of its citizens and non-French residents, however today they were out in force to ensure that order was maintained before, during and after the match.

'Rule Britannia... Britannia rules the waves... Britons never, never, never shall be slaves...'

Ronny Cutlass and ten of his cohorts were gathered outside a small bar in the shopping precinct adjacent to the underground car-park from which we had just emerged squinting into the bright afternoon sunshine.

Stripped to the waist and lager handed, Ronny and the boys were treating their audience, an even mix of Monegasgue nationals and heavily armed riot police, to West London's own version of the 'Last night of the prom's'.

'I thought you said there was a ban on alcohol son?' I said to Ugly John, as we pushed our way politely through the crowds, following Jogger who was striding resolutely ahead of us.

'That's what my mate said,' replied Ugly John frowning. 'It don't look like it though does it eh son,' he continued, rubbing his hands and licking his lips in thirsty anticipation.

'Where are you taking us?' said Baby Gap Brian, as we caught up with Jogger who had led us out of the precinct and down a narrow road along which was being driven an assortment of expensive, exotic looking Italian automobiles.

'The Condamine,' replied Jogger knowledgeably. 'It's the harbour. Worth seeing cos they'll be preparing the area for the Monaco Formula 1 Grand Prix which is next month.'

I'm not a big fan of F1, but I suppose down the years I've watched the Monaco GP enough times on TV to allow various parts of the legendary circuit to indelibly imprint themselves in my subconscious.

The swimming pool, the pedestrian bridge bedecked with adverts for Gauloise cigarettes, the old fortified town of Monaco-Ville built high on the rock which looked down on the rest of the Principality, it all looked so familiar now.

I closed my eyes momentarily and imagined the tyre burning screeches and high pitched engine whines of the cars as they raced past, their drivers jockeying for pole position along the notoriously treacherous circuit knowing that victory in this the most glamorous of all F1 events would guarantee them lasting fame, untold wealth and the amorous advances of scores of impossibly beautiful women that were drawn to the annual event.

The imaginary sound of F1 was replaced by the very real sound of the sirens belonging to several police vehicles that sped past us.

'Fuck me,' said Ossie, putting his fingers in his ears, 'that's loud enough to make anyone think war has just broken out,' he continued, as we walked along the red asphalt area adjacent to the marina which Jogger informed us was where the pits would be housed for the Grand Prix.

'Maybe war has just broken out,' said Baby Gap Brian, who had stopped walking and was now staring out across the harbour, shading his eyes from the sun and looking for all the world like an old seafarer... or was it Uncle Albert from Only Fools And Horses.

'What's the fucking point of coming all the way out here and having a row?' said Ossie, as he pointed at a blue hulled yacht which dwarfed everything else in the harbour. 'Look at the size of that thing,' he continued, not waiting for a reply to his previous question, 'I wonder if it's Abramovich's?'

* * *

As we began to walk up the winding path which led from the harbour, up the side of the rock and into Monaco-Ville, I thought about what Ossie had just said. He was right, what was the point? "You do it for the reputation of the club," I remembered Del Goss saying years ago when we'd travelled up to Preston for a glamorous 2nd Division fixture.

Del had instructed everyone to unscrew and steal every single light-bulb from the carriages of the 'football special' we had travelled to the match on; when we alighted at Preston station our orders were to throw the light-bulbs on the floor at the feet of the horses on which police officers, who were to provide us with an escort to Deepdale, were mounted.

It was like a scene from a Wild West movie, horses and bodies everywhere. Chelsea 'ran' Preston that day and which ever way you looked at it the 'reputation' of the club had most definitely been enhanced. A couple of people got arrested, but that was all. In those days as kids, we dealt with the police by raising the middle finger of our right hands from a safe distance and then doing a runner.

If you were unfortunate enough to get arrested, you maintained the right to remain silent until the opportunity to do a runner presented itself again and then you ran.

If you ended up in the station, the worst punishment you would receive would be at the hands of an adult relative who would box your ears in gratitude for having been dragged away from an evening in front of the telly.

Today, reputations were not enhanced by going up against the police. Little in the way of provocation was needed in any country for the police to march in and crack the heads of those whom they believed to be the ringleaders of any type of civil disturbance... and believe me, they seem to really love this aspect of their work.

As we tramped slowly through lush green gardens coloured with a variety of plants whose names I had no idea of, but whose scents filled the air with a bouquet of tranquillity, I wondered if the police had tired of the

nationalistic anthems of Ronny Cutlass et al and had exercised unreason-
able force to silence them.

"The reputation of the club", eh... and where would Del Goss be right
now I wondered? Probably having a few gentle beers with his cronies in
one of the 'dry' bars down in the Condamine, telling stories about the old
days... about trips to places like Preston and Blackpool... about kids like
me who were too young and too naive to know any better.

*   *   *

Once inside the walled town we walked across the grey cobble stoned
square that edged Prince Rainier's whitewashed palace and made our
way over to some medieval ramparts that overlooked the western half of
the Principality.

The vantage point was superb and afforded us views of both Monte
Carlo with its internationally famous Casino, and Fontvielle an area of 40
Hectares that had recently been reclaimed from the sea and was now
home to, among other things, Stade Louis II home to the Principality's
only professional football team L'Association Sportive de Monaco FC.

From up here the stadium, which was opened in 1985, resembled a
giant open air opera house. Its verdant pitch, which was laid well above
street level and set on top of a multi-purpose sports complex that apparently incorporated an Olympic sized swimming pool, looked like an oversize roof garden.

Three sides of the stadium were covered with the far end open and
capped off by a row of arches which give it a Romanesque appearance.

'60 million quids worth,' quipped Jogger, knowing that we were all
marvelling at the stadium. 'It took six years to build and can withstand
earthquakes measuring up to 7.5 on the Richter scale,' he continued
eruditely, pushing his sunglasses back up the bridge of his nose in the
manner of an elderly professor. 'Y'see the arches? They allow the sea
breeze to ventilate the stadium during the summer when it gets really hot.
That's why they have so many world class athletics meetings here.'

'Fuck me,' I whispered in Ossie's ear, 'this geezer knows a lot about
everything doesn't he.'

Ossie nodded but said nothing as we waited for Jogger to complete
our informal education on matters related to AS Monaco FC.

'That's why the cabbie in Nice hated 'em so much then!' exclaimed
Baby Gap Brian, after Jogger had told us that the club, which was now
bankrolled by the royal family, was able to attract the cream of managerial
and footballing talent because income tax did not exist in Monaco.

The club had amassed seven French titles since it was founded in 1924 and its distinctive red and white shirts had been worn by household names such as Fabien Barthez, Emanuel Petit, Thierry Henry, David Trezeguet, Lilian Thuram, and Glenn Hoddle.

Both Arsene Wenger and Jean Tigana had enjoyed success as managers here before fortunes on the pitch waned and the club, without the lucre provided by competing in Europe and unable to survive on the income generated by average gates of 8000, teetered on the brink of oblivion as it flirted with bankruptcy

Royal heir apparent, and ever present supporter, Prince Albert stepped in at the head of a consortium of local businessmen and AS Monaco FC, who had been relegated briefly to the Second Division for exceeding the French FA's limit on debt, were back in business with ex Chelsea midfielder Didier Deschamps, who had recently taken over as coach, remaining at the helm of an exciting young side.

Jogger also told us that the clubs shirt sponsors, a financial group called Fedcominvest, had initially offered to pay off the clubs debts but the deal had been vetoed by the royal family who were concerned about some of the personnel involved in the Russian based company's business dealings.

'Bleedin Russian rouble billionaires they get fucking everywhere,' said Baby Gap Brian, tutting and shaking his head as we walked back across the square towards a bar called La Pampa Glaciers, where we'd agreed to meet Young Dave and the others.

'Just as well,' I said, relishing the prospect of getting my hands on another ice cold beer, 'otherwise the way things were going we'd have been worrying about the cost of a return ticket to Plymouth next season rather than Prague.'

* * *

The waiter placed a large bowl of chips on the table in front of Big Chris and pointed at his watch. 'At seex thirtay vee are clo zed... no more bier, vee also vant to go to ze game.'

'All right mate, mangetout... mangetout,' said Big Chris, grabbing a handful of chips. 'You'd better bring us un autre dix bier's then my son,' he continued, stuffing the chips into his mouth and holding up both hands to give further clarification of how many beers were required.

The waiter nodded and forced a false smile. To him we were all the same. We were no different to Ronny Cutlass and his cohorts shouting the odds down in the precinct. As far as he was concerned he was witnessing at first hand the specifically British culture of binge drinking. However, even though the concept of drinking to excess baffled him, he was still more than happy to relieve us of our Euros provided we continued to behave in a relatively sober manner.

'Blimey Big Chris I'm impressed,' said Chicken Plucker, reaching into the pocket of his jacket for his Marlboro's. 'You couldn't ask him where the toilet is could you?... I'm bursting.'

'Oi garçon... son. Ou 'est le khazi mate ?' asked Big Chris, deliberately acting the oaf and keeping us all entertained into the bargain.

'Khazi... vot ees zis khazi? Ees eet a how you say... a tooreest attraction? I don't know zis khazi.' The waiter shook his head and looked around the table hoping that someone would enlighten him.

'Toilet mate... I need the toilet,' said Chicken Plucker, standing up and patting down his pockets in order to determine where he'd put his cigarette lighter.

'Ahh ze toilette,' said the waiter, raising the index finger of his right hand. 'Seet down von moment yes... I will get you ze coin for ze door... ees just around ze corner yes.'

The waiter pointed down the side street onto which La Pampa Glaciers backed and then scurried back into the bar whilst a relieved looking Chicken Plucker sat back down in his chair and finally lit up his cigarette.

This was Chicken Plucker's first away trip this season. He used to be a permanent fixture on the Chelsea scene, but now work commitments prevented him from getting to as many games as he'd like to get to.

According to Young Dave, Chicken Plucker was somewhat of a haute cuisine celebrity these days. His legendary Plucker Sauce, a piccante accompaniment for braised leg of pork, had been championed on TV by Gary Rhodes and was allegedly soon to be made available in packet form on the shelves of the nations supermarkets.

Chicken Plucker, christened Andrew by his parents, had held down a wide variety of jobs before talking his way into the job of saucier at Young Dave's restaurant. He'd washed dishes at the Ritz, been a Red Coat at Butlins and as a five year old been the cute little kid in the mild green Fairy Liquid adverts.

The monicker Chicken Plucker had been bestowed on him by Young Dave, in whom he'd confided that the worst job he'd ever had was plucking chickens on his Auntie May's farm one school summer holiday.

Young Dave didn't deal in Christian names, they were for normal people. All his friends had nicknames, most of which he'd come up with himself, and Andrew was to be no different.

* * *

'Thank fuck for that,' said Young Dave, tossing his mobile phone onto the table and picking up his beer glass. 'That was Yohan the woodcutter... he'll be up here with three tickets in five minutes... he wants a ton fifty for 'em.'

'Who the fuck is Yohan the woodcutter?' said Ugly John, looking at his watch. 'There's only an hour and ten to kick off,' he continued, smoothing his hands across his temples.

'Fuck knows,' I said, 'but I bet he used to work for Young Dave.'

'He's a bloke that used to work for me...,' replied Young Dave, in answer to Ugly John's question.

'Don't tell me he used to be a lumberjack and his names Yohan,' interrupted Big Chris.

'Yeah... how d'ya guess that?'

'Well... er you call him Yohan the woodcutter.'

'That does it,' I said, scraping my chair back along the floor and standing up. 'I'm goin for a top ten hit... this khazi must be pretty good, Plucker, Baby Gap and Lemon still aint come back yet.'

I walked into the bar to get one of the 'special' tokens required to gain access to the toilet. As the waiter handed me the token I glanced out of the window and saw Young Dave cuff Big Chris across the top of the head. He did it in the way a proud father would when quelling an outbreak of insubordination and insolence amongst his youngest children... and it made me smile.

*   *   *

'Jeeeesus Christ!' I exclaimed, as I pushed open the toilet door and walked into a small recessed alcove in which Baby Gap Brian, Lemon and Chicken Plucker were bent up double and laughing so hard they were crying. 'What the fucks going on here then?'

'It's the... ha... ha... it's the kha... ha ha khazi,' shrieked Bay Gap Brian, pointing at the door and trying to regain his composure.

'What about it?' I said, putting the token in the door lock mechanism and turning the handle.

'Ha... ha, it's a special khazi mate... you'll see.' Baby Gap stood up and wiped the tears from his eyes and pushed Lemon and Chicken Plucker, who were both still laughing uncontrollably, out through the main door and into the street.

I opened the door with some trepidation thinking that perhaps the lads had sabotaged the toilet in some way but everything seemed normal, apart from the fact that there was a lot of water on the grey flagstone floor. I sniffed the air and grimaced as the pungent fumes of the chemicals used to disinfect the toilet irritated my nostrils.

'Just like any other khazi,' I thought to myself, as I dropped the kids off at the pool and watched a large Trapdoor spider make its way slowly across the floor towards my foot. 'Maybe that was it... the spiders eh... nah... what's funny about that?'

I looked up at the ceiling, at the walls and at the cistern behind me... nothing. Unless I was about to be devoured by some monster that lived in the toilet pan, and was currently hiding behind the u-bend, there was nothing to be suspicious about other than the fact that I could still hear Baby Gap Brian and Lemon giggling outside in the street. I finished off my business, sorted myself out and pressed the chrome lever on the side of the toilet which I assumed would activate the flush mechanism. Wrong! Well sort of. Travelling around the world has taught me a few things. One of these being that you should always expect the unexpected when answering the call of nature.

The thing was though that you wouldn't necessarily expect to have to be on your guard when using a public lavatory located across the square from the Prince's Palace in one of the richest places on God's earth.

Fair enough elsewhere. In India I'd often found myself nervously squatting over a hole in the ground, my modesty concealed by a couple of sheets of rusty corrugated iron, having to keep my eyes peeled for the hands of thieving dacoites, scorpions and rats the size of a rugby balls... to say nothing of the snakes.

'Jeeesus Christ... What the f f f...' As I depressed the chrome lever the toilet thankfully flushed, but as it did so the seat began to revolve and water began to bubble up over the rim of the stainless steel pan cascading over the lip and onto the floor.

I pushed the lever again in the hope that this would switch off this novel and futuristic self cleansing mechanism but this only served to make matters worse. The toilet seats sedate revolutions began to gather momentum spraying the water out in a wider arc which encompassed my jeans clad legs.

'You wankers ha ha... oops,' I shouted, laughing and then checking myself as I opened the toilet door expecting to see my friends but instead being greeted by the sight of a massively overweight woman dressed in black leggings and a loose fitting T-shirt across the front of which was emblazoned the slogan Jesus Saves.

'Hey sir, you finished with the John now?' drawled the woman, in what sounded like a Jerry Hall style Texan accent.

I looked over my shoulder and noticed that the toilet had once again returned to its static state.

'Yes m'am,' I replied mimicking her intonation.

'Praise the Lord,' she said, breaking wind loudly as she pushed past me.

'He won't help you love,' I muttered, as I stepped out into the street to be greeted by the still laughing Baby Gap Brian.

Baby Gap was all for hanging around to see if the fat American woman's faith in God would save her from the terrible fate that lay in wait for her in the toilet but Young Dave was shouting after us and beckoning us to return to the bar as his friend Yohan had just arrived in some style astride a pearly white heavily chromed Harley Davidson motorcycle.

'He looks like that bloke Ponce off the old TV series about the Californian highway patrol men... er CHIPS... yeah that was it,' observed Roger Socks.

'You mean Ponch,' said Lemon.

'Nah Ponce is right... he looks like one of the faggots off the Village People, look at him,' said Big Chris, as we watched Yohan and Young Dave engage in an animated discussion which concluded with three match tickets being exchanged for 450 Euros.

'Monaco veel fuck your Cockernee asses tonight,' said Yohan, as he pocketed the money, mounted the Harley and gunned its engine.

'Nothings gonna fuck my fat arse tonight,' chortled Big Chris, as we watched Yohan roar away across the square, the revving engine all but drowning out the shrill female screams that could be heard coming from the general direction of bar La Pampa Glaciers soon to be world famous toilet.

*   *   *

'*Champions League... we're havin a laugh... Champions League... we're havin a laugh.*'

Young Dave and I were stood on yellow plastic bucket seats along with the 1400 other Chelsea supporters hemmed into Sector H of Monaco's Stade Louis II.

The stadium, which had looked impressive as we'd surveyed it from the giddy heights of Monaco-Ville's ramparts, felt distinctly odd. It was full and yet there were less than 18,000 spectators in attendance for this evenings fixture.

Artificial, that was the adjective I was looking for. If Milton Keynes were a football stadium it would be Stade Louis II. To me the evident dislocation between investment and architecture seemed chasmic.

In the past I have been known to indulge in passionate expletive ridden monologues focussed on the shortcomings of some of the grounds I've set foot in however here, in this 'state of the art' complex built to cater

Baby Gap Brian ... flowered up and alone in amongst the Monaco
massive ... April ... 2004

for a country whose population numbered a mere 30,000, words failed me.

If the stadium was artificial then the pre-match atmosphere generated by the home supporters could at best have been described as synthetic. The red and white banners of the static Monaco 'ultras' gathered in the flat fronted stand behind the goal opposite us hung limply in the lifeless but balmy evening air.

It was only when the players took to the field of play that Monaco's supporters animated themselves, getting behind their team by rapping above their heads inflatable plastic red and white tubes which made a grating noise similar to the sound a ratchet makes.

'In your Monaco slums... in your Monaco slums... you root in the dustbins for something to eat... you find a dead lobster, you think it's a treat... in your Monaco slums.'

Our chant was not only ironically entertaining but served to drown out the irritating noise being made by the Monaco supporters. Looking around the stadium there were pockets of blue dotted sporadically across the red and white canvass. In the sector adjacent to ours there was a group of about 100 Chelsea fans un-segregated from the home support but the police, who were conducting security operations in front of us in an admirably low key fashion, seemed relatively unconcerned.

Geordie Jase and Lemon had found their way into our pen and as the seating was unreserved had managed to clamber across to where Young Dave and I were stood which was directly under the large electronic scoreboard behind the goal.

Chicken Plucker, prompted by a text message, waved to us from the bottom corner of the stand to our left which was comprised mainly of media and hospitality boxes. Ugly John rang me to say that he and Jogger were safely ensconced in the far end with the Monaco 'ultras'. Big Chris and Roger Socks were apparently somewhere in the stand to our right but at that moment, as kick off approached, I had no idea where Baby Gap Brian and Ossie had secured their vantage point.

'Ranieri's blue and white army... Ranieri's blue and white army.'

* * *

'Marco Ambrosio... Marco Ambrosio.'

The stand in keeper turned to acknowledge our chant and was applauded loudly. Tonight he was playing behind the defensive quartet of Melchiot, Desailly the captain, Terry and Bridge. In midfield were Parker, Lampard and the man who seemed to save his best Chelsea performances for this competition Claude Makalele.

'Super, super Frank... super, super Frank... super, super Frank... super Frankie Lampard.'

As we chanted Lampard's name, Young Dave received a text from Chicken Plucker saying that he was sat next to Frank Lampard senior and I finally spotted Ossie and Baby Gap Brian away to our right in the midst of a group of plastic baton waving Monaco fans.

Gronkjaer, who'd made such an impression when he'd come on against Arsenal in the 2nd Leg at Highbury, started the game along with the twin striking partnership of Crespo and Gudjohnsen.

Ranieri's tinkering options on the substitutes bench comprised of Sullivan, Huth, Geremi, Joe Cole, Mutu, Hasselbaink and surprisingly Juan Sebastian Veron who had been plagued by injury and concerns over his fitness for much of the season.

As the game kicked off the Monaco supporters finally found their voices and got behind their team who responded by immediately testing the Chelsea defence, with both Evra and Rothen running at Melchiot and Parker down the left hand side.

'He looks sharp that Giuly... frighteningly quick,' said Young Dave, as we craned our necks to see the action which was mainly taking place in

Chelsea's half of the pitch.

'Morientes worries me... oooh... shit... see what I mean,' I replied, burying my head in my hands as Giuly crossed to the talented Spaniard whose shot from the edge of the box was blocked by Desailly.

'Come on Chelsea... Come on Chelsea... Come on Chelsea... OH SHIT!'

With barely quarter of an hour gone Monaco opened the scoring. Melchiot who was being given a torrid time by Rothen brought his tormentor to the ground with a scything tackle for which he was booked.

In the manner of that most famous of all players to wear a number 25 shirt, Rothen clipped the free kick across the box, our flat footed defence failed to clear the ball and the unmarked Prso sent a looping header beyond Ambrosio into the back of the Chelsea net.

'Bollocks!' I said, shaking my head. 'It's been coming aint it eh.'

'Chelsea... Chelsea... Chelsea... Chelsea.'

Momentarily stunned by the goal, the first the team had conceded on foreign soil in this seasons competition, we were soon in good voice again and our support galvanised Chelsea who began to press forward with Makalele and Lampard starting to boss the midfield.

'We are the famous... the famous Chelsea.'

Chelsea responded by stepping up another gear.

'Go on Eidur... go on son,' I shouted, as the Icelander latched onto a Scott Parker pass and then seemed to stumble over the ball.

'Fuck it... no go on... Hernan... Yessss!... Goal... Fucking brilliant ha ha.'

Eidur Gudjohnsen had somehow managed to squeeze the ball across the goal mouth to Hernan Crespo who took one touch before side footing the ball into the net.

Crespo's celebration of the goal was as good as any I had seen. He vaulted the pitchside advertising hoardings, sprinted across the running track and ran towards us with his arms flailing and lank hair trailing behind him. It reminded me of the way Joe Allon, a Shedite cult hero and one of many strikers who'd tried and failed to fill Kerry Dixon's golden boots, had celebrated scoring his first goal for the club.

'Hernan Crespo... Hernan Crespo... hello... hello Hernan Crespo.'

After a shaky start and the concession of an early goal, Chelsea were on level terms. Crespo had given us a priceless away goal and suddenly we were all in a party mood.

'Are you watching... are you watching... are you watching Arsenal,' we chanted, hoping that our voices could be heard by any Arse fans who might be watching back at home.

I could just about see Claudio Ranieri, I couldn't see his face but I imagined he'd be smiling right now. You only got to see those close up emotional images on TV. The day after the Arsenal game I'd read in the paper how Ranieri had wept tears of joy on the Highbury pitch after Chelsea's famous victory.

Amidst all the celebratory pandemonium in the Clock End at the final whistle in that game, I'd missed out on seeing that... but then where would I rather have been? Sat in front of the telly watching replays of the action from every angle whilst listening to old Mr Bojangles himself, Ron Atkinson, mixing his metaphors with Des Lynam, or right here in the thick of it, living and breathing every sparkling moment? No contest.

'We love you Chelsea we do... we love you Chelsea we do...we love you Chelsea we do. Oh Chelsea we love you.'

Chelsea began to play with more and more confidence. Crespo should have increased our advantage from a great Lampard cross but instead he volleyed the ball over the bar.

'It's in the bag this lads,' said Lemon, as we applauded the players from the pitch at half time.

'Let's hope he keeps the same players on the pitch for the second half eh,' said Geordie Jase, fingering the small enamel Chelsea lapel badge that he was sporting proudly on his jacket.

'Yeah lets eh,' said Young Dave, offering me a Silk Cut which I gratefully accepted. 'Looks like your 3-1 forecasts out of the window son,' he continued, winking at me as he passed the cigarette packet to Lemon.

'Thank fuck for that,' I replied, raising my eyebrows and turning my head to look up at the huge electronic scoreboard behind me.

'If she don't come... I'll tickle her bum with a lump of celery... celery, celery.'

I laughed as I looked up and saw sticks of the green vegetable go sailing up into the night sky wondering what the Monegasques might make of this quaint Chelsea tradition. Soup, most probably.

* * *

'You are having a fucking laugh aren't you? What the fuck is Ranieri playing at?' said Young Dave, scratching at his forehead as the Chelsea players emerged from the tunnel to our right with Veron on as a second half substitute for Jesper Gronkjaer.

'Dunno son,' I replied, shrugging my shoulders. 'Their number 4 did a good job of shutting Gronkjaer down... but Veron's a different type of player.'

'Yeah, he's different all right,' said Geordie Jase, 'he's fucking rubbish, that's what he is man.'

Whilst I thought Geordie Jase was being a bit hard on the Argentinean playmaker I was prepared to give Tinkerman the benefit of the doubt.

The second half started in much the same way as the first half had, with Monaco, now attacking the goal in front us, pushing up and putting Chelsea's defence under pressure. Twice they almost retook the lead; firstly when Ambrosio made a spectacular save from a header at a corner, and secondly when Desailly cleared a Morientes shot off the line with the keeper beaten.

'*Marcel... Marcel Desailly... Marcel... Marcel Desailly.*'

'Thank fuck for the Rock eh... he aint lost the magic,' I said, slapping Young Dave across the back as our support heaved a huge collective sigh of relief when the ball was booted up-field.

The respite was only temporary though and Monaco continued their stern examination of Chelsea's defence.

'Great tackle Makalele,' said Lemon, as the tigerish midfielder effected a brilliant sliding tackle on Zikos to prevent him crossing what would have been a dangerous ball across the Chelsea five yard box.

'Fuck me... that's dodgy,' I said, as Zikos stood up from the tackle and appeared to punch Makalele on the back of the neck.

'He's gonna go for that,' said Young Dave, as we watched Makalele fall dramatically to the floor.

'*Off... Off... Off,*' we shouted, as the referee brandished the red card at Zikos and then the yellow at Makalele.

The Monaco players and supporters were incensed at the decision. We just laughed and cheered.

'I didn't see it mate, did you?' I asked the question to no-one in particular, but the general consensus was that Makalele had deliberately got Zikos sent off.

'Oh well... fuck em,' I said, clapping my hands together. 'That's it now, this should be a piece of piss.'

Chelsea went on the offensive and Deschamps substituted Monaco's goalscorer Prso and made his team adopt a more cautious formation.

'Go on Eidur... fuck I can't see... shit, that looked close,' I said, as Monaco's keeper sprinted out of his goal to make a great save.

'*Eidur Gudjohnsen... Eidur Gudjohnsen... ooooh.*'

The chanting of the strikers name broke off as he headed Veron's corner fractionally over the bar.

'Jimmy's coming on, Claudio's going for the win lads,' said Young Dave, as we looked over to the Chelsea bench and saw Hasselbaink take off his tracksuit in readiness for action.

'Who's he taking off? I asked, trying to see the number on the fourth officials indicator board.

'Looks like Scotty Parker dunnit,' replied Lemon.

'Yeah, he's making his way over eh... you're having a bleedin giraffe aren't you!' I exclaimed, as the fourth official indicated that it was in fact Mario Melchiot who was making way for Jimmy Floyd Hasselbaink.

'Oh Jimmy, Jimmy... Jimmy, Jimmy, Jimmy Floyd Hasselbaink.'

'He's pushed the gamble button,' said Young Dave, as we tried to make sense of Ranieri's decision to move Scott Parker from midfield to right back which also meant switching Veron from the left to the right flank.

'We've lost our shape,' said Geordie Jase knowledgably. 'Look, instead of stretching them wide and taking advantage of the fact their down to ten men we're playing 4–3–3... it's fucking stupid.'

Geordie Jase was right, even though Hasselbaink had almost scored twice, Chelsea looked increasingly ragged. Giuly, Monaco's captain, was using his electric pace to good effect and exposing Parker's shortcomings as a full back and it was no surprise when Ranieri substituted Parker with Huth in an attempt to shore up the defence.

'Fuck me someone stop him... get in there Marcel!' yelled Young Dave, pointing at Giuly who'd skilfully held off the Chelsea captains challenge and passed the ball to Morientes who had run into a great position on the edge of our penalty area.

'For fucks sake... NO!'

Morientes hammered the ball into the back of the Chelsea net and sent the home support into raptures.

'That's fucking bollocks Claudio,' roared Lemon, as we watched Ambrosio, who'd had absolutely no chance of making the save, pick the ball up and lash it angrily up field.

'Just ten fucking minutes... against ten fucking men... wankers,' said Young Dave, his voice ridden with angst.

'Come on Chelsea... Come on Chelsea.'

There was still plenty of conviction in our chanting but unfortunately it wasn't enough to raise the morale of the team and I sensed that Didier Deschamps knew this. He sent on Nonda for Giuly and seconds later Monaco had a 3–1 lead. Maybe Ambrosio could have done better when Nonda stabbed the ball past him, who knows.

I stared disbelievingly at the scoreboard; which ever way I looked at it... there was no getting away from the fact that Monaco had mugged us 3–1. At the final whistle I sat down in my seat and rubbed the palms of my hands backwards and forwards along my thighs and shook my head as I watched the players trek disconsolately down the tunnel.

Same old Chelsea, maddeningly unpredictable, we'd thrown it all away. Claudio Ranieri's tactics, which two weeks earlier had seen off Arsenal and earned him column inches of praise from the voracious Fleet Street football hacks, had been unfathomable. If Peter Kenyon had been sharpening the axe again over the last couple of weeks then Roman Abramovich may well have seen enough this evening to be persuaded to deliver the final coup de grace himself.

Match Result

L'Association Sportive de Monaco FC 3 : Chelsea FC 1

*   *   *

'Roman Abramovich... Roman Abramovich.'

We were still waiting for the stewards to open the security gates to allow us to exit the stadium when Roman Abramovich, flanked by several burly looking minders, walked past our sector and made his way over to the players tunnel. He waved to us acknowledging our support but the haunted expression on his face was that of a man who's pride had been wounded by the monstrous deficiency of his teams second half performance.

Five minutes after Mr Abramovich had made his way down the tunnel. Chelsea's CEO, Peter Kenyon also walked past our sector but this time the chanting was less appreciative.

'It's gonna take something special for that geezer to win over the hearts and minds of the Chelsea faithful,' said Young Dave, as we shuffled down the steps and made our way dejectedly out of the stadium.

'Beckham?' said Geordie Jase, kicking an empty coke can along the floor.

'Beckham and Ronaldo,' I replied, checking my mobile phone for text messages and wondering what Abramovich and Kenyon might be plotting next.

*   *   *

Several beers and a packet of cigarettes later I'd reached the 'what's the fucking point?' moment of self pitying gloom. The journey back from Monaco to Nice had been uneventful and our conversation peppered with giveaway expletive riddled expressions highlighting our frustration at what we had witnessed.

Tactically Ranieri had thrown the baby out with the bathwater. So often criticised for being over cautious and playing to the Italian, 'catenaccio', defensive counter-attacking blueprint which had yielded a club record number of clean sheets and away victories, Tinkerman had speculated

It looked like Young Dave, Chicken Plucker, Lemon and Geordie Jase were going to be stranded in Monaco until Yohan the woodcutter (far right) gave them a lift back to Nice aboard his forklift truck.

wildly on being able to return home from Monaco with a victory that would almost certainly have guaranteed Chelsea's passage back to Gelsenkirchen.

'You can't just blame the gaffer,' said Baby Gap Brian, pretending not to notice the palpable charms of waitress who was loitering at the far edge of our table.

'Well you can... but the players have to shoulder some of the responsibility don't they,' sighed Ossie, the smile on his face which had been ever present since we'd entered Le Havane being replaced by a frown.

Ossie had a point. Chelsea's capitulation had been spectacular. Whilst I expected Claudio Ranieri to admit liability for the defeat, I hoped that the players would share the burden of accountability.

'2–0... that'll do it eh,' continued Ossie, folding his arms and sitting back in his chair.

'I reckon we'll either win 5–0 or it will be a bore draw,' offered Ugly John, leaning across the table and taking a closer interest in the discussion.

'Agreed... yeah I can see that,' said Baby Gap Brian, tapping his fingers on the table in time with the Latino music thudding from Le Havane's impressive soundsystem.

I watched as girls ebbed and flowed from the bar area to the dance floor where they would dance the Salsa with frightening proficiency. The big rich sound had an infectious quality to it, and the rhythms were impossible to dislodge from the brain. Slowly but surely the depression began to lift.

'It's like dancing by numbers innit,' I remarked, trying to follow the succession of steps that a Jennifer Lopez lookalike was trading with a small muscular albino man who bore an uncanny resemblance to Ugly John.

The albino, sensing he was being watched, looked over in our direction and smiled as he weaved his hips and gave 'J-Lo' his best moves leaving me in no doubt that he found our bemused looks profoundly satisfying.

* * *

STINKERMAN, proclaimed the *Daily Mail*'s back-page headline, but I was too exhausted to contemplate reading a blow by blow account of how Chelsea's Champions League train had been derailed by the folly of Claudio Ranieri.

I looked at the glazed expression on Ugly John's face as he wrestled with the forces of sleep, trying to keep himself awake until our flight was called and I wondered if he felt the same way that I did.

I could handle the physical exhaustion and the hollow hangover headache, I could handle the taunts of the Arsenal supporters always quick off the mark when it came to revengeful text messages, and I could handle the glorious unpredictability so synonymous with Chelsea Football Club.

But right now I felt that I, and every other fan who'd paid out good money to see the game, had been cheated and I couldn't handle that at all.

'Maybe we we're all a bit hasty giving Eriksson the cold shoulder,' said Ugly John, as we made our way through the departure gate.

'*We do need Eriksson... we do need Eriksson,*' I sang, in a low voice.

'Ha you fickle bastard ha ha,' chortled Ugly John.

'And you're not?' I replied, trying to stifle a yawn as we boarded the plane.

'Not really, I always said Eriksson was the right man for the job.'

'Bollocks!'

'It ain't bollocks it's the truth... well almost.'

'Ranieri's finished ain't he... even if we turn the tie around at the Bridge.'

'Even if we win the Champions League mate.'

'Even if he finds life on Mars my son.'

TWO WEEKS LATER

A fortnight ago as I'd traipsed silently, head hung low, through passport control at Gatwick airport, the grim realization of what I'd witnessed the night before had all but corroded my confidence in Chelsea's ability to turn things around in the return leg at Stamford Bridge.

The acidic nature of the defeat in Monaco coupled with the immediate pillorying of Claudio Ranieri for his tactical gaffes, and Makalele and Desailly for their unsporting behaviour, had subsequently left me feeling sick to the pit of my stomach.

Two weeks later, as I stepped off the District Line train at Fulham Broadway and made my way through the station concourse passing by the massed lines of touts, whom at 5pm were more interested in buying than selling tickets, the heartburn caused by Ranieri's indigestible kamikaze strategy had been eased by regular and increasingly frequent doses of that special type of Milk of Magnesia which only football fans have access to... blind optimism.

Defeat in the Principality of Monaco had been followed by defeat in the slightly less glamorous environs of Tyneside. A spirited Newcastle United side, motivated by the prospect of qualifying for the Champions League next season, overturned an early Joe Cole strike to win 2–1 and condemn Claudio Ranieri to a further week of being roasted slowly over an open fire by the media.

The second half destruction of a competent Southampton side at the weekend had buoyed the mood and done much to re-float and steady the good ship Chelsea. The 4–0 victory, our first in six matches, had shown that we still had an appetite in front of goal and possessed the killer instinct required to savage any team whose defence might be prone to lapses of concentration.

The win was a confidence boosting tonic for players and supporters alike. The self belief was back; but despite this, the 'sharks', as Ranieri liked to refer to the nations football journalists, were still circling for the kill in a pool that was getting bloodier by the minute.

Regardless of the wall of silence built ever higher around the Stamford Bridge boardroom, the Sunday papers were full of stories about Ranieri's imminent sacking and the installation of Jose Mourinho as the new head coach.

Ranieri looked to me like a man who was tiring of the struggle. A feature of his endearingly idiosyncratic performances at the press conferences that followed defeats earlier in the season had been the polite denial of having any knowledge of Peter Kenyon's curtain twitching pursuit of other potential coaches, most notably Sven Goran Eriksson. Yesterday though, he'd admitted to knowing the name of his successor.

However, not withstanding the fact that Claudio Ranieri had now self styled himself as a 'dead man walking', and despite the morale sapping loss of Damien Duff to a dislocated shoulder, the team had continued to talk up their prospects during the final countdown to the return leg with Monaco and I'd continued to brainwash myself into believing that anything was possible.

"We done the Arsenal didn't we... so we can do these cunts," Sir Larry had said to me in the drinker last night, as I'd fuelled my optimism with a late night brace of Stella's.

"We will need to do our best performance of the season and Monaco maybe their worst", was the more articulate and realistic observation of Claudio Ranieri at yesterday's press conference.

The facts, which ever way I looked at them, were very simple and straightforward to understand. It was up to the players now; Ranieri's position was both irrelevant and immaterial. In just under three hours time they would have the opportunity to bathe themselves in glory by once again upsetting the odds and winning through to play in the final of the most prestigious club competition in the world... a final that would be contested against FC Porto, the team ironically coached by Jose Mourinho.

*　　*　　*

On match days the One Bar was a veritable cornucopia of confusion. Customers queued three deep at the stainless steel bar waiting to be served by impishly pretty girls wearing thong revealing low slung hipster jeans.

Friends and acquaintances huddled together in tightly knit groups talking loudly across each other, their excited chatter fracturing as they passed bottles and pint pots above their heads to those fortunate enough to be sat on the low level sofas positioned under the TV screens at either end of the bar.

The occasional sound of glass breaking on the pitted oak floor was met with raucous cheers and a disapproving glare from Tara the landlady who always kept a watchful eye on proceedings from the safety of an alcove near the toilet door.

Gemma, the skinny ribbed waitress who always worked alone, remained calm under pressure as she weaved her way across the bar carrying two bountiful plates of Thai food. 'Number 25,' she brayed, in a voice which rose sonorously above the drone of pre-match banter.

'Over here love,' I shouted, holding up the wooden spoon I'd been given when I'd ordered my food.

'We could do with him tonight,' said Ossie, rubbing his hands as we watched Gemma make her way over with our food.

'Who?' I said, winking at her before gratefully relieving her of the plates.

'Number 25 son,' replied Ossie, cocking his head to one side and admiring the abstract design tattooed on the small of the girls back as she pushed and jostled her way back to the bar.

'Gianfranco Zola... yeah, not half,' I said, pausing to eat a couple of forkfuls of stir fry noodles which I'd sprinkled liberally with soy sauce. 'This game would've been made for the little fella eh,' I continued, reminiscing for a brief second about the gifted striker who'd we'd had the pleasure of seeing play again for Cagliari last month.

Ossie was right. Even now, in the twilight of his career, I would rather have seen the wizard Zola working his magic on the Stamford Bridge turf than a mercenary like Crespo whom, despite scoring the occasional 'big' goal, never once looked like he was proud to wear the blue shirt of Chelsea.

The One Bar's sound-system, which was normally silent pre match, crackled loudly into life, fizzing, popping and buzzing with static. Everyone, including Ossie and I, looked up with expectant faces wondering what aural jewel was about to be unleashed on our eardrums.

The unmistakable two-tone ska beat of the Harry J. Allstars classic instrumental, 'Liquidator' erupted from the speakers. Traditionally played at the ground just prior to kick off along with 'Blue is the colour' and 'Blue day', 'Liquidator' had a big rich sound and a freestyle *clap, clap, clap, clap... Chelsea* section that was impossible to extricate from the senses.

Only Keegan, the bizarrely named geriatric looking British Bulldog bitch, remained motionless. With one lazy eye open she surveyed proceedings from the comparative safety of the corner of the bar adjacent to where we are sat, waiting patiently to be offered a scrap of chicken or beef from those sat nearby.

Hip Hop Dan (far left) steps up with Gate 17 for the visit of Monaco ... four hours later he was crying tears as big as October cabbages.

*   *   *

After we'd finished our food we tortuously made our way through the bar to join Young Dave and the others. There was insufficient space for all of us to be together in the main bar so Young Dave had led his west country cohorts out through the rear exit, down the shallow stairwell and into the One Bar's cottage style beer garden.

I paused to have a chat with the ubiquitous Vegas Dave, apologising profusely that I'd once again forgotten to return the snide DVD copy of the Football Factory he'd lent me a several weeks ago.

Like me, Vegas Dave had become increasingly confident over the last couple of days that Chelsea would 'do the business' tonight.

'Lampard for the first goal son,' he said, raising his eyebrows and nodding at me. 'I've had a nifty on 'im... luverly.'

'Might have some of that myself,' I replied, knowing that I wouldn't. I hadn't gambled a solitary penny since I'd fleeced myself laying off the Wallaby egg chasers against the Kiwi's in the Rugby World Cup. I'd thought about it a couple of times, but I'd already decided that the next bet I was going to have would be on the outcome of England / France game at Euro 2004... although I hadn't yet formed an opinion on which team I was going to lay off.

I shook hands with Vegas Dave promising that I'd return the Football Factory DVD back to him by the weekend. As I made my way down the steps into the walled beer garden I remembered that I'd lent the DVD to Fuck Off Colin the night before the first leg of the semi-final... and guess what? I hadn't seen FOC since.

Not to worry; if old Fuck Off had vanished into the ether I could always buy another copy from Goofy the Gook, the crazy Chinaman who peddled pirate DVD's around all my local drinkers. 'Footborr Factollee,' as he called it. You could have a good old laugh with Goofy the Gook.

'What's your best selling title?' I'd asked him last Friday night when he'd made his customary closing time appearance in the Gamecock.

'Rove Actuary,' he'd replied, grinning maniacally to expose a crooked set of decaying teeth that clearly hadn't seen a toothbrush in decades.

'Ah Love Actually... I've seen it though... what else've you got then?'

'Rove Actuary... numbah one, numbah two... Kirr Birr, numbah thlee... Tloy... you buy all thlee, I give you speciar plice.'

'Ah er Kill Bill and er... mmm Troy,' I'd said, after pausing for a while to figure out what Goofy was trying to sell me from the black bin liner he had tucked under his arm.

'Yeah... Goofy the Gook, no problem,' I muttered to myself, as I made my way over to where my fellow displaced Gate 17 cohorts were stood grizzling about the unseasonably cold damp weather and the ever increasing possibility that the heavens were about to open once again.

* * *

'Anyone need seats... seats for the game,' drawled the tout, his cold eyes and fleshy mouth suppurating with corruption as he scanned the pavement for people willing to pay the £300 he was asking for a ticket.

'Scum,' hissed Ossie, as we crossed the Fulham Road and made our way through the crowds that were congregating in ever increasing numbers in the Chelsea Village courtyard immediately outside the stadium.

If I'd been a first timer, had it not been for my senses of smell and hearing I could have come to the conclusion that Chelsea Village was just like Monaco's Stade Louis II; a manufactured haven for the shallow and the bland where everything... players, managers and probably even the supporters if they protested too much, was disposable.

But fortunately, my senses of smell and hearing were very much intact. As we walked slowly through the teeming mass of people swathed primarily in the blue and white of Chelsea, the smell of burgers, hot dogs and onions sizzling in week old fat combined with that of piping hot fish and chips soaked in vinegar to create an atmosphere that was inherently English.

'Hat, scarf and a badge... wear your colours.'

'Programmes... programmes.'

Vendors shouted to make themselves heard above the general homogenous big match hubbub.

'*We are the famous... the famous Chelsea...*' The chant coming from inside the ground was picked up by everyone outside creating a stereo effect that Dolby would have been proud of. As we shuffled up to the back of the small queue that had formed at the turnstile entrances to the upper tier of the Shed, I looked up at the fresh looking neatly pointed brickwork and sighed.

Despite the superficiality of its modern façade, the 21st century version of Stamford Bridge still felt like home. Of course I missed not seeing the WELCOME TO STAMFORD BRIDGE hoarding flanked by the two traditional Chelsea lion club crests that used to be mounted above the entrance to the Shed. Of course I missed not clicking through the rickety old turnstiles and clambering up the endless flight of tired old concrete steps which led me to my own personal nirvana. Of course I missed the playful rivalry between the white wall, middle, left and tea bar sections of one of the most famous and charismatic ends in world football... but you have to move on.

'Before you were born son,' Young Dave would say to his thirteen year old lad Dan when quizzed about the electric fence brainchild of Ken Bates or the monkey chants that greeted the arrival on the pitch of the first black players to play for the club. Dan was a smart kid with an enquiring mind who was always asking questions based on snippets of other peoples conversation he'd overheard in the One Bar.

Dan came to most of the home games these days and with him he brought a crossover urban street style fashioned on his hero Eminem. Hip Hop Dan, as he had become known, had an eclectically strong grip on popular culture which transcended race colour and creed and mirrored the marketing mans vision of what the new Chelsea was all about.

'Oi Marco... are you with us mate?' shouted Young Dave, snapping me out of my daydream as we made our way up to the turnstile.

'Yes mate... yeah, course I am,' I said, rummaging in my jacket pocket for my match ticket.

'Forty nine bleedin quid eh!' exclaimed Ugly John, as he pushed me through the turnstile and handed his own ticket over to the operator. 'That's the most I've ever paid to see a match at the Bridge... and look at the way they've priced up the new season tickets... it's bloomin ridiculous I tell ya.'

Ugly John had a point. Kenyon's concept of keeping price rises to a minimum was an interesting one. This season £715 had entitled me to see 19 premiership matches and any domestic cup ties, including replays, played at the Bridge. Next season the price had been set at £750 for premiership matches only.

'You'll still be here mate,' I said, looking at this evenings Chelsea team which was being displayed on the TV monitor mounted on the wall at entrance to the toilets. 'Just like the... fuck me Jimmy's playing... er rest us,' I continued, interrupting my own reply to voice my astonishment at Ranieri's team selection.

Hasselbaink had vilified Ranieri's tinkering in the press and despite the fact the manager claimed not to read the sports pages of the popular press I was still surprised that he'd selected the Dutchman for his starting line up.

'Maybe his mother told him to pick Jimmy,' said Young Dave, pointing out Big Chris and Roger Socks who had just made their way through the turnstiles followed closely by Ossie and Baby Gap Brian.

The joke was that Ranieri's mother would question his team selections in much the same way that everyone else did. Duff was the man for her, but sadly tonight he would be a spectator in the stands praying like the rest of us that Jesper Gronkjaer would be able to prise open the Monaco defence and deliver a couple of telling crosses for Eidur or Jimmy to lash into the net.

The team was attack minded enough, it had to be. With Makalele banned, Joe Cole was given another starting chance to earn himself a place in Chelsea folklore. The full team was, Cudicini in goal; Melchiot, Bill Gallas, Terry and Bridge in defence; Gronkjaer playing wide of Geremi, Lampard and Joe Cole with the seasoned Chelsea strike partnership of Hasselbaink and Gudjohnsen expected to do the business in front of goal.

I didn't want to think about the players on our bench, because if they had to become involved it most probably meant that Ranieri was having to switch to Plan B... and if Ranieri was having to do that then the chances would be that Chelsea were failing in their endeavours to haul back the two goal deficit.

*   *   *

'And it's super Chelsea... super Chelsea FC... we're by far the greatest team the world has ever seen...'

The entire ground, barring the far section of the East Stand Lower which was playing host to the travelling supporters of Monaco, unified in its support of the team drowning out the prissy Champions League fanfare that heralded the arrival of the players on the pitch.

'One man went to mow... went to mow a meadow... oooh'

The chant was interrupted in the first minute breaking up into collective gasps and cursing, as Hasselbaink, with Chelsea surging forward from the kick off, picked up a loose ball and rattled a shot straight at Monaco's Italian keeper Flavio Roma.

With Chelsea attacking the Shed End goal in the first half, we were perfectly positioned to see the best of the action. But for me we were too low down; even though we had a diagonal view of proceedings it just wasn't the same as watching the game from our usual vantage point in the Mathew Harding Upper.

It rankled me that Chelsea had bowed to UEFA's wishes and, as with the Stuttgart match, closed off a large section of the stand. The crowd of just over 37,000 was vocal enough, but several thousand extra voices could have made the atmosphere even more intimidating.

'Chelsea... Chelsea... Chelsea...'

The game was being played at an electric pace with Monaco swift to counter attack every Chelsea move that they broke down.

'It's our night mate... I'm telling you it's our night,' said Young Dave, as Morientes fluffed a chance to put the visitors ahead.

It was the second time Young Dave had made this hopefully prophetic statement. The first had been when we had taken our seats and been treated to David Bowie's classic track Heroes booming at an ear drum bursting level from the tannoy.

'We can be heroes... just for one day,' we'd sung along with the chorus, hoping that it was loud enough for the players to hear as they went through their final preparations in the dressing room. Young Dave and I had both simultaneously declared that Heroes was our favourite song of all time and he took this as a presage from the great god of football that Chelsea were on the cusp of a magnificent victory.

'Go on Forrest skin em,' I shouted, as Gronkjaer held the ball up by the touchline on the far side of the penalty area.

'Fuck me... fuck!' I stood up and held my breath as he curled the ball invitingly across the crowded box looking for the head of Jimmy or maybe Eidur. But he found neither and the ball looped under the bar and into the net.

For a split second, no one could quite believe it... and then the ground erupted.

'GOAL... yes... ha... ha.' I leapt in the air and hugged Baby Gap Brian and Ossie who were sat next to me. Young Dave and Hip Hop Dan turned and clenched their fists, delirious smiles on their disbelieving faces, whilst Roger Socks and Big Chris embraced each other like long lost brothers.

'Ooh arrr Jesper Gronkjaer... ooh arrr Jesper Gronkjaer...'

I felt sorry for Ugly John and Lemon who were sat on their own at the other end of the Shed; sublime moments like this were best shared with those whom you regularly shared the self flagellating pleasure of watching the gloriously unpredictable boys in blue.

With 20 minutes gone Chelsea were 1–0 up on the night but still 3–2 behind on aggregate.

'I'm telling you son it's definitely our night,' said young Dave for a third time, as Terry blocked a Morientes goal-bound shot and deflected the ball onto the post.

'Jeeeesus... Jeeeesus Christ!' I cried, as I watched Hasselbaink beat the Monaco keeper with a cross that Gudjohnsen headed awkwardly against the crossbar.

The team, spurred on by a full repertoire of Chelsea terrace anthems, continued to put Monaco's goal under increasing pressure. Their defence looked jittery and I became more and more convinced that if we kept our shape and our heads then it would be just a matter of time before we got the crucial second goal.

If Gronkjaer's goal had been a misplaced cross, their was no doubting the fact that he was thinking about putting the ball in the back of the net a short while later when he found himself in a shooting position on the nearside edge of the box.

'Go on Forrest... oooh... Frankie... fuck, hit it... fuck, what a blinding save... CUNT!' I along, with thousands of others turned the air expletive blue as Gronkjaers miss-hit shot found Frank Lampard in the middle of the penalty area. Super Frankie chested the ball down and volleyed it first time, but the keeper saved spectacularly.

'I know... I know... it's definitely our night,' I said, patting Young Dave on the back and taking the words from his mouth as Monaco counter attacked once again only for Morientes, who had Gallas beaten for pace, to drill the ball wide when it would have been easier to score.

With only one minute to go to half time the indefatigable Lampard sent us into blue heaven. Melchiot, whose spindly legs and braided pony-tail made him the unlikeliest looking of footballers, cut cleverly into the Monaco penalty area and pushed the ball to the advancing Gudjohnsen whose inch perfect pass found Lampard... GOAL!

Chelsea were 2–0 up on the night and as things stood, with the tie level at 3–3, Crespo's away goal in Monaco meant that all of a sudden a return to Gelsenkirchen was back on the cards.

Our celebrations were loud enough and long enough to have been heard in Sloane Square. At the restart the fourth official held his board up signalling that there would be a minimum of three minutes added time.

'*Super, super Frank... super, super Frank... super, super Frank... super Frankie Lampard...*'

'Are we gonna drive over there?... I fancy a stop off in Amsterdam,' said Young Dave, putting a cigarette in his mouth in readiness as Ossie and Baby Gap Brian made an early beeline for the toilets.

'*Are you watching... are you watching... are you watching Arsenal...*'

'Yeah, why not son... oh my God... no, fuck NO!'

With just a few first half seconds remaining Monaco pulled a goal back. From where we were sat it was difficult to see what happened; Morientes chipped the ball beyond the flailing arms of Cudicini and it appeared to hit the woodwork a couple of times before being knocked in by a Monaco player who was goal hanging at the near post.

The Chelsea crowd in the Mathew Harding stand booed loudly but the goal stood. There was barely time to restart the game before the referee blew his whistle and pointed at the dressing room signalling that an eventful first half had come to an end.

Chelsea now needed another goal just to force the tie into extra time.

As the twin scoreboards showed a replay of the goal the whole ground began to reverberate to the sound of booing. Ibarra had jumped for the ball and deflected it over the line with his arm... hand ball surely... but it was too late now. All I could picture as I made my way to the toilets was the red half of North London cheering wildly as the ball hit the back of the Chelsea net.

*   *   *

'*Ranieri's blue and white army... Ranieri's blue and white army.*'

The rallying call greeted the players as they emerged for the second half.

'Can we still do it Marco?' said Hip Hop Dan, with an imploring look on his young face.

'Course we can son... course we can,' I replied, ninety-five percent of me believing that overall victory was possible and the other five percent succumbing to a creeping nagging doubt that my gloriously unpredictable Chelsea were going to throw it all away.

Chelsea set about the task of balancing the aggregate score with renewed vigour. Deschamps had been forced into a substitution that necessitated a defensive reshuffle which saw Ibarra, the scorer of Monaco's goal, move from midfield to right back.

In the same way that Monaco had exposed Ranieri's tinkering two weeks ago Chelsea, and Wayne Bridge in particular, now sought to do the same.

'Go on Bridgey... go on son... Eidur, Eidur... fuck it... ah BOLLOCKS!' Having leapt out of my seat when Bridge knocked a great ball through to Gudjohnsen, I held held my arms up expectantly as Eidur's miss-hit shot bounced back to Gronkjaer... and then buried my head in my hands as 'Forrest Gump' volleyed a first time effort into the Mathew Harding Stand.

The cruel god of football had handed the knife he'd been sharpening to Ibarra and instructed him to plunge it into the metaphorical stomach of Chelsea during injury time in the first half. With a full half hour still to play in the second, he got Morientes to deliver what would be the final mortal blow to my teams heart.

Lampard had just gone close with a shot, but then from the resulting Monaco counter attack Rothen slotted a wide angled ball to Morientes who lashed the ball into the back of the Chelsea net.

The goal was met with a stunned disbelieving silence from all but the small band of Monaco supporters away to our right who twirled their red and white scarves above their heads whilst ecstatically chanting the name of their team.

Fatally wounded, Chelsea's Champions League lifeblood spilled onto the Stamford Bridge pitch. Ranieri tried desperately to staunch the flow by substituting Geremi, Hasselbaink and Melchiot for Parker, Crespo and Johnson but the damage had already been done.

Long before the final whistle was blown, empty spaces had begun to appear in the stands as the stone cold certainty of Chelsea's imminent elimination from the competition hit home.

At the death, I applauded the Chelsea players from the pitch. Last to leave was a tearful Gudjohnsen, consoled sportingly by Didier Deschamps.

Match Result
Chelsea FC 2 : L'Association Sportive de Monaco FC 2
AS Monaco FC win 5–3 on aggregate.

* * *

I shook the hands of my Gate 17 companions and watched them depart, queuing for the tube didn't appeal to me right now so I remained. I joined in a half hearted rendition of *'Ranieri's blue and white army...'* but it did little to raise my spirits.

As I sat back down in my seat I looked on with a mixture of despair and envy as the Monaco players went over to their own supporters and conducted a very public celebration of what had been an outstanding achievement.

Away from home Monaco had done what Chelsea had failed to do, come back from two goals down. At home Chelsea had failed to defend a two goal advantage. It was that symmetry thing all over again... and which ever way I looked at it there was no escaping the fact my Champions League odyssey was over.

Grown men and children wept openly whilst women tested the effectiveness of their waterproof mascara. I felt like crying, but what was the point in that? At times like this tears are not enough.

I support Chelsea, the flamboyant millionaire upstarts from the Kings Road whose gloriously unpredictable style of play isn't really suitable for the weak or faint of heart.

'Close but no cigar,' I muttered to myself, taking one last look around the factory of broken dreams before making my way slowly out of the stadium.

EPILOGUE

I hadn't looked a pretty sight when I'd checked myself out in the mirror earlier in the morning. Balding and unshaven, I'd looked like a disillusioned member of the Anthill Mob who'd traded in the rigorous demands of Wacky Races for a life of miserable suburban solitude... which, being totally honest, wasn't too far wide of the mark.

The season was over now. As I sat on the low wall outside the front of my house, basking in the midday sunshine whilst waiting for Sex Case to pick me up and give me a lift to the airport, I felt myself being swathed by the comforting cloak of nostalgia.

Glorious unpredictability... who would ever have believed it eh? Meeting Vegas Dave in the middle of the Nevada desert... beating Liverpool in the final game of last season to secure our passage into the Champions League... Roman Abramovich investing a kings ransom in the club I hold dear to my heart... being ever-present on the train journeying towards European glory that was so cruelly derailed... witnessing Wayne Bridge's goal first hand when we finally overcame our Arsenal hoodoo... finishing second in the Premiership, and finally waving goodbye to Claudio Ranieri the man who in my eyes had made it all possible.

At times, football can be a vindictive business. When Ranieri had been appointed as head coach, I'd been amongst the first to criticise his methods and chant the name of Vialli. Now though I viewed him as a man I would be proud to call my father.

'One Ranieri... there's only one Ranieri... one Ranieri, there's only one Ranieri,' we'd chanted, as we bade farewell to Tinkerman on the final day of the season.

* * *

When I looked at the team, the biggest irony lay in the fact that the player who, over the course of the past few seasons, had probably been subject to more verbal tongue lashings than any other, was the same player that had

Chelsea convert Geordie Jase heads home with his Louis Vuitton case
bursting at the seams with Stone Island casual wear

been primarily responsible for giving us supporters the adrenaline rush and fillip that we needed, when we'd needed it most.

Discarded now, but it was Jesper Gronkjaer, yeah Forrest Gump, the man who was known to his team mates as Dracula because he was afraid of crosses, that had made the telling difference in those matches of critical importance.

The goal against Liverpool at the end of last season, the super-sub performance against Arsenal at Highbury, the stunning goal that gave us all hope as we battled at the Bridge to overcome Ranieri's Monaco debacle, one in the onion bag in the 1–1 draw Old Trafford and his final piece de resistance in the last game of the season which consigned an already doomed Leeds United to the anonymity of the Nationwide League.

'Run Forrest run... ha ha.' I wondered if he would come back to haunt Chelsea one day and as I did so I was nudged back to reality by the beeping horn of Sex Case's trusty old Vectra which had pulled up outside my house.

*   *   *

The prophylactics placed in the path of true love are all too easily ruptured when the great god of football has a say in the outcome. The thing was though that the great god of football hadn't reckoned with the glorious unpredictability that associates itself with the followers of Chelsea Football Club.

My impatient lust for glory had seen me purchase a return ticket for an Air Berlin flight to Düsseldorf the day after we'd knocked Arsenal out of the Champions League. I'd been so convinced that a divine wind was blowing Chelsea back to Gelsenkirchen that I'd weighed out my money in advance just to make sure that I'd be able to get there if all the other travel alternatives didn't come together.

Sadly, instead of a divine wind Chelsea only mustered an insufficient evening breeze. The night after we'd been eliminated from the competition, just as I was considering tearing up my flight ticket and tossing it in the bin, I'd decided to place my last remaining chip on the great roulette wheel of love.

118 118 was my number, and it came up trumps.

'Yeah... er is Tiffany there?' I'd said nervously, as I dialled the number of the Irish Pub in Dusseldorf which I'd secured through directory enquiries.

'This is she... who is this?' had been the inquisitive reply.

An hours worth of catch-up dialogue later and I'd secured myself a ticket for the Champions League final and three days in the company of a delectable barmaid who would hopefully 'get it' if I was given a sporting chance.

*   *   *

On the way to the airport my mobile rang, it was Young Dave.
  'Listen Marco, just a quick call to wish you all the best with Tiff.'
  'Yeah, cheers mate... nice one, how ya doin?'
  'Not bad son. Listen, have you heard the news?'
  'No mate, what's happened?'
  'Aintcha heard?'
  'What mate... about Ranieri?'
  'No son?'
  'What... about Beckham?'
  'No son?'
  'Well don't keep me in suspense mate... what the fuck's happened?'
  'It's just been on the news son... Big Chris has gone on diet.'